Shoo, Jimmy Choo!

The Modern Girl's Guide to Spending Less and Saving More

Shoo, Jimmy Choo!

The Modern Girl's Guide to Spending Less and Saving More

by Catey Hill

Money Editor of nydailynews.com and Recovering Shoe Addict

Foreword by Wes Moss CFP®, of *Money Matters*

STERLING

New York / London
www.sterlingpublishing.com

To Jay: Thank you for your constant love and support (and patience!). I could not ask for a better partner in life.

And to Lindsay: The grace and steadfastness with which you handle your career, finances, and personal life are an inspiration to me each day.

STERLING and the distinctive Sterling logo are registered trademarks of Sterling Publishing Co., Inc.

Library of Congress Cataloging-in-Publication Data

Hill, Catey.

Shoo, Jimmy Choo! : the modern girl's guide to spending less and saving more / by Catey Hill.

p. cm.

ISBN 978-1-4027-6669-5

1. Women–Finance, Personal. I. Title.

HG179.H469 2010

332.0240082–dc22

2009019523

2 4 6 8 10 9 7 5 3 1

Published by Sterling Publishing Co., Inc.
387 Park Avenue South, New York, NY 10016
Text © 2010 by Catey Hill
Illustrations © 2010 Mary Lynn Blasutta
Distributed in Canada by Sterling Publishing
$^{c}/o$ Canadian Manda Group, 165 Dufferin Street
Toronto, Ontario, Canada M6K 3H6
Distributed in the United Kingdom by GMC Distribution Services
Castle Place, 166 High Street, Lewes, East Sussex, England BN7 1XU
Distributed in Australia by Capricorn Link (Australia) Pty. Ltd.
P.O. Box 704, Windsor, NSW 2756, Australia

Manufactured in the United States of America
All rights reserved

Personal names in anecdotal examples have been changed to protect the identities of their holders.

Sterling ISBN 978-1-4027-6669-5

For information about custom editions, special sales, premium and corporate purchases, please contact Sterling Special Sales Department at 800-805-5489 or specialsales@sterlingpublishing.com.

Contents

Foreword

By Wes Moss, CFP®

What does it take to be happy? After years of meeting and advising hundreds of wildly different people—Democrats, Republicans, doctors, teachers, lawyers, utility workers, engineers, writers, the list goes on—I've seen that a significant part of being happy is having financial security. And almost all of these happy people have one thing in common: They took an active role in smartly managing their money, career, and financial future—*and they started doing it at a young age.*

Shoo, Jimmy Choo! shows you how to do just this. In my years as a CFP, I've seen that happy people generally know how much money is coming in and how much is going out every month, and how to fill the gap in between. They have an informed, solid plan for retirement. They buy homes they can afford, using traditional mortgages and paying down the principal every month, and end up owning their home outright by the time they retire. They pay off credit card debt and loans in a timely manner. These are key principles necessary for a secure financial future, and these are just the principles that Catey Hill highlights for young women in *Shoo, Jimmy Choo!*. Not only can Catey's fundamental principles literally be worth hundreds of thousands of dollars in your pocket, they can help make you one of those happy people . . .

Shoo, Jimmy Choo! is a timely book, but even timelier is that Catey had the foresight to sit down and begin writing this book long before it was cool to *not* "keep up with the Jones." This "keeping up with the Joneses" mentality led Americans into massive debt. In fact, the average American was spending nearly every penny they were making. Many Americans bought homes, cars, clothes, gadgets and many other things they simply could not afford. Many Americans saved almost no money. And look where it got us . . . In a day and age where this massive consumer debt, combined with things like Wall Street's complex financial instruments, has driven our country into the worst recession since the 1930s, it is clearly time to get back to basics. And that's why I recommend *Shoo, Jimmy Choo!* to young women: It takes you back to basics with practical, easy-to-follow financial advice that will set you up for a financially secure—and happier—future.

PART I:

Style, Diet, and Fitness...
for Your Finances

AN INTRODUCTION TO SAVVY MONEY MANAGEMENT (AND WHY YOU NEED TO START, LIKE, *NOW*)

You don't have the pocketbook of Ivanka Trump. Not even the pocketbook of good ol' K-Fed. In fact, you're not even close. That's right, you're nearly B-R-O-K-E. Scraping the bottom of your purse for quarters, eating Ramen noodles right before payday B-R-O-K-E. Or, more likely, you're buying hot new patent-leather flats, getting fabulous biscotti highlights, all on an overextended credit card (and no savings to speak of) B-R-O-K-E. And it makes you wonder... How did a cute, employed girl like yourself end up having to hock her skinny jeans on eBay just to pay the rent?

Or maybe you're not quite B-R-O-K-E, but you don't have much in your retirement fund, you don't really understand investing, or you don't have a solid plan for your financial future. (And ladies, a solid plan does not include waiting to save money until you make more money, marrying Barron Trump, or winning the Mega Millions.)

Well, girls, I've got you figured out. And more than that, I've got the solution to your financial woes. Whether you're plugging away at a $25,000-a-year job, or living beyond your means despite a $100,000 salary, I can set you on the path to financial security.

Yeah, yeah, you've heard that promise before. What makes me different? Well, I was just like you—slaving away at a job that didn't pay me enough, buying shoes I couldn't afford on my credit card, and with no savings to speak of (other than the $20 emergency bill I stashed in the lining of my purse in case my hot date turned psycho). Then I got a job at Forbes, and it scared the crap out of me. I realized that unless I set my finances straight, I was never going to wrangle myself out of my not-so-glamorous financial situation, let alone ever get to stop working (and believe me, if you met my former boss, you'd understand why this scared the crap out of me). So I tweaked my spending habits, learned how to save and plan for my future, and now I'm on the path to becoming a pretty wealthy woman. But don't worry, I still have a great wardrobe and plenty of shoes. . . .

This book tells you how I did it—in three simple steps (plus tons of tips on how to get the best free and inexpensive goodies, because, ladies, I know you need your mani-pedis and highlights). It gives you tips gleaned from hours spent with certified financial planners, economists, and financial writers and editors, as well as reams of research. You will find all of the must-know pointers that I've collected from months and months of work at Forbes, and from my current job as the money editor for the *New York Daily News* online. I've also included real-life success and horror stories from women like you, who have battled their financial demons and (mostly) survived intact to tell about it.

Ladies, if you have credit card debt, save less than 13 percent of your income every month, have no in-case-of-emergency fund, or are certain that you'll marry rich and *then* fix your finances, you can't afford not to read this book. And here's the kicker: I won't make you give up your passion for pedicures, your love of lingerie, your hankering for handbags, or whatever else you can't live without buying. You may have to buy fewer of these items, but I'll show you how to have it all. If I, a shopaholic who can't pass a day at work without scouring eBay for the latest Prada bag, who absolutely refuses to wash her hair with any shampoo other than Kérastase, and who can't stand the sight of her butt in anything other than Paige jeans, was able to become financially secure, so can you.

The Money Makeover
*How to Determine if Your Finances Need a
Little (or Not So Little) Touch-Up*

When you think about retirement and savings, what comes to mind? If you're anything like I was, retirement is something you did with last year's handbag, and saving is something you did with your calories before Thanksgiving dinner. Your idea of an emergency fund is a $20 bill shoved in the back of your panty drawer, your retirement plan consists of praying that the CEO gets canned and you miraculously land his seven-figure-a-year job (and that fabulous corner office while you're at it), and your investment strategy, well, I am not even going to go there. You're a smart, together girl, but your finances are another story.

Or maybe you're not that bad. You're one of those girls who is already pretty good with money but could use a little financial touch-up. You're pretty sure that your retirement fund is invested smartly, that your savings will last should you lose your job, and that you manage your taxes well, but you wouldn't mind knowing a little more, just to be sure.

Whichever group you land in, or if you're somewhere in the middle, this chapter will help you decide whether you need a complete money makeover or just a little nip-tuck, and you'll find out if *Shoo, Jimmy Choo!* is the book that will make it happen. It will then give you a brief—and painless, I promise—kick in your (financial) butt with a lesson on why you need to deal with your finances, like, *now.*

SIGNS THAT YOU NEED THIS BOOK

Here are ten signs that you need a financial makeover:

1. *You have no concrete plan for a secure financial future.* And, girls, by concrete plan I don't mean marrying a rich man, winning *Deal or No Deal,* or landing a major role in a TV show. I am referring to a plan that includes saving for retirement, debt reduction, and building emergency savings.
2. *You have significant debt and no solid plan to get out of it.* A solid plan does not, I repeat, does *not* include winning the lottery, ignoring your bills in the hope they will disappear, or thinking that you'll start paying your debt off once you get a better job. A solid plan includes specific strategies and timetables for erasing your debt.
3. *Less than 13 percent of your income goes to your retirement savings (or worse, you haven't even thought of saving for retirement).*
4. *You have only a small in-case-of-emergency fund, or none at all.* The $12 you keep tucked in your wallet so you can bribe the valet when you need to make a quick escape after a lunch with your mother is *not* a sufficient in-case-of-emergency fund, not even close. I'm talking at least three months' pay stashed away (somewhere other than in the back of your panty drawer).
5. *You pay only the minimum, or a little extra, toward your credit card every month.*
6. *You don't understand the difference between a Roth IRA, a traditional IRA, and a 401(k) . . .*
7. *. . . Nor do you know the best ways to invest in these retirement plans.* (And, ladies, if you haven't heard of an index fund, don't think you know how to invest in your retirement plan.)
8. *You get a huge income tax refund each year.* I know you feel like you've won the lottery when that check comes in, but it's actually not

the best idea. The dreadful IRS is keeping your money all year when it could be in your little hands every paycheck!

9. *You don't have the insurance you need.* Every single one of you needs health insurance. (Yes, that means you!) You also need either renters or homeowners insurance. If you have a car, you need auto insurance. It's also a good idea to have disability insurance (or at least know what it is, for a start). And there are a few other types of insurance that you may need, depending on your individual situation.

10. *You don't have a clue about where your money goes each month (but it sure goes somewhere).* Now, this is a situation I am intimately familiar with. My clothes used to be held hostage at the dry cleaner's for months because I'd never have the cash to get them (and naturally, that meant I'd have to buy a new dress on my credit card). I simply could not understand where my cash went. Sound familiar?

Maybe you've read finance books before and they were just too dense. Maybe they seemed totally disconnected from your life. Maybe you just couldn't realistically follow their advice. Well, that's where this book is different. It's written for you—a smart, chic girl—in a way you can relate to. I'm in my twenties, and used to have the same financial problems you're dealing with now—that pesky credit card jumping out of my wallet a little too often (I call it the Plastic Plague), the but-I-can't-afford-to-contribute-to-my-401(k) mentality, the nagging I-hope-nothing-goes-wrong-because-I-certainly-don't-have-any-savings voice. But I changed my entire financial situation. I'll be set to retire, quite well, I might add, at the age of sixty-five. If I get fired, I can live comfortably for months with no job because of my savings. I have numerous (smart) investments. I don't have credit card debt. And here's the kicker: I don't make a lot of money and I don't have a sugar daddy (though if you know of any . . .), yet I can still say this. I took control of my finances on my own. And with this book, you can do the same, by following simple, doable steps that make sense in your real life (and that won't put you to sleep).

Look, girls, I know you're probably thinking that of course you'd like to save more money, get out of debt, buy a home, and eventually start saving for retirement, but financial planning never seems to stick when you try it. When you've attempted to be more financially disciplined, it went the way of your brush with Atkins—great for a week and then down the tubes. Believe me, I understand. I used to think that on my paltry salary there was no way I could ever save any money or pay more than the minimum on my credit card. I kept putting off saving for retirement by telling myself that I'd start doing it once I made more money. When I actually had money in my bank account, it never lasted. I'd blow it on a treat for myself (so, yes, my hair looked fabulous, but my bank account did not). But, ladies, I turned it all around. Sure, it took some discipline. And yes, I had to stop buying every single piece of clothing (and a few other things) I wanted. But now I'm no longer in credit card debt, I'm saving for retirement, and I have an emergency cash fund . . . and so can you.

Perhaps you're concerned that you don't know a thing about finance (except how to argue with your credit card company), or you're panicked because math was lost on you by the time you reached high school. Ladies, I get it. When I first started my job at Forbes, I would leave a meeting and have to race to my computer to look up the meanings of the financial terms people were casually throwing around. But you don't need to be able to solve the subprime mortgage crisis or the current banking fiasco in order to understand the financial concepts presented in this book. All the terms you'll come across are carefully and simply defined. You'll be surprised at how uncomplicated money management can be (and also realize how pretentious your banker date was when he tried to make it sound oh-so-complex).

So the point of all this: If I can do it, so can you. And here's why you need to. . . .

THE IMPORTANCE OF DEALING WITH YOUR FINANCES, LIKE, NOW

You may be sitting there thinking that Prince Charming will rescue you from your financial woes, that you'll deal with your debt when you make more money, or that you'll contribute more to your retirement fund, investments, and savings later in life. Every girl I know has told herself at least one of these lies. But let me tell you, it most likely isn't going to work.

First of all, Prince Charming? If the number of bad dates you've been on in your life hasn't rid you of that notion, I don't know what will. There are simply not enough rich, amazing guys to go around. And even if there were, can they really rescue you from your financial woes? You may be one of the lucky ones, but do you want to bet on it? Maybe it's just me, but betting on a man seems to lead to a sink full of dishes, a filthy house, and an extra ten pounds. (And, well, divorce rates continue to hover at about 50 percent.) And don't think Social Security is going to swoop in and help you out here. Have you watched the news lately . . . ?

Second, as for your misbegotten notion that you'll deal with your debt later, need I remind you that as you procrastinate, the interest on your credit card (and all those other loans) is compounding? Compounding interest on your debt is not good. It's kind of like what happens to your bum when you inhale Chips Ahoy a few times too many—it expands, rapidly, and then it takes a lot of work to fix it. Let's take a look at just how much interest payments can cost you.

Why You Hate Compounding Interest (or, How Your $1,000 TV Ends Up Costing You More Than $2,000)

Let's say you buy a $1,000 television set on your credit card, and *never buy another thing with this card.* Your card has an 18 percent interest rate and your monthly minimum payment is 2.5 percent of your balance (so your first month's payment is $25) or $10, whichever is greater. This interest rate and minimum payment are pretty standard for credit cards. You pay the minimum—no more, no less—each month. How much will this TV cost you? Drumroll, please . . . a whopping $2,115.41—more than double the TV sticker price. *You'll have paid more in interest than the actual cost of the television!* And it will take you more than twelve years to pay it off (and by that time, I'm sure you will have gotten a new one!).

Why You Love Compounding Interest (or, How Investing Only $144,000 Can Make You a Millionaire)

Then there's your retirement, savings, and investments. This is where compounding actually works in your favor. It's quite simple: The earlier you start, the longer your money will have to grow. (Translation: Start now and get rich with a lot less effort!) Being old and broke isn't a pretty sight. How on earth are you going to afford that much-needed Botox if you're scrimping by in your old age? And no, Prince Charming is not getting you out of this one, as we've already discussed. Who do you think you are, Melania Trump?

The table below illustrates the magic of starting to save early in life. Let's say you get an 8 percent return on investment (this is pretty standard for retirement fund returns over the long term). If you put $300 per month into your retirement account starting at age twenty-five, you'll be a millionaire at the age of sixty-five. If you wait until you're thirty-five to start contributing this $300 per month, you'll have only $440,445 upon retirement—less than half the money you'd have had if you had started ten years earlier!

Age That You Began Contributing to Your Retirement Fund	Total Contributions ($300 Per Month)	Amount of Money in the Retirement Fund at Age 65	Compounded Interest
25	$144,000	$1,007,212—you're a millionaire!	$863,212
35	$108,000	$440,445	$332,445
45	$72,000	$177,923	$105,923

The lesson—it doesn't take that much to become a millionaire, *if you start saving early in life.*

TIP: *Compounding works against you (big time!) when you are paying off your debts, and for you (big time!) when you are building up savings.*

So you need to get your finances together, like, *now!* And I'm going to show you how to do it. I've done all the homework for you—all the harassing of financial advisors, all the I-learned-it-the-hard-way life lessons, all the knowledge gleaned from years of working at leading financial and news organizations, including Forbes and the *New York Daily News*—to make sure I was giving you the best advice possible. It's all done, it's all in this book, and miraculously, it all boils down to three simple steps:

1. Identify and alter your spending style.
2. Put yourself on the Debt Diet.
3. Build up your financial fitness.

They're easy to remember: style, diet, fitness—probably already some of your life's priorities.

CHAPTER 2

Dress for (Financial) Success

How to Get What You Want out of Life . . . at Least Financially

This chapter is the financial version of the LBD (little black dress). You know how your LBD is the one thing in your closet that always prepares you for a date? No, it won't make the date go well, but it does lay the groundwork for it to be a much less traumatic experience (I mean, looking hot never hurts your chances with the man or woman of the minute). That's what this chapter does for your finances—it lays the groundwork for you getting your financial life together. By the time you finish this chapter, you'll be on your way to getting what you want out of your life, in the financial sense at least.

Before I jump right in and make you a millionaire (no exaggeration, girls, even with this crappy economy, you can get there!), you've got to do the LBD recon on your financial situation. Here's how it works. First, you need to understand what I call your financial now—basically just a snapshot of your current financial situation. Then, you've got to outline your financial future—all the goals you want to achieve that relate to your finances.

YOUR FINANCIAL NOW

To understand your financial now, you are going to create a financial snapshot—a picture of everything you own and owe at this moment. And, ladies, this is *not* a glamour shot; rather, it may be pretty scary, on par with a no-makeup-at-8-a.m.-and-hungover close-up.

Getting this snapshot requires two simple steps:

1. Gather your financial statements and organize them.
2. Find out FICO score.

I know this sounds intimidating. I mean, "gathering all your financial statements"? You can barely remember where you put your keys ten minutes ago. And acronyms, well they usually mean something far more complicated than you want to deal with. But this is really pretty easy, I promise.

Step 1: Gather Your Financial Statements and Organize Them

Now this might be a little frightening (kind of like opening your boyfriend's closet and getting assaulted with the sight of a gigantic pile of clothes and a very peculiar stench), but it's necessary. You have to know what you're dealing with. Do you know where all your assets are, or even what an asset is? What about how much they're worth? Do you know how much you owe in terms of loans, mortgages, and taxes? Even if you do or think you might, gather your financial statements and create folders for each category listed below. For example, in the Automobiles folder, you will have statements for your auto loans, purchase agreements, titles, warranties, repair receipts, and insurance.

- ❋ Automobiles
  - ❏ Auto loans
  - ❏ Purchase agreements, titles, warranties, maintenance and repair receipts
  - ❏ Insurance
- ❋ Bank statements (checking and savings)
- ❋ Investment accounts (excluding retirement)
  - ❏ Statements from mutual funds, stocks, bonds, CDs, money market accounts, etc.

- Credit card statements
- Mortgage
  - ❑ Closing statement and other purchase documents
  - ❑ Mortgage statements
  - ❑ Insurance (private mortgage insurance, homeowners insurance, etc.)
- Insurance
  - ❑ Rental, life, health, disability, etc.
- Retirement
  - ❑ All retirement account statements
- Salary/income
  - ❑ Pay stubs, checks, and other payroll items
  - ❑ Other sources of income
- Student loans
  - ❑ Original loan agreement
  - ❑ Monthly statements
- Tax returns
  - ❑ W-2s, 1099s, tax-related forms, etc.
  - ❑ If you plan to itemize deductions (see Chapter 14), put relevant statements and receipts in your files
- Other loans/debts
  - ❑ Include other kinds of loans, statements of money owed, etc.

Yes, I realize that you might not have these statements anymore—it's hard enough finding room for your shoes, let alone space for those ugly bills that fill your mailbox—but start saving them when they come in. For statements you cannot find, try calling the company. The lender or other creditor will usually be able to furnish copies of bills so that you can figure out what you owe them.

I know some of you probably receive electronic instead of paper statements (good for you, eco-conscious chicks!), but for this exercise, please print those statements and file them. It will make it easier for you to fill in the chart below.

Take a deep breath. You have officially just filed something that wasn't your perfect nails! And now, I want you to use the items you have on file to fill out the chart on pages 11–12, which will give you a financial snapshot of this moment in your life. It's not a perfect picture, but it's good enough for now. It's better to underestimate than overestimate, but try to be as precise as possible where you can.

Financial Snapshot
Date: _____

Assets If you can personally get cash for it, it's an asset. Sample assets below.	
CATEGORY	**CURRENT VALUE** **(If multiple items in a** **category, list separately)**
Cash	$
Checking account balance	$
Savings account balance	$
Investments (CDs, stocks, bonds, money market accounts, mutual funds, other investments excluding retirement accounts)	$
Retirement accounts (IRAs, Roth IRAs, 401(k)s, 403(b)s, Keogh, SEP-IRAs, other retirement accounts)	$
Market value of your home(s) (This is not what you paid for the home; it's what it could be sold for if you put it on the market today.)	$
Cash value of life insurance	$
Market value of other real estate/property (This is not what you paid for the item, it's what it could be sold for if you put it on the market today.)	$
Automobiles (Kelly Blue Book value; see kbb.com)	$
Money owed you (utility deposits, rental income, etc.)	$
Jewelry and collectibles	$
Value of the business you own	$
Miscellaneous (If you can sell it for a decent amount of money—be honest with your- self—you can put it in this column. Think about things like electronic equipment and furniture.)	$
TOTAL	$

Liabilities (aka Debts)

A debt/liability is money you owe. Include only debts that you can't cancel, such as credit card bills and auto loans (so don't include your home phone and gas bill because you can call and cancel these services). Insert the amount of money you still owe on these liabilities. Sample liabilities below.

CATEGORY	AMOUNT STILL OWED
Mortgages	$
Student loans	$
Credit card balances	$
Auto loans	$
Home equity loans	$
Other loans (i.e. 401(k) loans)	$
Taxes owed	$
Miscellaneous	$
TOTAL	$

Monthly Income

Calculate your take-home pay each month from all your sources of income. Let's say you receive $1,200 once a year after taxes are taken out. In this chart, you'd write $100 in the Monthly after-tax salary box. (This $100 was calculated by dividing $1,200 by twelve to determine your monthly income.) If you had other sources of income, you would add those to the $100.

CATEGORY	AMOUNT
Monthly after-tax salary	$
Interest earned	$
Dividends	$
Other (alimony, child support, rental income)	$
TOTAL	$

Ladies, I don't want you to panic over this chart yet. For now, we're just using it to help you get organized. So if you see a lot of debts in your chart, don't hyperventilate. Millions of girls like you have tons of debt; what with student loans, mortgages, auto loans, it's hard not to. And debt isn't necessarily a bad thing—buying a home is a great thing, if you can afford it. Student loans are often completely necessary. And the really good news is: You're young enough that you can improve your financial situation. Just knowing exactly where you stand in the financial world is the first step to getting where you want to be, but it's hard to plan when you don't know where your money is.

Step 2: Find Out Your FICO Score

Yes, it's an icky acronym, and a four-letter one at that, but the FICO score is one of the most important items to understand (and change) on your path to a secure financial future. Here are the key things you need to know about your FICO score.

What is a FICO score and why should I care?

Your FICO (FICO stands for Fair Isaac Corporation) score is basically your financial life story—whether you paid bills on time, how much debt you have, and more—all in a three-digit number. (Yes, someone has been documenting your whole life—you knew it was worth a story, didn't you? Too bad it's your financial life.) It tells anyone who would lend you money, such as a credit card company or a mortgage broker, or anyone who needs you to pay your bill on time, such as your landlord or the car dealership, how likely it is that you'll pay them back on time and in full. Ladies, if you want a credit card, cell phone, car, house, whatever, that lender is most likely going to want to know your FICO score. He doesn't want to get burned like your last boyfriend whom you conveniently "forgot" to repay after you found him cheating.

If your FICO score is high, you'll get a better interest rate on your credit cards and loans, saving you thousands of dollars in interest. (Ask yourself: Would you rather buy that adorable clapboard house you've fallen in love with, or throw those thousands of dollars at the fat cats running your credit card company?) I realize that interest may not seem that important to you. I mean, what's 11 percent or 18 percent, after all? That's nothing, right? But ladies, it is *expensive*. See the box below to discover how much a "little" interest can cost you.

Interest: How your $5,000 credit card bill ends up costing you more than $12,000

Let's say you have $5,000 in credit card debt. Your interest rate is 18 percent. You pay the minimum payment on your card each month, which is 2.5 percent of the balance (so the first month, you'll owe $125, which is 2.5 percent of $5000) or $10, whichever is greater. At this rate, it will take you twenty-six years to pay off the credit card, and it will cost you more than $7,000 in interest payments alone (a total bill of more than $12,000!).

Where did the credit bureaus get the information in my FICO score?
Your FICO score is based on your past financial behavior (or, as the case may be, misbehavior). Every credit card purchase, loan, bill payment, etc. is reported to a credit bureau. There are three credit bureaus—Equifax, Experian, and Transunion—and each of them has a record of your past financial transactions, which is used to compute your FICO score. You have three different FICO scores from each of the three different credit bureaus. The data is sometimes different from each one due to errors and/or differences in which companies report your financial behavior to which bureau. (Not all companies report your financial life to every bureau.)

How do I get copies of my credit reports and FICO scores?
To get a copy of your credit reports from Equifax, Experian, and Transunion, go online to annualcreditreport.com and request copies of these reports. You should check all three to ensure everything on them is correct. You are entitled to one free report from each bureau each year.

Then check out your FICO score(s) at myFICO.com. Getting all your scores will cost you around $50. If you are totally broke at the moment, just retrieve one of your FICO scores. You'll already have your credit reports, so you'll have a good sense of what the other FICO scores will look like.

What factors affect my FICO score?
- **35 percent:** *Whether you paid your bills on time.* The more bills you pay on time, the higher your FICO score. (And no, they don't care that you were in Mexico so you couldn't pay the water bill, or that you had exams, which made you forget to deal with your cell phone bill.) It only matters that you paid the minimum balance on time and that the company received the payment on time.
- **30 percent:** *Ratio of total debt to total credit limit.* Total debt is the amount owed on credit cards and installment loans, which are loans in which you pay a fixed amount at regular intervals (you have all of this information in your Liabilities chart on page 12). So let's say you have a $1,000 balance on one credit card and you owe $2,000 on another. Your total debt is $3,000. Your credit limit is the total amount of money all your credit card companies will let you spend. Let's say you have a $4,000 limit on one credit card and a $2,500 on another. Your total credit limit is $6,500. You can find out your credit limits from your credit card statements or by calling the credit card company.

     To get your ratio of total debt to total credit limit, divide the total debt by the total credit limit. In the above example, the debt-to-credit-limit ratio is 46 percent, which was calculated by dividing $3,000 by $6,500. The lower this percentage, the more it will improve your FICO score.

* **15 percent:** *Length of credit history.* This is how long you've had credit cards and loans. The longer you've had a credit history, the better your FICO score.

* **10 percent:** *Recent applications for credit and opening new credit accounts.* When you apply for a lot of credit cards or loans in a short amount of time, it lowers your FICO score.

* **10 percent:** *The ratio of credit cards to loans.* Lenders want to see a good mixture of credit cards and loans. This does not mean you should run out and get a loan! It's only a small part of your score, and if you have credit card debt, you should be worrying about paying that off, on time, rather than getting yourself into more debt.

What is a good FICO score?

Scores range from 300 to 850. Scores of 300–500 are awful. (As in, girl, consider an extended trip to debt boot camp.) Scores of 760–850 are the best. (As in, maybe you should be writing your own finance book.)

5 steps for improving your FICO score

If your throat closed up when you saw your FICO score, don't panic. Here are five steps you can (and should) take to improve your FICO score.

1. *Check to make sure there are no inaccuracies on your credit reports that could be lowering your score.* To do this, you first need to get all three of your credit reports. Visit annualcreditreport.com to do this. If anything shows up that's inaccurate—for example, a late payment that you weren't aware of, a loan you didn't take out, whatever—go back onto the credit bureau's Web site (experian.com, equifax.com, or transunion.com) to learn how you can file a claim. The credit bureau has thirty days to respond to your claim. If they decide to keep the inaccurate claim on your report, you will have to deal with the business that made the claim directly. Just call their customer service department.

2. *Going forward, pay all your bills on time.* Yes, I realize this is like asking you to make it into the office by 9 a.m. on the morning after your birthday, but I'm still going to ask it. Use online bill pay to schedule payments so you can't pay them late. And remember, paying your credit card bill on time only means that you have to pay the minimum on time. Of course, you should be paying more (see Chapter 5).

3. *Increase your credit limit by calling your credit card companies and asking them to raise it.* Since part of your score is your debt as compared to total credit limit, increasing your credit limit on one or all of your credit cards will improve your score. However, do not get a new credit card to do this! Just increase the limit on your current cards. And if you think increasing the limit will make you spend more, then don't even think about it. This is a strategy, not free reign to spend more!

4. *Don't cancel credit cards that you've had for a long time; just don't use them.*

5. *Don't apply for a bunch of new credit cards in a short amount of time.* So don't get three new cards in a month. Why do you need them anyway? (Actually, don't answer that. I realize that your definition of "need" may not be quite where it should yet.)

What if I don't have a FICO score?

This means you have no credit history, and it's actually not a good thing. If you have no history, lenders are far less likely to give you a loan or credit as they have no way of knowing how likely it is that you'll pay them back. The solution to no credit history: Get a credit card and pay it off on time. Just go on cardweb.com, find a low-interest card, and call the company to sign up. If you can't get a credit card, see Get a Secured Credit Card section in Chapter 5).

YOUR FINANCIAL FUTURE

Your financial future is made up of everything you want to achieve that requires money—buying a home, getting out of debt, saving for a vacay (Rio, anyone?), whatever you want out of life that isn't free. To achieve the financial future you want, you will need a financial life plan, which is simply a set of specific financial goals and strategies for achieving them. Yes, I know that sounds scary—you can't even stick with a guy or girl for more than a few months, and I'm asking you to create a financial life plan. But it's not that hard. You've collected all your statements and created a financial snapshot of yourself. You know your FICO score and are working on improving it. So let's look ahead. You're still young and you *can* get what you want out of life, at least financially. You just need to know a) what it is that you want, b) when you want it, and c) how much it'll cost you. Once you know that, each subsequent chapter of this book will show you how to get there. Plus, I've created simple charts on pages 20–23 to help you get started. Let's quickly look at the steps you'll need to take.

Step 1: Set Specific Financial Goals

These are any goals that will cost you money. Make each goal as specific as possible. Some examples include:

- *Buy a home.* Specifically, buy a two-bedroom apartment in X neighborhood in the next five years.
- *Save for retirement.* Specifically, retire at age sixty-five with enough income to have the same standard of living that I'm enjoying now.
- *Get out of credit card debt.* Specifically, pay off all of my credit cards (list all credit cards and interest rates here) in the next two years.
- *Pay off student loans.* Specifically, pay off all my student loans (list all student loans and interest rates here) in the next ten years.
- *Buy a car.* Specifically, buy a used Honda, no more than two years old, within the next year.
- *Quit my job for six months to write a book* (my personal fave!). Specifically, save up enough money so I can have the same standard of living for six months without the job that I have now.
- *Take a vacation.* Specifically, travel to Spain for a week next winter.

Step 2: List These Goals in Order of Importance to You

My only caveat is that if you are in credit card debt, or another high-interest debt, getting out of it needs to be at the top of your list. If your company offers a 401(k) that matches your contributions, you should put in money up to what they match as well as pay off your high-interest debt as quickly as possible. I will discuss this more in Chapter 9. Following the getting-out-of-debt goal should be the goals to build up an emergency savings fund, save for retirement, and buy a home. There is more on all of these goals in subsequent chapters, but for now just make sure they're included in your chart.

Step 3: Determine the Total Cost of Each Goal

In conjunction with reading this book, Bankrate.com, ShooJimmy Choo.com, and Google are your BFFs in determining the total cost of your goals. Use Bankrate.com to determine the cost of paying off interest-bearing debts (debts that you pay interest on, such as loans and credit cards) and how much you'll need to save for retirement. Google, along with this book, is good for other goals. Want to buy a home? Check out Chapter 13. Then Google home prices in your area and how much you will need for a down payment, closing costs, and other fees. That's the amount you'll need to save. Here are a few goal-specific costs to keep in mind.

Paying off interest-bearing debts (like loans and credit cards)

For goals like paying off loans and getting out of credit card debt, you've got to factor in interest payments as well as the original amount of the debt to figure out how much the goal will cost. When you are paying off debt, interest can add to the total cost of your goal *big* time. You may owe $5,000 on your credit card right this minute, but if you don't pay it all off, you'll owe that $5,000 *plus* all the interest you accrue. So the total cost of the goal will be significantly more than $5,000. Check out the Real Cost of Debt and related debt calculators on Bankrate.com or ShooJimmyChoo.com to help you figure out the total cost of your interest-bearing debts. You will enter the current amount of debt you have and the number of years over which you want to pay it off, and the calculator will tell you the total cost of your debt and how much you will need to spend in monthly payments to pay it off.

Retirement planning

Use the retirement calculator in the Money section of AARP.org to figure out how much you'll need for a comfortable retirement. Estimate the information to the best of your ability, remembering that as a woman your life expectancy is about eighty years and your average yearly return on investments in the long-term will likely be about 8 percent.

Decide How Many Months It Will Take You to Achieve Each Goal

I know you already included a timetable in the goal itself, but it's good to have it in a separate box as well, just to reiterate the point. (And no, retiring next year and jetting off to Aruba probably won't happen—but maybe retiring at forty-five will.) You will revise these goals as you get further into the book, but for now, write them all down. The timing may have to be tweaked once you figure out the amount of money you can realistically put toward your goals each month. At the moment, choose what you think is a realistic timetable for each goal, which you can revise later.

Determine the Monthly Cost of Your Goals

Establish how much it will cost you *each month* to achieve each goal, as well as any strategies that will help you succeed. Once you know the total cost and the number of months in which you want to achieve a goal, you can determine the monthly amount you need to save to get there.

For getting-out-of-debt goals (goals that require you to pay off debt like loans and credit cards), you can do the math on your own. Let's say you'll need $2,400 total (that includes all the interest you'll owe) to pay off your credit card within two years. So $2,400 ÷ 24 months = $100 per month. So you'd have to pay $100 per month to achieve the goal.

For savings goals (goals that require you to save money like retirement investing, placing a down payment on a home, or taking a vacation), use a savings calculator such as the one on Bankrate.com or ShooJimmyChoo. com to determine the amount you'll need to put aside each month. You can't calculate the monthly payments on these goals like you did with the getting-out-of-debt targets because of interest. Since your savings and investments are earning interest (and if they're not, well, ladies, keep reading this book!), the monthly amount you actually need to save might be less than you think. For example, if twenty-five-year-old Jane wants to have $1 million upon her retirement at age sixty-five, she won't have to literally put $1 million in the bank. In fact, if she puts $300 per month into her retirement account until she retires (assuming an 8 percent interest rate, which is pretty standard on long-term retirement accounts), she'll be a millionaire at age sixty-five even though she's contributed only $144,000!

TIP: *Remember that your strategies for accomplishing your goals need to be as specific as possible. As in, "I will have $100 automatically deducted from my checking account each month and sent directly to my Roth IRA at Charles Schwab." If you don't outline both the amount of money you need and your strategies for accumulating it very specifically, you know you'll let something slip. (Yes, ladies, you will let your savings slip, the same way you justify "just a few Oreos" when you're on a diet—by telling yourself that it won't hurt "just this one time." But when is it ever "just this one time?")*

You will need to update your strategies each year or whenever you have a life event that affects your finances. For example, you now may be focused on paying off your credit card debt. But once you do pay it off, you'll have more money to start working on other goals. This will mean that you'll need to update your strategies to reflect this new financial situation.

Now look at the Sample Financial Goals Chart on pages 20–21, and then create your own chart using the worksheet on pages 22–23.

Sample Financial Goals Chart
January 1, 2010

GOAL	TOTAL COST OR SAVINGS NEEDED	TIMING (Number of months until I achieve goal)	
Get out of credit card debt Specifically, pay off MasterCard (balance $1,000; interest rate 18 percent) and Visa (balance $2,000; interest rate 15 percent) in full by January 1, 2011.	$3,190 (includes interest owed)	12	
Save for retirement Specifically, save enough money so I can retire at age sixty-five and still enjoy the same standard of living that I now enjoy.	$1,000,000	480 (That's forty years.)	
Have an emergency savings fund Save enough to live comfortably for six months with no job.	$18,000	36	
Buy a home Save up for a down payment so I can buy a two-bedroom apartment in Marietta in the next five years.	$33,000	60	

Total Needed Each Month to Achieve Goals (Year 1): $340 per month

MONTHLY AMOUNT NEEDED TO ACHIEVE GOAL (Include specific dollar amounts—as in, "I will put away $_____ each month to achieve this goal.")	WHERE TO GET HELP
Set up automatic bill pay from my checking account each month in the following amounts: Each month, from January 2010—April 2010, pay: $250 on MasterCard, $50 on Visa. In May, pay: $25 on Mastercard and $275 on Visa. By June, the MasterCard will be paid off so: Each month, from June 2010—December 2010, pay: $300 on Visa (in month of December will only owe remaining balance).	**Online help:** Visit Bankrate.com for a variety of debt calculators including the Real Cost of Debt calculator that will help you calculate the total cost of debt and the monthly payments needed to pay off that debt. **In this book:** See Chapter 5. A good strategy for dealing with credit card debt is to pay the maximum amount you can afford on the highest-interest card and the minimums on the other cards each month on time until all are paid off.
Automatic withdrawal from my paycheck of $40 (the amount my employer will match) into my 401(k). Secondary goal: Once I have paid off my credit card debt (in one year) and have saved at least ½ of my emergency fund, I will contribute $300 each month to my Roth IRA via automatic bill pay. (Note: The monthly amount needed must take into account the interest you will accrue.)	**Online help:** Use the retirement calculator on AARP.org to figure out how much you'll need for retirement. **In this book:** See Chapter 9. If your employer matches your 401(k) contributions you should contribute, even if you have a bunch of debt to pay off.
After I pay off my credit card debt and put up to what my employer will match in my 401(k), I will set up automatic transfers of $474.95 into my ING savings account each month (assumes a 3.5 percent interest rate on savings).	**Online help:** Visit Bankrate.com for a savings calculator. **In this book:** See Chapter 11.
After I pay off my credit card debt and save for my emergency fund and retirement each month, I will set up automatic transfers of $505.08 per month into a money market account (assumes a 3.5 percent interest rate on savings).	**Online help:** A down payment is usually up to about 20 percent of the purchase price of the home. You'll want to search online to find home prices in your area. You'll also need to save for closing costs and a few other costs. Visit Bankrate.com for a savings calculator. **In this book:** See Chapter 13.

You can find financial calculators on ShooJimmyChoo.com.

Financial Goals Chart
Date: _____

GOAL (Remember that if you are in high interest debt, paying that off needs to top your list, followed by building up an emergency fund, saving for retirement, and buying a home.)	TOTAL COST OR SAVINGS NEEDED

Total Dollar Amount Needed Each Month to Achieve Goals: _____

TIMING (Number of months until I achieve goal)	MONTHLY AMOUNT NEEDED TO ACHIEVE GOAL (Include specific dollar amounts—as in, "I will put away $_____ each month to achieve this goal.")

As you read through this book and learn more about your financial goals and strategies for achieving them, you will revise the Financial Goals Chart, so complete it in pencil. But don't skip this step just because you'll make revisions later. It's still important to start with some goals now. Setting goals keeps you motivated and focused. And, ladies, you know you're going to need that focus and motivation. You need something to distract you when you pass that adorable little shift dress in the window at H&M. You need to be able to ask yourself "House or dress?" and then answer "House!" and keep on walking. Set these goals, and keep them in mind as you follow the advice in this book.

Workin' the Web

Want to learn more about managing your money? Check out these Web sites for help with everything from debt management to retirement to your career.

1. CateyHill.com

My personal Web site, featuring links to cool features and articles (and the occasional sample sale tip for those of you who have been saving!), my blog, and more. If you'd like to ask me a question or send me a comment, click on the "Contact" link on CateyHill.com.

2. ShooJimmyChoo.com

The official site of Shoo, Jimmy Choo!, complete with financial calculators, money management tips, and more to help you spend less and save more.

3. Bankrate.com

This comprehensive personal finance site includes news, advice, and financial calculators related to home equity, investing, autos, debt management, insurance, and more.

4. FiLife.com

FiLife.com is devoted to improving your entire family's

financial situation. This site includes information and advice about budgeting, banking, insurance, debt, and more.

5. **Mint.com**
A free online budgeting and money management site that will help you get your budget in shape in no time at all.

Other sites that are worth checking out: CNNMoney.com for the latest money news and personal finance guides; Kiplinger.com, SmartMoney.com, and Fool.com for solid personal finance advice; MsMoney.com, LearnVest.com, and GoGirlFinance.com for women-centric money and career advice. Also, check out WiseBread.com for a list of the top personal finance blogs.

PART II:

(Spending) Style

AN INTRODUCTION TO YOUR SPENDING STYLE (AND WHY IT MAY BE *SO LAST SEASON*)

Why have your efforts to get yourself out of debt and build up savings not worked? You've seen the advice, listened to your friends, and still, chunky bangles and skinny jeans beckon you from that gleaming store window. Savings, retirement plans—these just aren't you. You're more of a closet-stuffed-with-shoes, love-to-eat-out, can't-resist-a-sale kind of girl. Okay, I realize most of you aren't this extreme, but can you really tell me—with a straight face—that your spending doesn't get a little out of hand, at least some of the time?

So you spend a little much sometimes. You love your latte in the morning, your *Vogue* on a Saturday afternoon, your happy hour drinks with the girls. What's the big deal? Ladies, if you ever want to get rid of your boss, forever—no more hiding your computer screen for fear that the boss will realize your obsession with Perez Hilton; no more late night, coffee-fueled briefs; no more 7 a.m., oh-lord-I'm-so-hung-over wake-up calls—you're going to need to start saving for retirement. If you ever want to buy a house, stop paying astronomical interest on your credit card, have a big in-case-of-emergency or in-case-I-get-fired-for-arriving-late-again fund, you are going to have to save. And to save more, most of you will have to spend less. To reiterate, *for most of you, the first step to getting out of debt and/or saving for your goals is to spend less.*

So that's what Part II of this book will address—first, figuring out what you spend money on and why, and then determining how you can spend less. I'll show you why you "needed" that chocolate suede mini and the stacked Louboutins to match, why you "deserved" that mani-pedi when you finished that brief at the office. Then I'm going to show you how to stop "needing" these things so much. (I know, you're thinking it's going to take electroshock therapy to rid you of your spending urges, but I can assure you, it's nothing that drastic.) Part II delivers everything you need to know about your current spending style, from what you buy to why you buy it, and then tackles how to change this style into something truly fabulous—a spending style that will help you meet your financial goals from pages 22–23.

Basically, controlling your spending for good is like trying to lose weight for good—you'll never be able to do it unless you know how and why you eat. Think of all those weight-loss gurus you've seen on *Oprah*. They all say the same thing: You have to deal with your core issues before you'll ever successfully lose weight and keep it off.

It's the same thing with spending. You have to get to the root of why you spend. Until you confront the inner demons that drive you to designer shoes, you'll never be able to get yourself out of debt and begin saving.

There is no one-size-fits-all solution, and that's why all the advice you've seen in the past, all the budget guidance, has all failed. It's like shoes and dresses: No matter how hard you try, one size simply does not fit all. That's why I'm going to show you how to determine your unique spending style and then alter it in two easy steps.

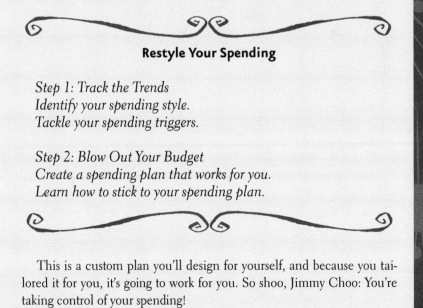

Restyle Your Spending

Step 1: Track the Trends
Identify your spending style.
Tackle your spending triggers.

Step 2: Blow Out Your Budget
Create a spending plan that works for you.
Learn how to stick to your spending plan.

This is a custom plan you'll design for yourself, and because you tailored it for you, it's going to work for you. So shoo, Jimmy Choo: You're taking control of your spending!

CHAPTER 3

Take on the Trends

How to Track Down the Demons That Drive
You to Designer Shoes

You have a fashion style all your own. Remember that fabulous day when you paired the leg warmers with your vintage '80s mini before anyone else caught on to the trend? Or how you revamped last season's little black dress by pairing it with this season's burgundy patent-leather flats? Well, it's not just your fashion choices that give you a distinct style; it's also your spending choices—what I call your spending style.

But no matter how un-fabulous it may turn out to be, it is crucial that you determine your unique spending style, as it's the first step toward controlling your spending and moving toward financial security. This chapter will help you do just that. It's going to do with your spending what you already do with your wardrobe—take on the trends with gusto, tossing the ones that just don't work for you, transforming others so they do. First, it will guide you through how to track the trends in your spending, from how much you spend to what triggers you to spend, and develop a solid blueprint—your own personal style guide—of your spending. Then, it will give you tips on how to turn those questionable trends on their head—and make them work for you.

I know some of you out there think you have your spending under control already. You think that you don't spend that much money—I mean, *you* don't buy too many clothes, *you* don't eat out at every meal—but I can almost guarantee you that there are items you can cut out (and not miss too much). So keep reading. After all, it's likely that you'll close this chapter with the realization that your former spending style was *so last season.* And that's one style error you don't want to make! So let's get started.

IDENTIFY YOUR UNIQUE SPENDING STYLE

To understand your spending style—what you spend money on and what triggers you to spend—I'm going to have you keep a spending diary. But before I get into how to do that, you need a lingo lowdown: definitions of a few terms that will help you understand your spending habits. I know you thought you were finished learning finance terms when you passed Economics sophomore year, but bear with me. Just keep your eye on the prize—that cute little house you're going to buy or that fabulous vacay you're going to save for—and learning these terms won't be so bad.

Lingo Lowdown

There are two types of expenses you will be tracking as you determine your spending style: necessities and discretionary expenses. The latter is broken into two categories for easier tracking. Here is how the categories work:

Necessities
These are expenses necessary to living or loans/debts that you can't get out of.

- Rent/mortgage
- Insurance (medical, dental, vision, homeowners/renters, etc.)
- Taxes
- Automobile (loan payments, insurance, gas, regular maintenance) or transportation (for example, bus or subway passes)
- Credit card debt payments
- Other debt payments

- Student loans
- Other loans (i.e., home equity loans)
- Retirement savings
- Investments
- Savings
- Utilities (electricity, gas, heat, water, phone, TV/Internet)
- Phone
- Child support
- Alimony
- Groceries
- Medical expenses

Discretionary expenses
These are expenses that are not part of your basic needs, things like clothing/accessories, beauty products, eating out, fitness, hobbies, subscriptions, pets, toiletries, gifts, and dry cleaning. To help you track these expenses, I'm going to divide them into two basic categories.

- **Day-to-day discretionary expenses.** These are categories of expenses that you buy pretty frequently, usually *at least weekly or once every few weeks.* Examples may include eating out/snacks, clothing/accessories, beauty (hair products, makeup, nail polish), pets (food, grooming), household (candles, cleaning supplies), and entertainment (movies, magazines, books, bars/drinks).
- **Incidental discretionary expenses.** These are items that you purchase fairly infrequently, *usually only once per month or less,* and tend to be more expensive than the items in your day-to-day expenses. For example, vacations, gym memberships, TV and Internet, haircuts and highlights for your hair, holiday gifts. (I know, you might not consider highlights an incidental expense since you *cannot* deal with mousey brown hair, but they really do fall into this category.)

See, only three terms and they were pretty painless. There may be some overlap between these expenses. That's okay. The goal of this exercise is not to figure out every single thing you've ever and will ever spend money on. It's to make you aware of big categories that your spending falls into.

To track each of these types of expenses, you'll need to do the following:

- Write down all the necessities you spend money on each month, such as rent, utilities, et cetera, as well as the motivation or emotion behind a purchase, and other relevant information. You'll find instructions and charts that will help you track your necessities on pages 34–35 and 36–37 and on ShooJimmyChoo.com.
- Keep a spending diary for one to two weeks to help identify the "little things" (i.e., day-to-day discretionary expenses) you spend money on and the emotion, motivation, and other relevant information for each. You'll find details on how to do this in the next section, as well as a sample spending diary and a blank spending diary for you to fill in on pages 36–37 and on ShooJimmyChoo.com.
- Write down all the incidentals you spend money on, such as a vacation, highlights, gym membership, et cetera, as well as the emotion, motivation, and other relevant information behind each purchase. The information and charts on pages 34–35 and 36–37 and on ShooJimmyChoo.com will help you track your incidentals.

Track Day-to-Day Discretionary Expenses

To determine all the little things that you buy (i.e., your discretionary day-to-day expenses) and why you buy them, you will need to keep a spending diary for at least a week, writing down everything you purchase as well as the emotion, motivation, and other relevant information for the purchase. Choose a typical week—not the week you are on vacation, for example. It's better to do this for two weeks, but I know that might be asking just a little too much. You do have a life outside of your finances after all. The blank diary on pages 36–37 will help you do this. For now, don't track necessities or incidental expenses. So if during this week you pay your rent or another bill that qualifies as a necessity, don't worry about including it in this chart. Just concentrate on day-to-day spending.

How to fill in the diary

This spending diary will track everything you spend money on *and* whom you were with, your mood, and anything you feel is relevant to that spending. If you lend your girlfriend fifty cents so she can get some gum, insert it into the calendar. Then write the emotion or motivation behind the purchase or action. For example: "Lent Susie 50 cents, felt obligated to give it to her." If you need that 75-cent Snickers from the vending machine for your 4 p.m. sugar fix, put it into the calendar: "75-cent Snickers, famished and bored at 4 p.m., boss gave me nothing to do today." Or, if you buy a gorgeous pashmina when you are feeling crappy, your emotion/motivation might be: "Retail therapy. Felt like crap after Heather got a promotion. At least now I look better than her." The emotion/motivation box should include anything you feel relevant to the purchase, from the people you were with to your mood.

This spending diary is key to helping you understand what you personally spend money on and why you spend it. So don't skip this step! You may think you know all those little things you spend money on, but believe me when I tell you, you probably don't. (No one *needs* to spend hundreds of dollars a year on mani-pedis.) Controlling spending is the key to achieving those financial goals, so bear with me.

If this sounds intimidating, keep in mind it's just one week (or two, if you can manage). Remember that time you didn't eat bread for a week? Or when you actually made it to the gym every day by 7 a.m. for the full week before spring break started? Compared to that, this will be a cinch.

How the Spending Diary Can Change Your (Financial) Life

Maybe you're feeling a little skeptical about this whole spending diary thing, telling yourself that it's not that important to do. Maybe you think you have a solid handle on your pocketbook and simply don't need to keep a spending diary.

Tsk, tsk, ladies. I've heard these excuses before (and yes, that's exactly what they are—excuses!—just like the little lies you tell yourself about why you have to wait to start your exercise plan, why you need a new dress and shoes to match, and why you can't live without La Mer). And guess what? I'm so over these excuses! Almost every single one of you could benefit from keeping a spending diary, and to prove it to you, I've collected a few testimonials from my girlfriends who did just that—and changed their financial lives forever.

"Well, to be honest, I wasn't sure it would do anything. I'm not a crazy spender. But it actually did a lot. When I looked back at the diary after two weeks, I realized how much little stuff adds up! I was spending way too much on crap that I didn't even need. And once I saw that—how much the trips to the Coke machine and to Duane Reade and other stuff like that were costing me—I cut it way down. From just changing those little behaviors, I'm saving more than $600 per year at this point. And you know what? I really don't miss that stuff very much at all."—Alex

"At first, I was kind of dreading being one of Catey's 'spending diary guinea pigs' when she was writing this book. It seemed like a giant pain in the butt. I'm so glad I just sucked it up and kept the diary. Turns out, I had a mean going-out-to-lunch habit, which I knew, but what I didn't realize was just how much it was costing me. This, combined with ridiculous Friday and Saturday nights out, was draining my bank account. You know, I knew all of this was happening, but I didn't fully realize how much money was flying out the door. When the evidence of the cost of all this was in front of my face, I made a promise to myself to cut back, and I have. Yeah, I still do those things, I sometimes still spend too much, but that spending diary opened my eyes. I have spent so much less recently because of it."—Lee

"It was enlightening. You think you know yourself, you think you know what you buy. But wait until it's all sitting on a sheet in front of you. It shocked me how much it all added up to. Now I am so much more aware when I spend money."—Sarah

Sample Day-to-Day Discretionary Expenses Chart

DAY	TIME	ITEM BOUGHT	AMOUNT SPENT	CATEGORY	
MONDAY	8 a.m.	Coffee and muffin	$4	Food/Drink	
	12 p.m.	Lunch	$12	Food/Drink	
	4 p.m.	Snickers	$1	Food/Drink	
	7 p.m.	Dinner and drinks	$45	Food/Drink	
TUESDAY	8 a.m.	Coffee	$2	Food/Drink	
	10 a.m.	Bagel	$3	Food/Drink	
	3 p.m.	Diet Coke and banana	$2	Food/Drink	
	6 p.m.	US Weekly	$4	Entertainment	
WEDNESDAY	8 a.m.	Coffee and muffin	$4	Food/Drink	
	12 p.m.	New shoes	$40	Clothing/accessories	
	4 p.m.	Chinese takeout	$11	Food/Drink	
THURSDAY	8 a.m.	Coffee	$2	Food/Drink	
	12 p.m.	Lunch	$11	Food/Drink	
	1 p.m.	Makeup	$12	Beauty	
	7 p.m.	Dinner, drinks (and more drinks)	$120	Food/Drink	
FRIDAY	8 a.m.	Coffee and muffin	$4	Food/Drink	
	12 p.m.	Dinner and drinks	$65	Food/Drink	
SATURDAY	12 p.m.	Brunch	$15	Food/Drink	
	3 p.m.	Mani-pedi	$35	Beauty	
SUNDAY	10 a.m.	Breakfast	$25	Food/Drink	
	12 p.m.	Clothes	$75	Clothing/accessories	
	7 p.m.	Movie	$10	Entertainment	

Total Weekly Spending: $502
Estimated Yearly Spending: $26,104 ($502 X 52 weeks)

MOTIVATION/EMOTION	CAN SPENDING BE REDUCED?
Need coffee in a.m. Am a monster without it.	Yes
Went with Jill. She had some great office gossip so we went out.	Yes
Afternoon starvation. My lunch was tiny.	Yes
Met up with Katie and Susie. Wanted company after crappy workday.	Yes
Need it in the morning, bad.	Yes
Need it to tide me over until lunch.	Yes
Starving, forgot to eat lunch.	Yes
Couldn't resist the cover—Eva is preggers!	Yes
Need it in the morning, bad.	Yes
Boring day. Killed time by shopping during lunch.	Yes
Too tired to cook.	Yes
Need it in the morning, bad.	Yes
Forgot to bring my lunch, again.	Yes
Crappy day, boss yelled at me. I look like crap so got some new makeup.	Yes
Felt obligated to meet the girls. Somehow dropped $120!	Yes
Need it in the morning, bad.	Yes
Dinner and clubbing! Didn't spend too much money—that new lip gloss made me look hot and the boys were buying.	Yes
So hungover, dying, needed greasy breakfast.	Yes
Still feel like crap; have date tonight so need mani-pedi, at very least.	Yes
Awesome date. I bought us breakfast since he paid for everything last night.	Yes
Shopping with Jill, caught her up on my date, bought outfit for next date.	Yes
Met sister for a movie, was so tired but felt obligated to go since haven't seen her in a week.	Yes

Day-to-Day Discretionary Expenses Chart

DAY	TIME	ITEM BOUGHT	AMOUNT SPENT	CATEGORY	
MONDAY					
TUESDAY					
WEDNESDAY					
THURSDAY					
FRIDAY					
SATURDAY					
SUNDAY					

Total Weekly Spending: $_____ (Add up the "Amount Spent" column)
Estimated Yearly Spending: $_____ (Multiply weekly spending by 52)

	MOTIVATION/EMOTION	CAN SPENDING BE REDUCED?

How many times have you told your man, "Honey, it's the little things that matter"? How he takes out the trash without you having to ask him, how he gives you a kiss when you come in the door? Well, girl, you need to learn to practice what you preach, because you're right—it is the little things that matter. And they matter big time to the fine folks at American Express.

I'm sure you noticed from your spending diary that little things really do add up. But just in case that didn't sink in, let me take a minute to show you. Let's say you buy one fashion magazine a week on impulse. You are wasting:

> $4 per week
> $208 per year
> $1,040 over five years

Yes, fashion magazines can be a waste, when you simply don't have the money for them, that is. I know you think you need to know about the latest Theory blouse, but you don't need to pay to know about it. Remember that thing called the Internet—your BFF when you need to procrastinate at work? Well, it houses about a million fashion Web sites overflowing with incredible Theory blouses and tips on just how to wear them. Try that route, because throwing away just $4 per week on those magazines (or similar items) adds up. And that's just $4 a week. I know that when you checked out your financial diary, you saw more than $4 a week of waste.

Let's say you waste $50 per week on items you don't need:

> $4 latte before work (you "needed" it—you're a monster without coffee)
> $4 magazine
> $3 nail polish (you "needed" to have it, you had a date)
> $6 lunch on the go from the office
> $5 snacks from the vending machine at work
> $2 muffin to tide you over until dinner
> $8 adorable gold bangles (you "had" to have them, they match your earrings)
> $2 lent to Ellen (its only $2 so you won't remember to ask for it back)
> $7 coffee and muffin with Lisa
> $9 drink after work (the day was rough, you "needed" it)

TOTAL: $50 per week

About $200 per month (depending on the actual length of the month)
$2,600 per year
$13,000 over five years

That's right, ladies: Wasting just $50 a week (and see how easy that money went?: no huge purchases, nothing that extravagant), will cost you $13,000 over the next five years. If you had put that money ($2,600 each year for five years for a total of $13,000) into some kind of interest-bearing account (let's say with a 4.5 percent annual interest rate), you would end up with more than $14,500. That's right, $1,500 plus for sitting on your butt, living like you usually do, and just letting your money sit there. So you can lose $13,000, or pad your bottom line with $14,500. It seems like a simple choice to me.

Pinpoint Incidental Discretionary Spending

Now it's time to track your incidental discretionary expenses, which are those items that you purchase fairly infrequently (usually only once per month or less) and that tend to be more expensive than the items in your day-to-day expenses.

To do this, I want you to think through your spending over the last year. Go back through your credit card statements and bank statements. Think about discretionary items that the day-to-day spending diary would not have caught: things like vacations, beauty (haircuts/color, facials), fitness (gym membership), gifts (birthday, holiday presents for friends and family), and big clothing purchases (such as a new winter coat).

Estimate the yearly cost of these items. Then break this out so it's a fixed amount per month. So if you took one vacation in June that cost $1,100, in the monthly column you'd insert $92 ($1,100 ÷ 12 months). This monthly column will help you budget. You will also want to look at the motivation/emotion, category, and timing of each expense. On a separate sheet of paper, you should make note of any items you expect to change in the coming year. For example, incidental discretionary expenses that you anticipate having in the coming year but that were not reflected in this chart or items that you will no longer spend money on.

Sample Incidental Discretionary Expenses Chart

ITEM	COST PER MONTH	YEARLY COST	MOTIVATION/EMOTION	
Gym	$105	$1,260	Had to get in shape so I signed up. Never go though.	
Gifts	$200	$2,400	Christmas presents for family and friends.	
Hair cut/color	$200 (I get this done every two months for $400, so I put it in here as $200 per month.)	$2,400	Am so picky about my having the perfect highlights; key to my look. Could shop around though.	
Vacation	$92 (I went on one vacation; it cost $1,100. Divide that by twelve months and you get roughly $92 per month.)	$1,100	I deserve a nice vacation once a year. I work really hard! Could go somewhere less expensive though.	
Major clothing purchases	$200	$2,400	New winter coat—$200 New tote—$200 Diamond studs—$2,000	

Total Yearly Incidentals: $9,560

CATEGORY	COULD YOU SPEND LESS?	TIMING—WHEN THIS PURCHASE OCCURS
Fitness/health	Yes	Monthly
Gifts	Yes	November and December
Beauty	Yes	Every other month
Entertainment	Yes	June
Clothing/Accessories	Yes	Coat—October Tote—May Diamonds—January

Incidental Discretionary Expenses Chart

ITEM	COST PER MONTH	YEARLY COST	MOTIVATION/EMOTION

Total Yearly Incidentals: $_____

Monitor Your Necessities

Most of your money probably goes to necessities like rent, bills, and debt payments. Write down how much you spend on these necessities. The blank diary on pages 46–47 is a great way to do this. Also, see the sample diary on pages 40–41. For a list of sample necessities, see pages 44–45.

Once again, you will also be looking at the motivation/emotion, category, and timing of each expense. So once you have written down all your necessities, identify items that you could spend less on. For example, can you get a less expensive cell phone plan? To reduce your rent, can you get a roommate or move into a less swanky neighborhood? Then analyze the motivation/emotion behind your spending in these categories. For example, let's say you have a lovely apartment, but you

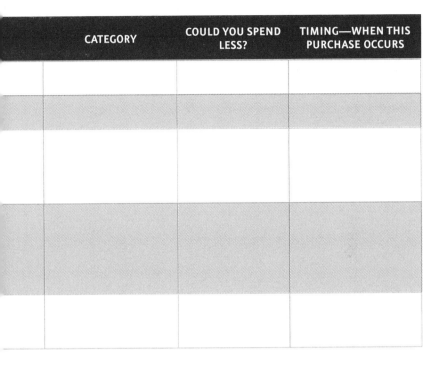

CATEGORY	COULD YOU SPEND LESS?	TIMING—WHEN THIS PURCHASE OCCURS

could live in a less expensive place. Why do you feel the need to spend so much on rent? Is it to impress others? Why do you need a lavish vacation? Do you feel that you deserve it? It might be hard to figure out a motivation/emotion for every item on your list, but try to do it if you can. Write down all of this information in the spending chart on pages 46–47—no judgment, yet.

As you fill in the Necessities Chart, for those items not billed to you monthly, try to figure out the monthly cost. For example, if your car insurance is $600 every six months (that's $1,200 per year), write in $100 per month ($1,200 ÷ 12).

Sample Necessities Chart

ITEM	COST PER MONTH	YEARLY COST	MOTIVATION/ EMOTION	
Rent/mortgage	$1,500	$18,000	Wanted to live in an amazing neighborhood near all my friends.	
Renters/homeowners insurance	$25	$300		
Electricity	$60 (January)	$720	Necessity. Could turn off the lights more.	
Heat	N/A—Landlord pays			
Water	N/A—Landlord pays			
Gas	N/A—Landlord pays			
Cable/Internet	$170	$2,040	Love to come home and watch movies. Takes my mind off the day, so have whole movie package.	
Home phone	N/A—Have only a cell phone			
Cell phone	$60	$720	Don't use all the minutes though since I mostly talk at night.	
Internet	See above			
Car payment/public transportation pass	$75	$900	Must ride subway; no way out of fee.	
Car insurance	N/A—Have no car			
Health, dental, and disability insurance	$65	$780	Get it through work; no cheaper plan.	
Other insurance	N/A			
Student loans	$145	$1,740		
Debt payments	$213	$2,556	Still paying off old credit card debt. No way out of it. Am paying as much as I can.	
Groceries	$200	$2,400	Often go a little crazy at the store getting many organic foods or trying the latest diet craze.	
Investments and savings	N/A			

Total Monthly Cost of Neccessities: $2,513
Total Yearly Cost of Neccessities: $30,156

	COULD YOU SPEND LESS?	IF THE BILL IS NOT A FIXED AMOUNT, NOTE MONTHS WHEN BILL WILL BE SIGNIFICANTLY DIFFERENT (i.e., electric bill higher in June, July, and August because of A/C)
	Yes	
	No	
	Yes	
	Yes	
	Yes	
	No	
	No	
	No	
	No	
	Yes	

Necessities Chart

ITEM	COST PER MONTH	YEARLY COST	MOTIVATION/ EMOTION	
Rent/mortgage				
Renters/homeowners insurance				
Electric				
Heat				
Water				
Gas				
Cable				
Home phone				
Cell phone				
Internet				
Car payment/public transportation pass				
Car insurance				
Health insurance				
Other insurance (list separately)				
Loans (list separately)				
Debt payments (list separately)				
Groceries				
Investments and savings (list separately)				

Total Monthly Cost of Neccessities: $_____
Total Yearly Cost of Neccessities: $_____

COULD YOU SPEND LESS?	IF THE BILL IS NOT A FIXED AMOUNT, NOTE MONTHS WHEN BILL WILL BE SIGNIFICANTLY DIFFERENT (i.e., electric bill higher in June, July, and August because of A/C)

HIGH ON STILETTOS: IDENTIFY YOUR SPENDING TRIGGERS

Now that you've filled in these spending diaries, it's time to identify your "spending triggers": factors that cause this unnecessary spending. This can be a time or day when you tend to spend a lot, certain people that seem to cause you to spend, or a mood that makes you want to shop. Maybe after a few drinks with the girls your credit card seems to jump out of your wallet ("Dinner's on me!"). Maybe in the morning before you've had your coffee, you just say, "Screw it, I need a treat." Maybe you shop when you've had a bad day. Maybe getting new shoes gives you a high (you know, the "stiletto high"—it's what you got when you slipped your little feet into those patent-leather Prada heels last year, and then had to buy them).

Look, ladies, you don't need Mr. Blahnik to help you deal with your boyfriend dumping you, and you don't need Paper Denim jeans to make you feel better about eating that extra slice of cake. (Yes, they do perk up your tush, but they also perk up Mr. MasterCard). Your morning macchiato is not a necessity, despite your boyfriend's exclamations to the contrary (yeah, I know, you've snapped at him pre-coffee one too many times). Your triggers—guilt, sadness, impulsiveness, whatever—are *not* helping your financial situation. And to improve this situation, you're going to need to understand what your spending triggers are.

This section will help you do that by providing a guideline for different types of spending triggers. To develop these categories, I talked to a lot of my girlfriends and found more spending triggers than I could count. But I narrowed them down to a few basic trends. Most of you will probably exhibit spending habits that embody a few of these patterns, so don't try to pigeonhole yourself into one. Just use these as a framework to help you see where your spending weaknesses are.

Emotional Spenders (ES)

You are an emotional spender if certain moods are your big spending trigger. You spend when you are happy/depressed/lonely/(insert emotion). Buying new stuff makes you feel better.

Take Sarah, for example. Last Saturday morning she had a huge fight with her boyfriend over the dishes. She felt like he wasn't doing his part around the house. Of course, this escalated into a gigantic drag-out fight. What does Sarah want to do to make herself feel better? Go shopping, of course.

Impulsive Spenders (IS)

You are an impulsive spender if you frequently buy on the spur of the moment without really thinking through why/if you need it. You weren't planning on getting something new, but you just "had to have the dress."

This is Cara. She passes by Bloomie's and sees in the window this outrageous, orange crocodile bag. "I have to stop here," she exclaims. "I love it, no one has this bag!" And despite the hefty price tag and the fact that this is completely impractical and doesn't match anything in her closet, she buys it. And this happens with her frequently.

Compulsive Spenders (CS)

If you are a compulsive spender, you spend all the time. You always have to have the newest/trendiest/best quality/coolest things. Buying gives you a high, every time you do it. Basically, compulsive spenders are shopping addicts. They just spend, spend, spend despite mounting credit card debt.

Take Lauren, for example. She has a six-figure salary and an amazing wardrobe—hundreds of handbags, a roomful of shoes, the best lingerie collection in the city—but creditors are constantly calling her house. She buys all the time: during her lunch break, after work, on weekends. She spends thousand of dollars a month on items she doesn't need and can't afford.

Absentminded Spenders (AS)

Absentminded spenders don't really pay attention to what they're buying. If you're an absentminded spender, you probably get your credit card bill and wonder, "How the heck did I spend that much? I didn't even buy anything." Almost all of you are probably absentminded spenders to some degree. You pick up a new nail polish at the drug store or a new top at the mall, and you don't think about it.

This is Katy's problem. She swears she doesn't buy anything—"I'm not like Lauren, always shopping." But somehow her bank account always seems to end up at zero right before payday. Katy doesn't spend her money mindfully. She'll grab a quick lunch and not think about it, or snag a few packs of gum she doesn't need at the checkout counter, and eventually it all adds up.

Social Spenders (SS)

These girls spend big when they're in a social setting; for example, around friends (or maybe just one friend in particular) or on dates. Perhaps you just can't say no to extravagant dinners with the girls, or one of your girlfriends always seems to get you to buy new shoes. Your spending occurs primarily in social situations.

Jen is an SS. She's pretty thrifty at home, buys the discount brands at the grocery store, and remembers to turn off the lights before she leaves the apartment, but as soon as she's with her girlfriends, it's a whole new story. A $200 blouse seems like a necessity—after all, it does make her look like she's lost ten pounds. A $30 brunch is nonnegotiable—how will she deal with her hangover without her girlfriends, brioche French toast, and several espressos?

"It's on Sale" Spenders (ISS)

You can't resist a sale. Shopping is like a sport for you. If you see a good deal, you can't just pass on by. Even though you don't really need an item, you tell yourself, "It's such a great deal."

Brandy has a closet full of items she doesn't wear, and nearly every one of them was on sale and "such a great deal" that she just had to have it. No matter how many times I tell her, "It's not a great deal if you never wear it," she doesn't seem to get it.

Reward Spenders (RS)

These spenders tell themselves, "I deserve this because I finished a project, had a hard week, did really well on a task . . ." You get the picture. If you're a reward spender, you reward yourself with stuff. When you finish the brief for the firm, when you go to the gym four days in a row, when you have a rough day, you buy something. Why? Because "you deserve it."

Lisa fits the RS profile to a T. Nearly every weekend she's at the spa. It's her reward for working so hard. She buys herself sweets when she's had a hard day. Buying things is how she treats herself, and it has gotten a bit out of hand.

Spenders by Category (SC)

If you're an SC, you can't resist certain types of things. You pass by the manicurist and you cannot say no to the allure of perfect nails (the Spender on Beauty), or you have to try the latest restaurant (the Spender on Food).

I am a coffee addict. Caffeine just makes me feel, well, normal. I'm pretty sure I used to keep that Starbucks near me in business. Pumpkin spice latte, caramel macchiato, here I came! And this was despite the fact that I had not one, but two, coffeemakers in my apartment. So, before I discovered the benefit of making my own coffee each morning, I would've classified myself as a Spender on Food, Specifically Coffee.

EMPOWERED BY YOUR SPENDING TRIGGERS

These are just broad spending triggers. You may be a mix of many types, or you may fit into one. But, the point is, you need to identify what triggers you to spend—whether it's emotions, specific people, the time of day, the weather, whatever. Let's look at the sample spending diaries, so that you can get a better idea of how to identify spending triggers.

Looking at the day-to-day discretionary expenses on pages 40–41, it looks like the woman who filled in the diary, let's call her Julie, is primarily a combination of a Social Spender (SS), an Emotional Spender (ES), and an Absentminded Spender (AS). She spends when she's with friends, when she's having a bad day or feeling guilty, and when she isn't really thinking about it. In looking at the incidentals chart, it looks like Julie is also a Reward Spender (RS)—she treats herself to a nice vacation—and a Spender by Category; beauty, fitness, clothing—she spends a lot on items such as haircuts, clothing/accessories, and a gym membership to make herself look better.

As you can see, Julie has a variety of spending triggers. So to help curb her spending, Julie should write down what these are: 1) friends, especially Jill (SS), 2) guilt (ES), 3) boredom (ES), 4) not paying attention (AS), 5) when I feel that I deserve it (RS), 6) stress (ES), 7) beauty (SC). Now Julie should rank these. Which triggers make her spend the most?

Knowledge is power—just knowing that these triggers exist will help Julie prepare for them. So if Julie is feeling stressed, she can know to avoid going shopping—she might buy something she really doesn't need! Now give this a try. Identify and rank your spending triggers, and write them in the following chart.

Spending Triggers Chart

SPENDING TRIGGER (Ranked from the trigger that makes you spend the most to the one that makes you spend the least.)	DETAILS (Note specifics about the trigger. For example, if you're a social spender and a certain person is the trigger, note that.)

Tips for Overcoming Your Spending Triggers

You've mapped out all your triggers. Now you need to make actual changes in your spending behavior. These tips will help you understand how to overcome the trigger situations.

First, for all you Spenders by Category—the foodie who is addicted to sampling the nuances of Asian fusion cuisine throughout the city, the fashionista whose name every salesgirl at Bloomingdale's knows, and all the rest of you (you know who you are!)—here are a few tips to help you curb spending in your category of weakness.

Foodies

If too much of your money goes to food, these tips are for you:

- Bust out the pots and pans that are gathering dust in your kitchen. Pots and pans: You know, those black Teflon things in the back of your cabinet that your mom gave you for your birthday. Use them to cook, instead of going out.
- Snack before you go out to eat and then just order an inexpensive appetizer. Added benefit: You'll probably drop a few pounds along the way.
- When you go out with friends, don't offer to split the bill evenly if you had less than everyone else. I know, you don't want to be that girl. But think of how much more depressing it will be when you're forty and living with your parents because you spent all your money on someone else's red wine and Gruyère.
- Plan your grocery list (with your financial situation in mind) before you are at the store.
- Don't grocery shop or go out to dinner famished. This usually means excessive eating or buying, otherwise known as: Hoover syndrome—an unfortunate condition that compels you to suck down all the food in sight.

Fashionistas and social butterflies

If too much of your money goes to entertainment and clothes, it's simple. You are going to have to cut back. Here are a few great ways to do it:

- Start by limiting the number of times you go shopping or go out. Go shopping only when you need something, and go out only when the activity sounds like you'll really enjoy it. I swear to you, staying home one Saturday night a month will not kill you. And spending a Sunday without a giant hangover is actually kind of nice. Also consider entertaining at home (house party!).

- The Post-it note trick: Wrap your credit cards in a Post-it note that says "Do I really need this?" This is your own personal mom-in-a-wallet—always there to point out what you shouldn't be doing.
- Shop around: Go to less expensive bars, restaurants, and stores; check around for a better deal on whatever it is you "need" to have, work the Web by scouring online retailers for rock-bottom prices.
- Take only a certain amount of cash with you: no debit card and no credit cards. When you run out of money, you'll be forced to go home. Another great thing about this plan is that you'll run out of cash before you do anything ill-advised (wine-fueled), like talking to the slimeball bartender who has been making eyes at you, having one more drink, you get the picture.

Posh ladies with swanky apartments
If too much of your income goes to rent:
- *Move*, or get a roomie! What else can I say? Find yourselves some roommates, or find a cheaper place. And don't consider yourselves above living with your parents rent-free. I know you and your mother can fight over something as inane as what the weather will be a week from now, but if your mental health can take it, not paying rent for a while is a good proposition.

Gabbers and TV junkies
If too much of your income goes to utilities, including cell phone and TV:
- Reassess what you really need. Could you reduce your cell minutes? Breathe, ladies, I'm not saying you have to give up the phone, but maybe, just maybe, you could handle talking a bit less or talking only when you have free minutes. Could you give up cable TV? Yeah, that does mean no more hungover Saturday afternoon marathons of five-year-old episodes of *The Real World*. But how many times can you watch Trishelle hook up with scumbags, anyway? Don't answer that.
- Shop around. See if you can find a better deal elsewhere. You're the kind of girl who is willing to scour the racks at Marshall's until you find the perfect Diesel jeans at the perfect price. Apply this dogged deal-finding to your other bills.
- Use less. Many of your utilities are based on usage. Try turning out the lights more often or using less water. If the water from your morning shower could be used to hydrate a small country, consider reinvestigating your needs. Who needs the pruny fingers afterward, anyway?

Cuties with cars

This might be a hard thing to cut out, especially if you need a car, but if you *do* spend too much on transportation:

- Know what you need and what you don't. Just remember, you don't *need* a Beamer, you don't *need* new rims, you don't *need* a weekly car wash and detail.
- Use less. Yep, try carpooling or (gasp!) public transportation. The less you use your car, the less you'll have to shell out for maintenance and gas.
- You know what they say about an ounce of prevention . . . it's worth a pound of cure. And in the case of your car, it's so true. Regular maintenance, oil changes, et cetera. keep your car running smoothly so you don't get hit with a giant repair bill that could have been prevented. In terms of your car insurance, careful driving can save you thousands of dollars.

Health-focused chicks

If you spend too much on health care:

- Know the real meaning of health. Health care means things that really have to do with your health. Your masseuse so does not count. Items that promote a "healthy" complexion, give you a "healthy" glow, promise "healthy, shiny hair," these don't either. You don't need them.
- Get regular. Getting your regular checkups are key to keeping health care costs down. Early detection of illness can save you a lot of money, so don't skimp on going to the doctor.
- Take care of yourself. Ladies, if you smoke, quit. I know it's hard to quit, but smoking kills, and it can cost you big bucks in terms of your health, not to mention the sheer cost of smokes. If you're overweight, try to lose a few pounds. If you drink excessive amounts of alcohol, try to cut back.

For all of you situational spenders—the girls who drown themselves in denim when they're upset, who reward themselves with Rebecca Taylor dresses after a hard day at work, and all the rest of you—here are a few tips, organized by spending trigger, to help you get those danger spending situations under control.

Emotional spenders

⚬ Awareness is key. If you're feeling down/happy/whatever your trigger emotion is, don't take your credit card with you, just bring limited cash.

⚬ Distract yourself. If you obsess about your bad day, of course you'll want some retail therapy, so try to distract yourself. Call a friend, go to the park, do something to take your mind off spending.

⚬ Try an activity that will make you feel better (or that you'll enjoy), but that won't put a dent in your finances. Go for a run, take a walk with your girlfriends, lay out in the park, or rent a movie.

Compulsive spenders

⚬ You just can't have a credit card with you, ever. It must remain at home, all day, every day. It is only for emergencies. And for you, I am going to define "emergency," because, rest assured, you will think that the zit on your nose requires you to get a facial. Emergency = life on the line. A zit does not qualify . . . not even close.

⚬ Take out only the amount of cash you will need and leave your ATM card behind. Only the cash that you really need, for purchases that you really need to make: You do not need the snakeskin stilettos, the double-tall latte, or the magenta lip gloss. You really don't.

⚬ You might want to freeze your credit card in a block of ice. Nothing like having to take a pickax to a block of ice on the kitchen floor to make you realize that your spending might be out of control.

Impulsive spenders

⚬ The Post-it note trick: Wrap your credit card or cash in a Post-it note that asks, "Do I really need this?" It's that simple: When you see your card, the note will make you ask yourself why you are spending.

⚬ Don't go "just window shopping." That's like saying, "I'll have just one bite of this cake." It's totally impossible. If you stay away from your trigger shops, you won't be able to spend in them.

⚬ Don't take your credit card with you. Just bring cash. You can't be impulsive when you have no money. The saleslady at Saks does not work on barter.

Absentminded spenders

⚬ Make the card or the cash hard to get so you have to dig for it when you need it. This will make you aware that you are spending. If your purse is anything like mine used to be, then this shouldn't be too hard.

- The Post-it note trick: See above.
- Don't bring your credit card or cash with you. Just bring your ATM card so that you are forced to go get cash when you need it. Having to drive all the way to an ATM makes you ask yourself if you really need those Burberry sunglasses or that gorgeous Laura Mercier cream blush.

Reward spenders

- Increase the length of time between the rewards you give yourself. If one week of work = one mani-pedi now, then make it two weeks of work = one mani-pedi. Keep increasing the steps to a reward until your spending is under control.
- Change the rewards altogether. Give yourself something that doesn't cost money or that costs little money. Do yoga after a hard day rather than drinks with the girls. I know, your throat just closed up trying to imagine the downward-facing dog in place of downing a drink. So maybe invite the girls to your house for BYOB drinks instead of going out.

Social spenders

- Socialize somewhere where you can't spend a lot of money. Potluck dinners with the girls are a personal fave. Or try hosting a clothing swap, hitting up a museum, or having a picnic in the park.
- Treat yourself in social situations like you are a compulsive spender: Bring only cash (and not too much!), no ATM card and no credit card.
- Let this social set know that you've put yourself on a new financial path and just can't spend like you used to. This will help them support you.
- And, of course, if you're so inclined, give them a copy of this book so they too gain financial security.

"It's on sale" spenders

- I love the Post-it note, ladies. It can work here to show you that just because something is on sale does not mean that you really need it.
- Try the guilt tactic: Make a list of the sale items you bought and don't wear, and keep it front and center in your wallet.

- If you see the sale sign in the window, don't go in. I know this is like seeing a croissant in the window when you've been on Atkins for a month, but try to just not go in there. It's easier to resist when you're not right next to whatever is most tempting to you.

Congratulations, ladies, you've just finished creating your own personal style guide—for your spending. You know what you buy, why you buy it, and whether you can spend less, and it's all on easy-to-read charts. Plus, you've got some great tips under your belt on how to resist your spending triggers. You are now armed with the knowledge you need to start making real changes in your financial future. Think about it: With all the extra money you'll have just from avoiding some of your spending triggers and spending a bit less on some of the unnecessary items on your charts, you'll be able to meet your goals from page 17 that much faster. But that's only the beginning. So read on, as the next chapter is going to elevate your (spending) style to a whole new level.

CHAPTER 4

Blow Out Your Budget
How to Build and Stick to a *Spending Plan*
(No Matter How Much You Love Shoes!)

Ahh, the blow out. It's the finishing touch on a perfect ensemble. Think about it: You can don the perfect Chanel frock, pair it with the sleekest Givenchy stilettos, round it out with the vintage YSL clutch, and top if off with those perfect diamond studs from your grandmother, but if your hair looks incomplete, well, it just throws the whole thing off. In swoops the blow out. It straightens, it shines, it volumizes, it va-va-vooms. Yes, it's the final bit of polish you need for the perfect outfit. And the final bit of confidence you need to head out the door looking and feeling like a million bucks.

What if you could do the same thing for your spending? Add in that final bit of polish that will take your (spending) style to the next level (refer back to those goals from pages 22–23). Well, now you can. See, you built the foundation for your spending plan in the last chapter, and now you just need the finishing touches. You need a blow out—for your budget.

The budget blow out will straighten out the kinks in your current spending. Here's how it works: Using all the information you now know about your spending from the last chapter, you'll create a customized spending plan (aka a budget) that will polish your spending to near perfection. And when this blow out is done, you can head out that door feeling truly in control of your spending and on a path to having (not just feeling like) a million bucks. So let's get started.

THE BACKGROUND CHECK—FOR YOUR BUDGET

By now you know what your spending style is, but this is only the beginning. You also need to know what your spending style should be, so you can know how to budget appropriately. For example, maybe you are currently paying way too much for your apartment. It's a necessity, but it doesn't have to be a *très* chic top-floor penthouse. The list below outlines what you should be spending, roughly, on major life items. But, ladies, if you're meeting all your financial goals (and make sure this includes paying off debt in a timely manner, retirement, and savings), you can skip this model-spending section. It's more to help those of you who still can't figure out where to cut spending.

I'm Debt-Free: What Should My Spending Style Be?

For those of you without debt (your mortgage and car payment don't count here), here is a rough guideline of how much of your income you should spend on these items. Remember that these are rough guidelines, so some of you will spend less in certain areas and more in others (i.e., if you live in New York City, San Francisco, or another expensive city, you may have to spend more on rent). These guidelines are here just to give you a general idea on where you can make spending cuts.

Rent/Housing: No more than 30 percent
First things first. *Ax* the "I need *my own* studio within walking distance of the best boutiques" mentality. You probably can't afford it. Maybe you can be more of a "several roommates in a less-exciting neighborhood" kind of girl. Which wouldn't be so bad . . . imagine how much less you would spend if you opened your door and the thousands of adorable shops in your current neighborhood weren't right at your fingertips. Rent/housing

also includes renters/homeowners insurance and other housing-related expenses.

Food: 15 percent

It's not just obscene amounts of calories that have the potential for destruction, it's also the obscene amounts of money you may be spending to consume them. Girls, if eating out is putting a major dent in your pocketbook (not too mention expanding your once-petite waistline), you have to rethink your priorities. Skip dinner out and just meet the girls for dessert, cook dinner at your house, or just stop hitting up swanky hotspots and dropping the cash like confetti.

Transportation/Car: 5–15 percent

This really depends on where you live. For those of you in big cities, you'll spend way less on this category because you don't need a car to commute. When you need a car for your job, of course you spend more. That being said, I highly doubt any of you need a little Mercedes coupe for your daily commute. Remember this category includes insurance, maintenance, and repairs as well.

Utilities/Bills: 5 percent

Cell phone, gas, electric, water, et cetera . . . it all adds up. Most of these are just necessities and the prices aren't negotiable. *But* your cell phone, that crux of your social life, the pipeline to you BFFs—its rates are negotiable. Shop around! And don't forget to check your minutes. I know your girlfriends have crises, but you need to budget your minutes for those sorts of emergencies or just use your landline, if you have one, so you don't exceed your minutes.

Entertainment/Clothes/Miscellaneous: 12 percent

So Prada and Chloe are probably out of the picture. For that matter, so are DVF and BCBG. If the only clothing item you buy all month is a cute little cardigan at Tory Burch, then maybe you can handle it. But if you're anything like me, you'll want the cute matching bracelets and headband and a gazillion other little items that will make it impossible for you to afford the cardigan. Miscellaneous includes expenses not specified in other categories.

Insurance and Health Care: 10 percent

Before I start, health care does not include new shampoo (even if it does say "for healthy hair") or cosmetics or anything like that. This is health in terms of medical care. (And no, your Dexatrim is *not* medicine, even if it does speed up your metabolism.) Health is medicine, doctor's bills, hospital bills, and health insurance.

Savings: 13–20 percent
This money should go into your retirement fund, emergency fund, or other savings for your life's goals. We'll discuss these in Chapter 9. You should try to put 13 percent, which should be the absolute minimum, of your income into savings if you are debt free. I suggest trying to get yourself up to the full 20 percent (or more!).

CASE STUDY: *Sarah makes $65,000. She brings home $3,800 per month after taxes. She should roughly be spending the following amounts in each category:*

> $1,140 rent (max)
> $570 food (max)
> $570 transport (max)
> $190 utilities/bills
> $456 entertainment/clothes/miscellaneous (max)
> $380 insurance/health
> $494 savings (includes retirement savings and contingency fund; *minimum*)

The $494 per month into savings is a minimum. Sarah should be trying to cut out other areas to increase this amount.

I Have Debt: What Should My Spending Style Be?

For those of you with credit card debt, student loans, and other debt (excluding your mortgage and auto loans), here is a rough guideline of how much of your income you should spend in these areas. Please see above for a detailed description of what is included within each category. Most of you should try to pay off your interest-bearing debts, including your mortgage and auto loans, as quickly as possible, and to do so you will likely need to reduce spending in other areas. So even if these guidelines say that you can spend 12 percent of your income on food, if you can reduce this amount and put the savings toward paying off your debt, then you should.

Rent/Housing: No more than 30 percent

Get your rent/housing costs down to the bare minimum. Find a roommate if you have to or move back in with your parents (yes, your mom's a pain, but believe me, the folks at MasterCard that want their money, like, *now* are far worse) and shop around for better insurance rates.

Food: 12 percent

Ladies, the less you eat, the skinnier you get, so cut those food costs ASAP and put the extra money toward your debt payments. Added benefit: You'll be the hottest girl on the beach this summer. Need I say more?

Transportation/Car: 10 percent

I know you love cruising around town on the weekends, but with the way your financial situation looks (hello, credit card debt!), you'd be better off leaving the car in the garage and spending all the cash you would have spent on gas on your debt payments. Check out Chapter 7 for more ways to cut spending in this category.

Utilities/Bills: 5 percent

Many of these bills may be hard to cut, but do what you can. Get a cheaper cell phone plan, use less water or electricity, whatever it takes to save some dough so you can pay off your debt more quickly.

Entertainment/Clothes/Miscellaneous: 10 percent (Reduce this area as much as you can and put it toward your credit cards or debt payments.)

Ladies, you should not, I repeat *should not*, be treating yourself to a fabulous vacation or buying yourself adorable new clothes or whatever other unnecessary items you buy when you have a pile of high-interest debt.

Insurance and Health Care: 10 percent

Do not forgo insurance and health care. That being said, see above for a little lesson on what constitutes health care (no matter how many times you try to convince me that mani-pedis are necessary for "healthy" nails, I am not going to let you slip that into this category).

Paying Off Debt: You should spend as much as you can afford—at least 15 percent of your income.

Pay as much as you can toward the highest interest debt and then the minimum payments on lower-interest debts. As soon as you pay off that super-high-interest debt, start paying off the debt with the second highest interest. But remember: Always pay the minimums on all your interest-bearing debts. See Chapter 5 for details.

Retirement Fund: Up to what your employer matches.

You do not want to forgo putting money into your 401(k) when your employer is matching the funds (this is called matching funds, and we will discuss in Chapter 9). Why is this a good idea? Because you can double your money, a pretty unbeatable financial proposition.

CASE STUDY: *Lauren makes $36,000. She brings home $2,000 per month. She should roughly be spending the following amounts in each category:*

> $600 rent (max)
> $240 food (max)
> $200 transport (max)
> $100 utilities/bills
> $200 entertainment/clothes (max)
> $200 insurance/health
> $460 paying off credit card debt (*minimum,* see Chapter 5 for details) and retirement fund

When your credit card debt is paid off, you should begin to increase your savings, eventually working to save 13 percent of your income, or more. I will discuss in Chapter 10 where you should put this money.

THE BIG "B"
(AS IN BUDGET, NOT BOYFRIEND!)

A budget is basically a spending plan—one that is often intimidating to women. They look at it like at a diet—something they know they need but something at which they are likely to fail. And so they ignore it. Not smart. First, it is likely that you'll need a budget, one that you stick to, to make all of your goals from page 17 happen. (Picture that sunny vacay in Rio right about now.) Second, a budget is nothing to be afraid of, as these next two sections will show you. It's simply a guide for your spending, framework that will help you spend less. Ladies, almost every finance book will tell you to create a budget and stick to it. And that's simply great advice. So let's dive in.

Making a budget requires the following. You'll need to track your spending each month by writing down every single thing you spend money on. Don't have a heart attack yet; there are a couple types of software that you can use to help you do this. Quicken (Quicken.Intuit.com) and Mint (Mint.com) now offer free basic budgeting software. I recommend that you try out the free Quicken budgeting program, and if you find that you need a more advanced program, you can buy the software. If you use online banking, you may be able to sync your credit and debit card statements with your budgeting software so that you don't have to kill yourself by entering everything manually. Also, some banks, such as Bank of America, are now offering free budgeting tools along with their online banking.

Unfortunately, these programs are not magical. They don't telepathically know your spending and insert dollar amounts into the spreadsheet. If you take out cash and buy a pair of shoes, your budgeting software doesn't update the spreadsheet with this information. *You* have to do the tracking and work. But this is *the best way* to ensure that you meet your financial goals. A budget is like a diet where you count your calories every day—you can't "forget to count" certain meals and snacks or you'll never hit your weight loss goal, just like you can't forget to count certain purchases or you'll never hit your spending goals. (And for those of you who know you'll forget, The Cheaters Way section is for you.)

Here's a budget worksheet that will help you start this process. It's easier to do this online, especially by using one of the software programs that syncs with your bank accounts, but the chart on pages 66–67 will give you an idea of what to expect. Before you begin developing your budget, take into account these budget tips:

1. *Set smart monthly budget amounts.*
   First, examine your spending diaries and look at all the categories in which you guessed that you could spend less. Then determine how much less you could spend. For example, if you currently spend $20 per week eating lunch out when you're at the office, could you cut this down to $10 per week? Set a realistic budget for yourself for each of the categories below. Also, look at your financial goals chart to make sure you are working to meet your goals with this budget.
2. *Tailor your budget each month.*
   Remember that expenses change each month. For example, your electricity bill may be higher in the summer when you pay for air conditioning. You will need to tailor your budget each month. Also, you probably don't take a vacation each month, so you don't need that expense in every month's budget.
3. *Make categories that work for you.*
   This worksheet is just a guideline. You should add or subtract categories depending on what works for you. For example, let's say you don't have student loans or a pet. You'll want to take those categories out of your budget.
4. *Be flexible throughout the month.*
   Expenses just pop up sometimes: Your car breaks down and you have to fix it, but that's not in your budget. What do you do? You'll need to cut spending in other areas that month to afford the maintenance (unless you've already read Chapter 11 and have the money to afford these repairs). This budget is merely a guideline. Life will throw you for a loop sometimes, so change the budget as needed.
5. *Pad your budget.*
   I usually assume about 10 percent more in expenses than I expect to actually spend. Money slips through everyone's fingers in one way or another, at least sometimes. This way, you have a little wiggle room for the unexpected.

SAMPLE BUDGET

CATEGORY	MONTHLY BUDGET TARGET AMOUNT	WEEK 1 ACTUAL SPENDING	WEEK 2 ACTUAL SPENDING
INCOME			
Salary			
Other			
TOTAL			
NECESSITIES			
Rent/mortgage			
Electricity			
Heat			
Water			
Gas			
Cable			
Home phone			
Cell phone			
Internet			
Car payment/public transportation pass			
Car insurance			
Health insurance			
Loans			
Debt payments			
Groceries			
Other			
TOTAL			
DISCRETIONARY EXPENSES (DAY-TO-DAY PLUS INCIDENTAL)			
Food (Including eating out, lunches, snacks; excluding groceries)			
Clothing/accessories			
Entertainment (TV, movies, concerts, etc.)			
Vacation			
Pets (Food, grooming, vet, etc.)			
Fitness/health (Gym, massage, yoga, etc.)			
Beauty (Makeup, hair, etc.)			
Household goods (Furniture, household products)			
Dry cleaning/laundry			
Gifts/donations			
Hobbies			
Other			
TOTAL			
INVESTMENTS/SAVINGS			
Amount put into 401(k), IRAs, etc.			
Amount put into stocks/bonds/mutual funds			
Amount put into savings			
TOTAL			

INCOME – (TOTAL NECESSITIES + TOTAL DISCRETIONARY EXPENSES + INVESTMENTS/SAVINGS) = BUDGET BALANCE

MONTH: _____

WEEK 3 ACTUAL SPENDING	WEEK 4 ACTUAL SPENDING	MONTHLY ACTUAL AMOUNT SPENT	DIFFERENCE BETWEEN BUDGET TARGET AND ACTUAL AMOUNT SPENT

If your balance is positive, you have money left over to put into savings, to invest, or to use for paying off debts. If your balance is negative, you do not have money left over for these things and may need to cut your spending further.

Remember that you will need to redo your budget each month, taking into account various expenses that will vary from month to month.

This budget is great, but it's way easier to do it online. Remember to check out the free budgeting software program offered by Quicken to get started.

The Cheater's Way

So you fell off the wagon. You splurged on that green Marc Jacobs pea coat (and by splurge I mean you spent your entire clothing budget for the year), or you went out to dinner with your girlfriends one too many times. You simply forgot to track everything you were supposed to. Ladies, I get it. Those rigid budgets where you track everything you spend all the time are pretty hard to follow. So for those of you who barely survived tracking your spending for a week, this plan is for you. I understand—a strict budget can be like a bout with the Zone Diet: great advice that you know could work— Jennifer Aniston's bikini bod is surefire proof—but never seems to stick for the majority of us. So if tracking everything every day is more than you can deal with, I've got a system for you. I call it the PAC plan.

    P—Prepare
    A—Automate
    C—Cash

Prepare

You created the spending diary and those other expense charts to become aware of where all your money was going and thus enable yourself to cut spending in certain areas. Now you need to use the knowledge and aware-ness you gained about your spending so you can be prepared for those spending triggers *before* they occur. Preparing for your spending is like getting ready for a big date: You have to anticipate what will happen and prepare accordingly. When he's taking you to dinner, you always remem-ber your breath mints. When you're going to spend the day at the lake, you remember to cut the carbs for a few days beforehand so you'll look hot in that adorable polka dot Shoshanna bikini. So why can't you apply this discipline to your spending? I'm not saying you can never impulse buy, but I am saying that you can anticipate your spending so you can stop it before it starts.

First, look at your financial goals chart and note how much money you will need to save each month in order to reach those goals. Then follow these tips:

- *Try to make some cuts in regular, infrequent expenses.* By regular, infrequent expenses, I mean those items that you pay for infrequently at regular intervals. For example, rent, gym membership, utilities, phone, TV/Internet—these tend to be the simplest to cut because it's easier to track the spending on them since you don't don't pay for them frequently and you get bills at regular intervals (whereas you can't plan as easily for when you'll eat out). That's just money you'll save every month without having to pay too much attention, whereas with those day-to-day expenses, you have to think about it more— "Did I spend X amount last week on groceries, so now I can spend only X amount this week on food?" You get the picture.
- *Know the categories that you overspend in.* Then pick a few categories and set concrete goals in order to limit spending in those areas.

To figure out these categories, highlight all the items on which you said you could reduce spending. Categorize them so that you can see the areas that you should focus on. Now make a concrete goal for reducing that spending (for example, cut beauty expenses by $40 per month). Try focusing on just a few categories if you can—I know it's really hard to deal with tracking expenses on a bunch of different items at one time. But if you know you just have to focus on how much you spend in a certain category, you might be able to manage tracking that.

Let's say, for example, that you are a beauty junkie—seventeen shades of nail polish, fourteen different eye shadows, twelve different shampoos, all just bursting out of your medicine cabinet. You tend to spend about $20 at the drugstore each week on beauty products. Make a promise to yourself that you will splurge only every other week, or that you'll spend only about $10 per week at the store.

- *Know your habitual expenses and set concrete goals on limiting spending on these items.* To do this, look at the things you purchase habitually, like a morning latte, the newspaper, or your gym membership, and assess which ones you can realistically go without or spend less on. Do you need the latte and the paper *every* morning? Do you use the gym enough to justify the expense (and don't start that "Oh, but I will go once I have time/summer starts/ [insert your lame excuse here]")?

Now make a concrete plan for cutting spending on these items. For example, if you decide you want to save $300 per month on living expenses, you might take in a roommate whom you charge $300 to live in your second bedroom.

Or let's say you want to save at least $20 per week and you're a latte junkie who spends $28 per week on your morning caffeine lifeline. You could cut out the lattes completely (your coworkers will just have to suffer for a few weeks while you wean yourself off them). Or you could just make coffee at home, saving yourself up to $28 per week. Alternately, you could drink only one or two lattes a week instead of one or two a day, saving yourself $20 per week.

● *Prepare yourself for your spending triggers so you can avoid unnecessary overspending that will sabotage your savings.*

When you look at the motivations for your actions, it will help you prevent overspending. Do you buy things for silly reasons (did that Missoni scarf really solve your mini-crisis with your BFF)? Do you buy to keep up with others? If you're just trying to keep up with your friends' lifestyle, ask yourself why it's so important to take those lavish vacations or partake in extravagant dinners with your friends. Will it really make any difference in your friendships? See pages 49–50 for more details.

Or let's say you waste money on snacks. You're starving while waiting for your girlfriends, so you have to buy a muffin. You require sugar at 4 p.m. so your boss doesn't find you asleep under your desk, so you dash to the office vending machine. Prepare by having food in your purse that you can munch on. You'll save a few bucks (not to mention a few calories!).

Automate

Ladies, this is my number-one piece of advice (as well as famous financial writer David Bach's) to help you ensure that you save every month: make it automatic. Have your employer institute direct deposit for you and then schedule automatic transfers for the day you get paid. You can set up an automatic transfer to pay your fixed bills, which could include loans, savings, credit card, for each period. The money will be gone from your account before you can spend it on other things. Pay the bills (utilities, phone, etc.) that aren't a fixed amount each period on this same day, if possible. Pay them all off so that there's no way you can spend this money on other things. Make a system for this that works for you. You can automatically pay your rent during one pay period, then take care of your bills the next. I add to my retirement fund with every biweekly paycheck. Either way, as soon as I get paid, the money is out the door to pay the bills.

Cash
Pay cash for everything else that you possibly can. Every week, withdraw exactly the amount of cash you are allowed to spend from your account. Purchase everything that you need with this cash. You'll be able to self-regulate by looking into your wallet and realizing, Gee, I have only X dollars left, so I need to watch what I spend for the next few days.

Now this obviously can't apply to every purchase, so you'll have to be extra careful when you do put things on your credit card. You'll need to realize that this is just like paying cash for the purchase, and compensate by making sure to take out less cash at the beginning of the following week.

Make a Plan That Will Work for You
If you try to do too much at once, you're likely to fail and quit trying. So cut spending in a few areas at first, and when you get used to these cuts, add in others. And don't overly deprive yourselves. If you love grabbing lunch with the girls, then maybe you don't have to go cold turkey. Just do it less often and make cuts in other areas. You need to create a balanced spending plan that doesn't completely deprive you. Remember, deprivation often leads to binging (remember when you scarfed that entire large pizza after your little stint on the South Beach Diet?), and binge-spending ends just like binge-eating—with you feeling guilty and annoyed at yourself.

Top Ten Items You Probably Waste Money On

1. **Clothes.** Where do I begin? Just because the DVF wrap dress was on sale does not mean that you could afford it. And you might not even be able to afford the on-sale Forever 21 dress you bought either.

2. **Shoes and accessories.** Why on earth did you need $100 red patent leather Mary Janes that match nothing in your closet? And for that matter, did you need to buy yourself starter diamond studs? The only thing those starter diamonds did for you is start your immense credit card debt.

3. **Food.** You read that the Perricone Prescription was the only way to lose weight. So you ditched all the bad foods in your cabinet and replaced them with salmon and veggies. Then, at 3 a.m. on day three of your diet, you begged the greasy Chinese place to deliver you forty dollars' worth of dumplings. After that, your diet was shot, so you had to refill your entire fridge and pantry with food you would actually eat. Does this money-draining scenario sound familiar?

4. **Alcohol.** Girl, I'm sure this doesn't need an explanation. You just paid to feel like crap the next morning. And you can't even remember if the previous night was fun. You slept in your clothes, so you now have to pay to get them dry-cleaned. Need I go on?

5. **Makeup.** Now I'm not saying you should go without, but I am saying that you do not need fifteen shades of designer lip gloss. I mean, Fiery Midnight? Even Gisele couldn't make that shade look good.

6. **Beauty treatments.** Shaving was too annoying, so you got laser. You heard that the Intraceuticals facial keeps skin glowing, so you ran out and got one (then got pressured into buying all of their other products). Between the waxing, facials, laser, massages, manicures, and the gazillions of products bursting out of your medicine cabinet, your credit card has gotten quite a workout.

7. **Your hair.** It all started many years ago when you were chasing Jennifer Aniston's perfectly highlighted buttery blond. Now you're over that, but you've moved onto needing the gorgeous

biscotti-almond of J Lo's hair or the rich chestnut color that Rachael Bilson has been sporting. And so here you are, thousands of dollars later . . .

8. **Cable TV.** Because if you don't watch *The City*, how will you be able to keep up with the gossip over lunch at work? And God forbid you don't stay up-to-date with *Dexter*, because then what will you use as your conversation starter with the hot bartender? Ladies, will the latest scoop on Dex really land you the bartender?

9. **The gym.** Now this doesn't apply to those of you who go regularly, but for the rest of us who have to turn away when we walk by the gym so we don't pass out from the guilt of never going, it's time to assess whether we really need that membership.

10. **Gas.** You love zipping around town in your little convertible, wind flying through your hair, a hottie by your side. Unfortunately, your bank account doesn't share this enthusiasm (though the friendly men that run OPEC sure do).

A CACHE OF CASH: SECRETS OF THE SELF-MADE RICH GIRL

I know that was a lot to digest. And you're probably a little freaked that you'll fail. But you can do this. And these tips will help you stay on your budget.

Tip #1: Go Green

And I don't mean a kelly green Bottega Veneta clutch. Green as in cash money—use it instead of plastic. Here's how:

- Leave the credit and debit cards at home.
- Pay cash for what you need.

This will keep you from spending money you don't have. Try shelling out ten $20s for those Stuart Weitzman strappy sandals instead of using your credit card, and then see how important they are to your wardrobe.

Tip #2: Feel Guilty

You need to put yourself on a guilt trip about relentless, unnecessary spending. Well, guilt trip might be a little strong. Think of it as a way to keep yourself mindful. This is the equivalent of putting a picture of a supermodel on your fridge—it makes you think twice before you dive spoon-first into the Häagen Dazs. A few ways to feel guilty:

- Make a list of things you waste money on and put it front and center in your wallet.
- Leave out the clothes or other items you never wear/use to remind yourself of the money you wasted.
- Tape a "guilty" note around your credit and debit cards. The note will say something to the effect of, "Do you really need this?"

Tip #3: Cheat a Little

Just because you looked at it or tried it out doesn't mean you have to buy it. The saleswoman at Neiman's may very well be attentive and sweet, but that does not mean you have to buy the Miu Miu kitten heels. Same thing at the restaurant, salon, or wherever. Remember, you don't need to buy six bottles of Aveda products because the stylist did a great job.

Tip #4: Procrastinate

One of my favorite tips from financial expert David Bach is this: For items that you want that are over $100, try to wait at least forty-eight hours before buying them. This is the cooling-off period, allowing you to think about whether you really want it (and what you might have to sacrifice in order to get it).

Tip #5: Sell It

If you haven't worn it or used it in a year, it might be time to sell it. Once a year, you should go through your home and clean out everything you don't use anymore. Then put it on Craigslist or eBay or have a yard sale.

Tip #6: Bank Smartly

Banking can cost you if you don't do it smartly. So here are the top tips for choosing the right bank.

- *Choose a bank that is FDIC insured (in the case of a credit union, choose one that is NCUA-insured).* This means that the U.S. government insures your account up to $250,000. If your bank goes under, the government will pay you back. If your bank went out of business and it wasn't insured, you could lose all of your money.
- *Look for low costs.* Banks charge different amounts—and some don't

charge at all—for such things as monthly fees for having an account (this can often be waived if you keep a certain amount in savings or use direct deposit), fees for each check written or deposit made, a fee if you go below a minimum balance or overdraft your account, ATM usage, opening/closing your account, overdraft protection, and more. If you have an account that has minimum balance requirements, make sure you understand how they compute the balance—it could be the average balance for the month, or it could be that if you ever dip below the balance required, you are penalized. Bankrate.com will compare banks in your area for you. Most banks charge for bounced checks, to stop payments on checks, and for overdraft fees, but these fees will vary for different banks. Shop around for banks with the lowest fees.

* *Choose a bank with the services that you need.* I suggest you look long and hard for a bank that offers free online banking (especially online bill pay). With online banking, you can pull up your account information from your computer so you can see your transactions, such as deposits, withdrawals, and more. Plus, you can pay bills online, set up automatic bill pay (they'll even mail the checks for you), move money between accounts, and more. Think about the other services you'll want—no-fee ATM withdrawals from out-of-network ATMs, for example. There are some banks that will pay interest on your checking account, so that's worth asking about as well. Most banks pay it on savings accounts (though you can probably get far better rates if you look—see Chapter 11). You'll want the highest interest rate you can get if you plan on using your bank's savings account. You want the services you need at the lowest cost possible. Shop around.

* *Convenience is key.* If you go to the ATM frequently, make sure that your bank has ATMs located conveniently throughout your area. If you like dealing with a person at the bank when making transactions, make sure that the banking center is easy to get to. ATM fees can be a killer, so having your bank's ATM nearby can be a huge money saver.

* *Consider a credit union.* A bank is a for-profit enterprise owned by investors; a credit union is a nonprofit enterprise owned by its consumers. Credit unions often offer better deals than banks because they pass along their would-be profits to customers in the form of lower fees, lower interest rates, and more. When you are shopping around for a bank, be sure to look into credit unions in your area as well.

- *Consider an Internet-only bank.* What is an Internet-only bank? This is a bank that exists online—you won't find a branch office in your neighborhood. ING (ingdirect.com) is a well-respected Internet-only bank.

Advantages of Internet-only Banking:

Because the Internet-only banks don't have to pay as much in terms of staffing, rent, and other fees, since there are not physical bank branches like a traditional bank, they often pass on some of those savings to consumers in the form of higher interest rates, free savings and checking, free online bill pay, unlimited checks, and more. Plus, for many of these banks, when you make an ATM withdrawal, you'll see it reflected in your account online very quickly, and you'll likely have online bill pay as well as the ability to manage your accounts online.

Disadvantages:

The main disadvantage is the ATM fees. Since Internet-only banks don't have any physical branches, you're going to be charged whatever fees the host bank charges. This is a big disadvantage if you go to the ATM frequently, and it could make this kind of bank not worth it for you. But remember that you can get cash back at many stores, like drug stores and grocery stores, when you use your debit card. And many Internet-only banks will give you some sort of monthly rebate for ATM fees. For instance, Compubank— compubank.com—gives four ATM rebates per month on its accounts. Other than direct deposits, you'll have to mail in your deposits, so it will take some time to see this money reflected in your account.

Top Tips for Money-Saving Banking

- *Don't overdraft your account.* This sounds simple, but it bears repeating because almost everyone has done it at least once. Overdrafting, trying to withdraw more money from your account than it actually contains, is one of the most costly bank errors you can make. Banks typically charge between $20 and $35 every time you overdraft. Overdraft protection ties your checking account to another account, so the bank pays the overdraft from that second account. But overdraft protection doesn't mean you are exempt from overdraft fees. The most common way banks offer you overdraft protection is by automatically putting the overdrafted amount on your credit card. This credit card likely has high interest rates, so this method can end up costing you big time. Sometimes the bank will issue a cash advance on this credit card to cover the overdraft. And this is *bad*. Repeat: B-A-D. See page 92 for the horrors of the cash advance.

Also, note that many banks offer free bounce protection. This is usually a bad thing, especially if you frequently overdraft. Here's how it works: If you overdraft, the bank may go ahead and pay the amount. But they will charge you a hefty fee and may keep charging you until you put money into your account to make up for the overdraft amount.

In order to avoid the damage overdraft protection and bounce protection can wreak, it's important that you know the amount of money in your account at all times. Of course, the best way to do this is to keep track of every withdrawal and deposit, as well as when they registered in your account (remember that deposits often don't hit your account immediately). You might have heard it called "living within your budget" or "balancing your checkbook," and you literally write down all your deposits and withdrawals into a register. You can usually find a register in the back of your checkbook; if you don't have one, you can create one yourself—writing down your beginning balance, subtracting any withdrawals, and adding in any deposits— remembering that these usually do not register immediately. Or, at the very least, go to your account online each day and check your balance. I use an online notification service that emails me when there is less than $100 in my account (you can usually choose the amount at which you want them to notify you, assuming your bank has this service). This is not a perfect system, but it does help.

* *Watch out for ATM fees.* These fees come in many forms. The ones you are probably way too familiar with are out-of-network ATM fees. You're stuck at some bar, need cash (where are those cute guys or girls you were sure would buy you a few drinks?), and have to go to another bank's ATM. And, of course, you get hit with fees for this service. And not just one fee—the out-of-network bank charges you a fee and then your own bank charges you a fee. Some banks charge

you a fee just for the ATM card, others charge monthly or yearly fees for ATM access.

Best Ways to Avoid ATM Fees

- *Plan ahead so you don't have to use an out-of-network ATM*
- *Choose a bank with many ATM locations so you'll almost always be near one of your bank's ATMs.*
- *Withdraw enough cash so you won't run out and have to use an out-of-network ATM.*
- *Avoid ATMs that cost a lot, such as those in casinos, convenience stores, hotels, and airports.*
- *Use an alternate form of payment if you are going to have to pay ATM fees. (Of course, you shouldn't use a credit card in this case unless you plan on paying off that balance in full and on time.)*

- *Choose the right bank.* See above for this one. Get the services you want at the lowest cost. Bankrate.com will compare banks in your area for you. Look out for unnecessary fees.
- *Consider using a deferred debit card.* This is a debit card that has a Visa or MasterCard logo on it, and you can also use it anywhere Visa and MasterCard are accepted. Many of you probably already have one of these as your debit card, though you might have a simple ATM card. Here's why I like them: Currently Visa and MasterCard cap your liability on these cards at $50 if your card goes missing and you report it within two days. Your ATM card can be stolen when it's in your possession the entire time, if someone puts a tracer on an ATM machine that you used or somehow steals your personal information and cleans out your account. If you use a deferred debit card, the situation can be remedied quickly.
- *Check your statements thoroughly.* Regularly scour your bank statements to make sure there are no mistakes. If you see anything suspicious, report it immediately. You usually have sixty days to tell the bank about a mistake. After the sixty days, they are not responsible for fixing the mistake.
- *Do your homework.* You can make sure your bank is in good financial

condition with Bankrate.com's Safe and Sound feature. Also, you should make sure that your checking and savings accounts at that bank are FDIC insured.

And there you have it, your own personal budget blowout—the finishing touches to your spending style. And this time around, it's a style that actually works for you. You now know how to monitor your spending so you spend less, and thus have more money to put toward your dreams (see pages 22–23).

But ladies, as you all well know, one blowout does not last the entire year. You will need to continually review and revise your budget, and the tips that will keep you on it, so that your budget changes with the changes that happen in your life. If you start making more money, have new goals, or another life change, the budget gets a little nip-tuck right along with the rest of your life. The Big B (as in budget) is a lot like the other Big B (as in boyfriend)—they both require maintenance in order to work the way you want them to.

So what's next on your path to the ultimate financial style? Why, a diet, of course, because oh, how things fit so much better after a little trim-down. The Debt Diet is coming up. . . . It's like a simpler version of Weight Watchers, but instead of dropping pounds, you'll drop the weight from all that looming debt.

PART III:

(Debt) Diet

AN INTRODUCTION TO THE DEBT DIET (AND HOW IT WILL TRIM DOWN YOUR DEBT——FOR GOOD)

I realize that calling this a diet has probably prompted a feeling of dread. Cue memories of throwing those chocolate chip cookies in the trash so you wouldn't eat them and then guiltily eating the ones on top right out of the can, or of literally losing your mind from trying to count the calories in everything you ate, or from struggling to avoid everything with sugar in it (and hence, pretty much everything that actually tastes good). However, this diet is far less painful and doesn't involve depriving yourself of sugar/fat/yummy food for the rest of your life, I swear. So here goes.

You now know what you spend and how to decrease your spending. What does that mean for you? It means you've freed up some cash. And guess what. You are not going to run to the nearest sample sale to spend it. You are going to dig yourself out of debt, especially high-interest debt. (Collective groan, I know, but when you don't owe anyone obscene amounts of money, you'll feel collective relief, I promise.)

You may be asking yourself why it matters if you handle your debt responsibly. Well, how you handle your current debt, including credit card bills and loans, could save you thousands of dollars in the future. It could mean the difference between getting a loan to buy a house or car, getting your dream apartment, or getting T-Mobile to give you a cell phone and *not* getting any of these things. It affects the interest rate you'll pay on your credit cards and other loans.

So that's the goal of the Debt Diet—to show you how to dig yourself out of debt responsibly. The Debt Diet will focus on the three types of debt that I've found plague you ladies the most: credit cards, student loans, and auto loans. (Other loans such as mortgages and home equity loans will be discussed in Chapter 13.)

But first things first, let's assess how much debt you have.

Step on the (Debt) Scale

The first step in almost any diet is to know your starting point—your initial weight—and then set goals to drop that extra flab. The Debt Diet starts the same way. So, let's step on that scale and get started. The debt scale will tell you whether you have too much extra flab—in this case, financial flab (aka debt). Think of it like this: Your bathroom scale tells you if you're carrying too many pounds; the debt scale tells you whether you're carrying too much debt.

Here is a chart to fill in so that you can figure out your financial flab situation. It will determine your debt-to-income ratio, which tells lenders how much debt you have relative to how much income you bring in. You can use the information you collected in the chart in the introduction to help you. Why do you care about your debt-to-income ratio? Because anyone who loans you money—for a home, car, cell phone, whatever—is going to care. Even if you can sweet-talk your man into giving you what you want, lenders aren't quite so easily swayed. They want to know whether you'll be able to pay them back in full and on time, and your debt-to-income ratio is a key part of how they determine this.

MONTHLY DEBT PAYMENTS	AMOUNT
Mortgage payment or rent	$
Home equity loan or home equity line of credit payment	$
Car payments	$
Student loan payments	$
Minimum credit card payments	$
Other monthly loan payments	$
Miscellaneous monthly debt (Don't include debts like your phone and utility bills, which you can cancel at any time. These are debts that are sticking with you no matter what, such as taxes you owe.)	$
TOTAL MONTHLY DEBT PAYMENTS	$
MONTHLY INCOME	
Take home pay (what you make after taxes come out)	$
Miscellaneous (i.e., maybe you get some kind of annual income; if so, divide the total amount by twelve to get the monthly income)	$
TOTAL MONTHLY INCOME	$
Debt-to-income ratio: Total Monthly Debt Payments Divided by Total Monthly Income	

Know your goal weight

You've stepped on the scale and know the weight of your debt—your debt-to-income ratio. Now you need to understand whether this is a healthy weight or whether it's diet time. Here are the guidelines for your debt-to-income ratio.

- Excellent (slim and trim—lenders probably love you): 30 percent or less
- Good (just a few diet tweaks—lenders have warm feelings about you): 31 to 36 percent
- Fair (too much flab—lenders are feeling pretty wary): 37 to 42 percent
- Needs some work (way, way too much flab—lenders will probably run for the hills): 43 percent or more

The goal here is to shoot for a debt-to-income ratio of 30 percent or less. Get those lenders to love you just as much as your girlfriends do! If you already have an excellent ratio but you have credit card or other high interest debt, you are going to have to do something about that. And if your score is lower than excellent, well, you have room for improvement.

Build a (Debt) Diet That Works for You

While the chapters in Part III will address the specific types of debt you might face and how to deal with each one, this section gives you strategies on how to deal with all of those debts together. Keep these in mind as you build a debt diet that will keep your (financial) flab at bay—once and for all.

Let's dive into a few of the most-asked questions on paying off all kinds of debt.

1. **Which debts should I pay off first?** Look at all the debts you listed in the chart on page 81. Put them in order of highest interest rate first. Pay as much as you can each month off the highest interest debt(s), and the minimum payments on the other debts until all are paid off.

2. **How much should I pay toward each debt?** At the very least, you always should pay the minimum on your debts. It's as simple as that. If you don't, your FICO score will dip, and you know what happens then—they're going to jack up your interest rates.

3. **Should I pay off credit card debt quickly, or put the money into savings?** In general, you should work on paying off your high-interest debts (for example, most credit cards) as quickly as you can before you put money into savings. Here is the simple rule: If the interest you'd earn from putting the money into savings is less than the amount of

interest you'd have to pay on the debt, then it's better to pay off the debt before you put the money into savings. For example, let's say you have a credit card with an 18 percent interest rate and you earn 4 percent on your savings. It's better to pay off the credit card as quickly as you can.

4. **Should I contribute to my 401(k), or pay off my high interest debts?** If your employer matches your contributions to your 401(k)—see page 132 for details—you should contribute up to what they will match even before paying off debt. (Though you should still pay the minimum on your debts.)

5. **Should I use my savings and/or 401(k) to pay off my credit card debt?** You should probably use your savings, but don't use your 401(k). Your savings are probably earning only an interest rate of 1 to 5 percent, while your credit card probably has a rate of 10 percent or higher. So it makes sense to use savings to pay off credit card debt. But if you take out a 401(k) loan to pay off your credit card debt, it can seriously hurt you. When you contributed to your 401(k,) you used pre-tax money, but when you repay the 401(k) loan, you will have to do so with after-tax money. This hurts! You'll learn more about this in Chapter 10, but for now, take my word for it. Don't do it.

6. **Should I use a HELOC (home equity line of credit) to pay off my credit card?** Maybe. It depends on the interest rate. If the interest rate you'll pay on the HELOC is lower than the rate on your credit cards, then it makes sense to use the HELOC to pay off your credit cards. However, you can lose your home if you don't pay back the HELOC. So it might make more sense to try to switch credit cards and get a lower interest rate.

7. **Should I declare bankruptcy?** Probably not. Yes, your debts will be forgiven, but the bankruptcy will stay on your credit report for seven to ten years (think of how old you'll be before this financial tarnish is wiped away. . . you could have wrinkles, mom jeans, and a couple of kids). It will wreak havoc on your FICO score, which will affect the interest rates you receive on credit cards and loans.

If you simply can't keep up with your debts and bills despite cutting spending and following the Debt Diet, in its entirety, there's help. First, ask a friend or family member if they can loan you enough money to take care of the situation. (But remember that mixing money and relationships can become pretty sticky, so make sure the loan terms, like when and how you'll repay the money, are clear from the beginning. Being broke is bad enough, and being broke and in a fight over money with your BFFs is even worse.) If that doesn't help, contact your lenders directly to see if they can work out a payment plan with you. Or contact the National Foundation for Credit Counseling at nfcc. org. They will help you out (for a small monthly fee). Bankruptcy should be a last-ditch effort to help you get out of debt. Beware of many debt-counseling services that advertise immediate solutions to your problems. They are often scams and may charge you an exorbitant amount of money.

Big "Fat" Lies That Keep You in Debt

I know finance is not always an easy subject to understand, so I'm going to translate the lies you tell yourself about getting out of debt into a language you might be more familiar with: the language of dieting.

Debt lie #1

I'll make more money in the future, so I'll wait to start paying off my debt until then.

In diet lingo: *I'll work on getting in shape once it gets closer to summertime.*

If you're anything like me, you procrastinate on your exercise plan, thinking that you'll just go crazy at the gym for two months before summer starts. You think that will be enough to get you in shape. The result: You can't stick to the crazy exercise plan (or you waited too long to start), and now you're going to have to spend the summer in a giant cover-up, much like the one you wore last year and threw out because you just knew that this summer would be totally different.

It's going to be the same thing with your debt—but worse—if you don't take action now, for the same two reasons. First, it's really hard to do debt boot camp and emerge free of financial worries after only a very short period of hardcore activity. Second, waiting to pay off your debt just doesn't work in your favor; it can cost you a lot of money—sometimes thousands of dollars. It's that pesky thing called compounding. Revisit that example from the introduction on page 6. And just in case you didn't turn back to that page (you know I'm on to you!), I'm going to remind you: Remember that the $1,000 television ended up costing $2,115.41 due to the power of compounding. It turned out to cost more than double the sticker price—and this person was making the minimum payments on her credit card.

Debt lie #2

I'll pay off my debt once I get married.

In diet lingo: *Once I get thin, I'll stay thin.*

I don't even need to explain this one . . . for all of you (like me!) who have done the cabbage soup, Atkins, Perricone, and a gazillion other diets, gotten really thin, and then wolfed Oreo's like it was going out of style, subsequently gaining back all the weight you'd lost, you know what I'm talking about. Marriage, like a diet, is not a 100 percent guarantee. Prince Charming often seems charming . . . but as we all know, looks can be deceiving. The divorce rate in America hovers around 50 percent, the man you fall madly in love with may not have the money to pay off your debt (we can't all be Julia Roberts in *Pretty Woman*), and having to narrow the already way-too-narrow dating pool based on a guy's ability to pay off your ever-mounting credit card bill is not going to improve your chances of finding—and actually remaining with—a man. Staying married is like staying thin: It's a big "fat" gamble.

Debt lie #3

It's only a couple of bucks.
In diet lingo: *It's only one piece of cake.*

One piece of cake every now and then is fine. One piece of cake when you've saved up your calories by eating light all day is fine. But one piece of cake every day when you haven't been eating healthy to compensate will create that lovely little muffin top. The same thing applies when it comes to your spending. Buying a treat every now and then is fine. Buying daily treats is cutting into the money you could have put toward paying off your debt.

Congratulations, you are on the path to a flab-free financial future. You stepped on the (debt) scale, know your debt weight, know your goal weight and have begun to build a diet that works to address these issues. You also know some of the diet-derailing lies that you may tell yourself when face-to-face with that Milly sundress. Things like, "Just this once" or "This dress looks so good, I'll definitely land a rich man who will pay it off." Just remember: The only thing those lies do is add unattractive (financial) flab. When you feel a lie brewing, cue up those goals from pages 22–23. Unless that little sundress is on the goals list (and don't add it now!), move away from the store window.

Now let's get to the nitty-gritty—how to deal with the major types of debt that may plague you, including credit cards, student loans, and auto loans. These next three chapters will address these topics and help you diet yourself out of debt once and for all. As you read through these chapters, keep in mind the Build a (Debt) Diet That Works for You section on page 82. It is the big-picture diet framework that will help you deal with all of these types of debts simultaneously.

CHAPTER 5

The Plastic Purge

How to Cure the Plastic Plague (aka Credit Card Debt)

AN INTRODUCTION TO THE PLASTIC PLAGUE

Your credit card. You and that little sliver of plastic have shared some good times together. Remember those gorgeous earrings, the smoking-hot pumps, the incredible meals, and that fabulous vacation? Ah, the good times. But, hello Dr. Jekyll and Mr. Hyde—that little sliver of plastic can turn on you in an instant. Like when you realized that there was no way you could pay off the gorgeous earrings, smoking-hot pumps, and fabulous vacation anytime soon. Or when you had to call Visa to get a new card because you wore out the magnetic strip on your old card. Or the fact that your credit card company has to remind you to pay your bill every month (and by "remind" I mean a bill collector has to call you repeatedly to get payment).

I realize that most of you aren't that bad. But if you're like many Americans, you aren't a credit card saint, either. You've got a bit of debt on your credit cards, and you regularly do not pay off your credit card bill in full each month. Sound familiar? If so, you've got a case of the Plastic Plague.

Basically, if you have credit card debt and don't pay off your balance in full and on time each month, you probably have the Plastic Plague. Luckily, I've got the cure. First, you have to cut unnecessary spending, as we discussed in Part II. This unnecessary spending is most likely the reason you have the Plastic Plague in the first place. So remember, buying little Toto a new winter sweater is not a basic living cost—he has fur, remember? And eating out every night is not a basic living cost either—you can cook, I swear. And second, you've got to create a solid plan to get yourself out of credit card debt. That's where this chapter comes in.

But before we begin, I just want to press upon you why it's crucial, critical, urgent (and whatever other synonym I can use here to convey urgency) to get out of credit card debt.

Plastic 101: Lingo Lowdown

Now, ladies, I know you are going to try to skip this part since you feel intimately familiar with your credit card, but just glance through it.

- Debit card: Works like a check, deducting the money right from your checking account. Often also serves as your ATM card. Debit cards with the Visa and MasterCard logo on them can be used anywhere a credit card is used. However, the cards deduct the money directly from your account, unlike a credit card.
- ATM-only or bank card: Lets users withdraw money, check account balances, and a few other transactions by entering a PIN number. ATM-only cards have more limited uses than many debit cards, as they cannot be used at many merchants since they generally require you to enter a PIN number.
- Charge card: Requires you to pay off the entire balance in full each month. Usually have an annual fee. Examples: Diner's Club, American Express.
- Major credit cards: Let you make purchases up to a preset limit. You are not required to pay off the balance in full

(in fact, they prefer that you don't! More money in their pockets!) Examples include: Visa, MasterCard, Discover.

- Retail cards: Credit cards for certain retailers (for example, an Old Navy credit card is a retail card). Often these have high interest rates, so be careful.
- Secured cards: See page 95.
- Smart cards (aka prepaid cards): You prepay a certain amount onto the card. That prepaid amount on the card is all you can spend.

WHAT A CASE OF THE PLASTIC PLAGUE REALLY COSTS YOU

That $5,000 charge may just end up costing you $12,000 . . .

"So what?" you might ask yourself, "I have some credit card debt. . . ." Well, let me just convince you that it's a big problemo. Look at how much things are really costing you when you don't pay them off.

Let's say you have $5,000 in credit card debt. Your interest rate is 18 percent. You pay the minimum payment on your card each month, which is 2.5 percent of the balance (so the first month, you'll owe $125, which is 2.5 percent of $5,000) or $10, whichever is greater. (Note that most credit cards compound their interest monthly, not yearly.) At this rate, it will take you *twenty-six years* to pay off the credit card, and it will cost you more than $7,000 in interest payments alone (a *total bill of more than $12,000!*). And this assumes you never buy another item on this credit card.

When you're using a credit card and not paying it off in full and on time every month, the price tag on those adorable Mary Janes doesn't really mean much. You'll pay the sticker price, *and then some, and then some more*, because interest isn't cheap. See the Why You Hate Compounding Interest section on page 6 just in case you need some more convincing. So it's expensive—very, very expensive—to remain in credit card debt. But you can dig yourself out of this debt, you really can. I've got a solid plan: something I like to call "plastic surgery."

PLASTIC SURGERY

It's time for plastic surgery—the only way to cure the Plastic Plague. There are three steps in the plastic surgery process: 1) prep for surgery, 2) strong-arm your surgeon, and 3) go under the knife.

Step 1: Prep for Surgery

You need to know what you're dealing with before you even start trying to get yourself out of debt. What are your interest rates, grace periods, minimum payments, billing cycle, and fees? Can you getter a better deal from your card company? To figure all this out, you'll need to—gasp—read your statement. You know how your credit card statement comes with all those papers? Those outline what kind of deal your credit card company is giving you. And you have to actually read and understand them.

The minimum that you need to know:

A. Grace period
How long you have to pay your bill before they start charging you interest.
This is the time from the credit card statement end date to the date when you owe payment. If you pay the entire bill before your grace period is up, they won't charge you interest. Hint: This is a good thing. But if you don't pay the bill in full during your grace period, guess what? The kind people at your credit card company will charge interest on the balance plus on every single additional purchase you make in the coming month. (And full means full—paying the minimum or a little more does not qualify you for the no-interest deal.)

Goals:
1. Know your grace period and understand that your credit card company can change it, so always check.
2. If your grace period is too short, shop for a card with a longer grace period.

B. Billing cycle
How the credit card company calculates your bill.
There are two types of billing cycles: 1) average daily balance and 2) two-cycle average daily balance. If you have the two-cycle average daily balance, you should switch cards unless you absolutely always pay off your bill in full and on time. The two-cycle average daily balance hurts people who carry a balance on their cards *big time*, because your card company calculates your interest based on two months of charges.

Goal: Make sure your card uses the average daily balance method to calculate your bill. If not, switch cards.

C. Interest rate

How much your credit card company charges you for the privilege of buying things on their card.

Your interest rate is the fee they're charging you for letting you borrow their money. It's usually expressed as a percentage, and it's most often called an annual percentage rate, or APR. If you always pay off your balance in full and on time, you'll never have to pay them interest. See pages 6–7 for an explanation on how interest works.

If you have a high FICO score, you should not pay more than about 10 percent interest. Even if your score isn't that great, you should still be able to get a rate of about 13 to 15 percent. Unfortunately, if your score is in the toilet, you might be pretty much at the mercy of the credit card companies.

Goals:

1. Get the lowest interest rate possible.

   If you have a bad interest rate on your credit card, you should a) call your credit card company and ask for a better rate (more on this later), and b) if they won't give you a better rate, shop around for a card that will. Cardtrack.com or Bankrate.com offer a list of credit cards and their interest rates.

2. Beware of interest rate hikes.

   Before new credit card legislation went into effect, credit card companies had much more leeway in their ability to raise your interest rates. Now credit card companies are required to give you forty-five days' notice before they hike up your interest rates. So guess what that means? You need to read those statements from your credit card company, since interest rate hikes happen all the time. The legislation also limits when credit card companies can raise your rates on your existing credit card balances (now, the companies cannot raise your rate in most cases unless you have not made your minimum payment for sixty days or a promotional rate's time has expired). You can read more about your rights under this new legislation at consumersunion.org. Monitor your statement each billing cycle to check your interest rates. If they increase, you know what to do: pick up the phone and complain.

D. Minimum payment

The minimum amount you are required to pay each billing cycle.

Usually this is calculated as a percentage of your outstanding balance (so, for example, if your minimum payment is 2.5 percent of your balance and your balance is $1,000, your minimum payment will be $25, or a minimum dollar amount, whichever is greater).

Goal: Always pay the minimum on time each month. Ideally, you'll want to pay your entire balance on time each month, but at the very least, pay the minimum so that your FICO score is not affected.

E. Annual fees
A fee you pay to the bank for the privilege of having its card.
If you have a card with an annual fee, you'll pay this fee even if you never use the card, so you need to assess whether these fees are worth it. Does the card have great rewards—that you actually use—that make it worth the annual fee? (And, ladies, "actually use" does not mean daydreaming about the first-class ticket to Hawaii that those Discover Miles promise. It means that you have already or soon will experience the plush, spacious, champagne-glass-always-full comfort of the first-class seat under your butt.) Does the fee give you a lower interest rate? If you don't pay off your balance in full every month, it might be worth the annual fee if it allows you to pay less in interest.

Goal: If you pay an annual fee but don't reap any rewards from it, it might be time to get a new no-fee card. Cardtrack.com and Bankrate.com offer a list of credit cards that you can choose from.

Other Not-So-Fun Fees and Tricks

Late fees
The amount you'll be charged for paying your bill late.
Late fees are usually a set amount of money that the company charges you when you make a late payment. This is in addition to the interest they'll charge you—yeah, they're jerks (ladies, feel free to insert your preferred synonym for "jerks" here).
Goal: *Avoid paying your bill late. Payment must be received (the date on which it was postmarked usually doesn't matter—they have to actually have it in their greedy little hands) on or before the due date.*

Cash advances

Using your credit card to get cash.

Swipe your little card and voilà—suddenly, you have cash in hand. Seems brilliant, right? Well, it's not. The cash advance is the most deadly part of the Plastic Plague. Just don't do it! First, the credit card company usually charges you a fee for this service. Oh, and then the interest rates are astronomical. And there is no grace period—you start paying interest immediately.

Goal: Avoid taking out a cash advance. If you are already paying astronomical interest on a cash advance, go on cardweb. com and look into getting a balance transfer to a different card with lower interest.

But let's say you are completely desperate. Given the choice between a cash advance and a payday loan, or some other dubious method of money-retrieval from the check-cashing store, it might make more sense to get the cash advance—it all depends on the fees. Go with the route that is least expensive.

Other fees

You may receive other fees from your credit card company. For example, if you go over your credit limit, they may charge you.

Goal: Monitor your credit card statement each month. If you see a strange fee on your statement, call your credit card company immediately.

Step 2: Strong-Arm Your Surgeon

Before every major surgery, the patient needs to be prepped—the toxins (unhealthy food, alcohol, and cigarettes) cleared out of her system so that the body is ready for the procedure. For your plastic surgery, this same rule applies: You have to clear out those toxins—in this case, high interest rates, and crappy credit cards—before you go under the knife and actually start paying off the debt.

Four tips to outsmart your credit card company
1. *Whine and complain (yes, it really works, at least on your credit card company—on your boyfriend, not so much).*

   Whatever you are paying in interest on your credit card, you can probably do better. If you have a high FICO score and not much debt, you should not be paying more than about 10 percent interest. Now, for the rest of you, you may have to pay a slightly higher rate, but not by much. Call your credit card company and threaten to transfer your entire balance to another company unless they lower your rates. Usually, they will do it, but if not, see Tip #2.

2. *Transfer your balance to a card with a better deal.*

You know that pesky Internet bill you pay every month? It's time to start getting your money's worth by visiting cardweb.com and Bank rate.com to shop for better credit card deals. Transfer your existing balance onto a card with lower interest rates, lower fees, and other perks. A balance transfer just means moving the money you owe from one card onto another card.

Look for offers with 0 percent APR for a year—*as long as you can pay off the debt in one year*—and low rates thereafter (13 percent or less), and no annual fees. And remember that this 0 percent is often just for the balance transfer, not for additional purchases. Read the fine print!

Some cards have introductory rates of 5 percent or less for a year, which is great, but remember that an introductory rate is just that: introductory. It will eventually readjust to a higher rate, and if you have a balance, it's going to hurt when it does.

Take a lesson from my friend Alex. She's become incredibly savvy at switching credit cards to pay the lowest amount of interest possible until she can eventually pay off all her debt. She marks on her online calendar when the introductory low rates will end and then sends herself automatic reminders (notice how "reminders" is plural) well before this date comes up to switch cards. She also keeps all the credit card terms and highlights any that she knows may come back to haunt her, like the fact that an interest rate is only for the balance transfer and not additional purchases. It's a bit of work, but it can save you tons of money. However, this is not free reign to put off paying your bill. It's simply a smart way to pay less until you actually pay off the bill.

3. *Make sure your card uses the average daily balance method, not the two-cycle average daily balance method.* Switch cards if necessary.

4. *Watch out for retail cards.*

These are credit cards offered through stores (your Neiman Marcus—translation: Needless Markup—card is a retail card), and they often have super-high interest rates. If you always pay off your balance on them, then it's safe to have them in your wallet. Otherwise, it's probably better to just say no—the 10 percent off you received on your hammered gold bangles probably isn't worth the astronomical interest you are now paying on them now.

Step 3: Going Under the Knife

Now for the harder part—you have to actually pay off what you owe. This part requires some work, but it's by no means impossible.

Five steps to pay off your credit cards

1. Gather all your statements.
2. Write down what you owe, what the interest rate is, and what the minimum payments are on each.
3. If you have debt on multiple credit cards, start paying off the card with the highest interest rate first. Pay as much as you can on this card every month. On the lower interest cards, pay the minimums.
4. If you don't have it already, set up automatic bill pay with your bank. Have your credit card bills automatically deducted from your account. This will help you avoid late fees and it will force you to pay the bills.
5. Once you have paid off that first card, you can start on the rest. Again, focus your attention on the cards with the highest interest rates, paying as much as you can on them, and pay only the minimums on the others until all debt is paid off in full.

On cardweb.com, you can enter your monthly minimums, balance, and interest rates and it will tell you how long it will take you to get out of debt. This is the best site for dealing with your credit card debt.

THE POSITIVE SIDE OF PLASTIC

It's actually a good thing to carry a credit card as long as you can be responsible with it. Credit cards help build your FICO score and can help you out in an emergency when you don't have enough cash. Note that a debit card withdraws money right from your account—it does not help you build up your credit score. So if you are a responsible adult without a credit card, you should get one. And if you can't be trusted with a credit card, I recommend that you get a secured card.

* Where do I apply for a credit card?

    You can apply for a credit card online at cardweb.com. Bankrate.
    com and cardtrak.com both offer listings of credit card offers so you
    can compare deals. You can also apply for a credit card at most banks.
    With all of these choices, shop around.

* I can't be trusted with a credit card or just can't get one, but I need to
  build up my credit score

    Option A: Get a secured credit card.

    For those of you who just cannot be trusted to have a credit card
    but need to build up your credit score, you might want to try getting
    a secured credit card. These cards appear on your credit reports like a
    credit card, but they usually allow you to spend only an amount that
    you have deposited in the bank in advance. However, it's different
    from a prepaid card in that you get a monthly bill, and you don't
    have to pay off the whole balance. These secured cards often have
    high interest rates, so you need to pay them off. Visit cardtrak.com
    and search "secured credit card" to find some options. Beware of
    high fees on these cards. It's important to shop around. Make sure
    that you use a card that shares its data with one of the credit bureaus
    so that when you pay on time, you can improve your credit score.

    Option B: Find someone who will cosign on a credit card with
    you.

    As a cosigner, this person promises to pay off your credit card
    bill in case you are unable to do so. But remember, they will be
    responsible for your debt if you get into trouble, so be certain that
    you'll be able to pay your bills.

PROTECTING THE PLASTIC

So yes, your credit card can be a positive force in your life, and not because
it will enable you to buy that cream pashmina you've been lusting after.
It can improve your FICO score, assuming you are responsible when you
use it. Unfortunately, it can also ruin your FICO score, even if it's not
your fault. Lost or stolen cards, mistakes on your statements—these can
devastate your FICO score. Here's how to protect yourself.

* How do I correct errors on my credit card statement?

    If you find an error on your credit card statement—a purchase
    you didn't make (I mean, as if you would buy Madden for X-Box)
    or some other error—call your credit card company immediately.

Their phone number is on the statement. If this doesn't resolve the problem, send a letter to the credit card company (remember to keep a copy for your records). They have between thirty and ninety days to fix the problem. You will not accrue interest on the charge during this time. (And, ladies, don't pretend that you didn't buy that Tory Burch bag . . . that is seriously illegal, and even the cutest handbag won't make prison orange look good.) Also, do not think that you can avoid paying the entire bill just because of one disputed charge.

* What do I do if my card is lost or stolen?

A couple (and by a couple you mean, like, six) glasses of wine, a barely remembered bar tab, and the next morning you can't find your credit card (and the bartender, though he remembers you and your girlfriends *quite well*, does not have your card). If this happens to you, call your credit card company immediately to report the lost or stolen card. If the card was stolen and you report it, you are responsible only for $50 in unauthorized charges. I recommend following up your call with a letter to the card company saying that the card was lost or stolen. You can find out the address on the credit card company's Web site. Also, with stolen cards, it's a good idea to contact the credit agencies—Experian, Transunion, and Equifax—and ask them to put a security or fraud alert on your account so that they can make sure no one applies for credit in your name. Visit their Web sites and follow the instructions on how to do this.

A thief doesn't even need your actual card to steal from you. They can get the card number by hacking into your computer or online accounts, obtaining a sales slip with the card number on it, or putting a tracer into an ATM machine. To protect yourself, don't leave credit card slips lying around, use a secure password with your Internet connection, and shop online only at reputable retailers. For more tips, check out the Federal Trade Commission's identity theft site at ftc.gov.

* Should I cancel old cards I no longer use?

Probably not. Remember that part of your FICO score is length of credit history—the longer the better. So just cut the card in half but don't actually cancel it, assuming that you don't have annual fees on it.

* When you need a therapist—for your credit card debt

You may have so much credit card debt that you feel you cannot deal with it without one-on-one help. First, ask a family member or good friend if they can loan you the money to take care of the situation. (Just remember that money issues can strain relationships, so make sure the terms of the loan, including how and when you'll pay it back, are clearly understood by everyone.) If that doesn't work, call a consumer credit counseling service like the National Foundation for Credit Counseling at nfcc.gov or 1-800-388-2227. They will help you out for a small monthly fee. Bankruptcy should be your last-ditch effort to get out of your debt mess. Beware of credit card counseling schemes—go right to the NFCC so that you know your credit card therapist is reputable.

Ladies, remember what a savvy shopper you used to be? You could sniff out the super-on-sale Catherine Malandrino dress even when it was surrounded by hundreds of other gorgeous, but not-quite-so-on-sale frocks. As you enact your plastic purge, you need to become a savvy shopper with your credit card terms (not your credit itself, ladies, your credit card *terms*). Get your interest rates as low as possible and fight for the terms that make sense for you, like the average daily-balance method. Dive in and start paying that credit card debt off, with the highest interest items taking priority, but always paying the minimums on all your cards.

Try to keep in mind that you probably aren't going to purge the bad plastic from your life tomorrow. Like any diet, this one takes some time to work. But you will see the progress each week if you stick to it. And by following the advice in this chapter, you can likely get out of credit card debt well before you get your first gray hair.

Finally, remember to focus on the big picture of your financial situation. You still need to control your spending and stay within your budget. You need to put your credit card debt into perspective with all your other debt, as we talked about on page 81. And whenever you feel frustrated or down about your finances, revisit those goals on pages 22–23. You can and will meet them if you stay on track. I am living proof of that—and soon you can be, too.

CHAPTER 6

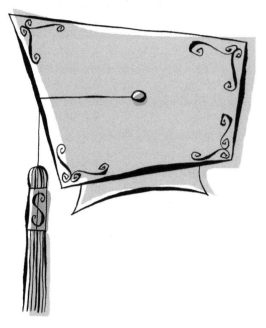

The Skinny on Student Loans
How to Pay Off Your Alma Mater for Good

So you finished college with only minimal liver damage. You've finally (after a few eventful years) lost the freshman fifteen—even if you actually gained the freshman thirty—and you can fit into your high school jeans when you fast for three days and wear Spanx. You managed to find a guy who didn't make you do a keg stand on your first date. Girl, you're on the right track with life (even if your mother isn't convinced), and the next step in your plan for world domination is paying off those student loans. Luckily, your interest on these probably isn't nearly as bad as the interest on your credit card. Still, the company that loaned you the cash wants their money.

HELP, I DON'T EVEN KNOW WHERE MY STUDENT LOAN PAPERS ARE!

It's funny—you know you have student loan papers but you have no idea where. Your parents have totally thrown up their hands in disgust when you asked them about it—"You're an adult now, sweetie; deal with it." What do you do? Go to studentclearinghouse.org and visit the Students & Alumni section, or visit nslds.ed.gov, enter your personal data, and information on your loans will come up. Sometimes the lender that you originally borrowed from isn't listed, but another lender is. Don't worry about it—those busy lenders buy and sell debt all the time. It doesn't mean you get a break, though. You still have to pay.

STUDENT LOANS 101

You need to read and understand the terms of your loan(s)—some light Saturday afternoon reading, let me assure you (hint: that was sarcasm)—because it's necessary. First, you need to know what type of loan you have and its terms: interest rates, loan term, monthly payments, etc. Then you should understand your repayment options, as well as your options for consolidating, deferment, and loan forgiveness.

Major Types of Student Loans

I imagine many of you are like my girlfriend Robin, who is sitting on a pile of student loan debt. Rob loves to learn—the many, many years of college, graduate school, and more graduate school are surefire evidence of that. Now she's earned a PhD—and a side of fatty debt along with it. See, Rob paid for college with loans. Then she paid for many years of graduate school with them. This isn't necessarily a bad thing, as school can pay off salary-wise in the long term. But you have to deal with this debt responsibly. And the first step in dealing with student loan debt is understanding the types of loans you have. (This section is also important for those of you who are considering going back to school and want to know your loan options.)

There are two main types of student loans: federal and private. Federal student loans, such as Stafford and Perkins loans, are guaranteed by the federal government and as such, tend to have relatively low interest rates. Private student loans, which often have higher interest rates than federal student loans, are usually administered by private financial institutions like a bank. Your interest rate on these loans depends on your FICO score.

Since the terms and conditions of private student loans vary widely depending on the lender and your personal financial situation, this section will concentrate on federal student loans. A great Web site for more information on these loans is studentaid.ed.gov. Here are the main types of federal student loans:

- Stafford loans

  Most of you probably have Stafford loans. These federal loans may be either subsidized, meaning that the government paid your interest while you were in school, or unsubsidized, meaning that you have to pay all the interest that accrued on the loans. In the 2009–2010 academic year, the subsidized Stafford Loan interest rate was 5.6 percent; unsubsidized was 6.8 percent. See staffordloan.com for more information.

- Perkins loans

  These are federal loans given to students with serious financial need. The federal government gives schools money so that the college can give out Perkins loans. This is one of the best student loans out there with a low interest rate of 5 percent.

- PLUS loans

  This is a low-interest student loan that your parents can get to fund your college or graduate education.

OPTIONS FOR REPAYING YOUR FEDERAL STUDENT LOANS

Now for the icky part: repayment. But not to worry—once you know your repayment options, you'll be able to find a plan that works for you.

You will have a grace period, usually six months from when you graduate, until you have to start repaying your student loans. You won't need to stick to one type of repayment option. Depending on your financial situation, you may want to pick an option that works better for you. To change your repayment plan, call and talk to your lender.

And remember, automatic bill pay is your BFF when it comes to paying back student loans—payments will be automatically deducted from your account each month so that you can't forget to pay them.

Standard Repayment

With the standard repayment plan, you pay the same amount of money each month and repay the loan in less than ten years. With this repayment option, you end up paying the least in terms of interest (unless you prepaid your loans), but your monthly payments will be higher than they would be with other plans. It can be difficult to swing these payments if you are just starting out and have a low-paying job.

Extended Repayment

If you have more than $30,000 in loan debt, you are eligible for extended repayment, which gives you up to twenty-five years to repay your loan. With extended repayment, you can either opt for fixed payments, which allow you to pay the same amount each month, or graduated repayment, in which case your payments start low and increase every two years. This plan has lower monthly payments, but the cost of your loan will be more than with the standard repayment option because you'll pay more in interest.

Graduated Repayment

With this plan, your payments start out low and increase every two years, and you have up to ten years to pay off your loan. If you're currently in a low-paying job but expect your income to increase, this plan may work for you.

Income-Contingent and Income-Based Repayment

With both of these plans, your monthly payments will be calculated on the basis of your income, family size, and the total amount of your loans (though each uses a slightly different method of calculating your payments), and you will have up to twenty-five years to pay off your loans. The income-based repayment plan is better for most people than the income-contingent plan. See finaid.org for details.

Income Sensitive Repayment

Your monthly payment is a fixed percentage of gross monthly income, usually between 4 percent and 25 percent. You must reapply for this repayment plan every year.

Calculators on finaid.org will help you compare the different repayment plans. Also, the following example from ED Financial will help you visualize the differences in repayment options. Let's say you have $30,000 in student loan debt and a 6.8 percent interest rate. Here's how your monthly payments and total interest paid will vary with each repayment option.

- Standard repayment
  Term of loan: ten years
  Monthly payments: $347.27
  Total interest payments: $11,324.04
- Graduated repayment
  Term of loan: ten years

Monthly payments: Start at $245.75, get higher as months go by, and end up at $509.58

Total interest payments: $13,380.41

How much more expensive this option is: You paid $2,056.37 more in interest with this plan than with the standard repayment plan.

- Extended repayment (with fixed monthly payments)

  Term of loan: twenty-five years

  Monthly payments: $208.22

  Total interest payments: $32,462.41

  How much more expensive this option is: You paid $21,138.37 more in interest with this plan than with the standard repayment plan and $19,082 more than with the graduated repayment plan.

Ideally you should repay your loan as quickly as you can to avoid paying more interest, so if you can afford it, the standard repayment plan is the way to go. Remember that you can always prepay your loans, which will cut the amount of interest you end up paying even more. But don't prioritize prepaying this debt over higher-interest debt like your credit cards. Talk to your lender to learn your options and ask him or her to do side-by-side comparisons of the repayment plans for you so that you can see monthly payments, interest payments, length of repayment, and total cost of the loan for all of your options.

SHOULD I CONSOLIDATE MY LOANS AND HOW DO I DO IT?

First of all, what the heck is consolidation? Answer: It's when you combine all of your student loans into one massive loan, and thus one monthly bill. (Note: If you have private student loans, do *not* consolidate them with your federal student loans.) The interest rate on this new bill will be the average of all the interest rates on the individual loans, but it will never go higher than 8.25 percent. The idea of one massive loan may sound scary, but it's really not.

Here are the advantages to consolidating.

- Only one monthly payment to deal with.

  I recommend having it automatically deducted from your bank account (if you can afford to) so that you are never late with payments.

- Repayment options that work with your financial situation, such as lower monthly payments.

For example, you may be able to extend your repayment term from ten to twenty-five years with the extended repayment plan. You can also get a repayment plan that works with your income situation (the income contingent plan). This will lower your monthly payments, though it will also increase the total cost of your loan since you'll pay more in interest. Note that the above repayment options may also be available if you do not consolidate, so check with your lenders.

- It's free to consolidate your federal student loans.
- You can lock in a fixed interest rate.

  If it's a good rate, this can save you a lot of money in interest payments over the years.
- You may qualify for renewed deferment benefits.

  Check with your lender—consolidating your loans may make you eligible for an extension on the date by which you would have needed to repay your loans.

There are also possible disadvantages.
- Consolidating can affect whether or not you can get a deferment or loan forgiveness. See page 104.
- If you consolidate and then take an extended repayment plan, you will pay more interest in the long run.
- The interest rate might be higher on the consolidated loan than the average rate of the individual loans. If this is the case, consolidation is not to your advantage.
- If you consolidate your loans during the six-month grace period, you will have to start paying back the loan immediately.
- If you've already paid off a large chunk of your student loans or have only a few years left before you'll need to begin repaying your loans, consolidation may not be worth the effort.

Ask your lender to explain the pros and cons of consolidation to you. You should also check out the online loan consolidation calculator at SallieMae.com or the Department of Education's Web site at loancon solidation.ed.gov. If your loans are from a private lender that doesn't offer consolidation, ask him or her to explain all of the different repayment options to you.

The ideal time to consolidate your loans is after you graduate college but before your grace period ends, because in that time period you can get a lower interest rate. The only downside to this is that you have to start paying back your loans immediately—your grace period is up. You can consolidate your loans at any time, though you can consolidate only once. There are, however, two exceptions: If you go back to school and get new student loans, or if an outstanding loan was excluded from your original consolidation.

THREE WAYS TO PUT OFF PAYING OFF YOUR FEDERAL STUDENT LOANS (OR AVOID HAVING TO PAY THEM AT ALL)

Don't take this as a carte blanche to just put off repayment. If you can start paying off your student loans right now, then you should. However, I know it's tough out there, so this section will guide you through loan for-giveness, deferment, and forbearance, which will help you put off paying (or better yet, allow you to avoid having to pay off) those loans until you're on better financial ground.

One note before we begin investigating these options: don't just assume that you'll be eligible. You'll have to contact your lender or debt consolidator to determine your eligibility.

1. Loan Forgiveness

The federal government will forgive—which means it will cancel all or a part of (poof, it's gone, never to be seen again)—your loan for certain kinds of volunteer work (Americorps, Peace Corps, VISTA), military ser-vice, or if you teach or practice medicine in certain communities.

For a complete list of loan forgiveness programs, visit FinAid.org.

2. Deferment

Deferment means just what it sounds like: putting off paying off your loans for a while. Deferment is preferable to forbearance. You can qualify for a deferment for these reasons, among others: economic hardship (and the fact that you cannot afford that gorgeous, black Tibi A-line dress is *not*, I repeat, *not* an economic hardship), unemployment, military deployment, enrollment in school, certain internships, national service.

If you have an unsubsidized Stafford Loan, you will have to pay interest during your deferment, or the interest may be added to your total loan balance, but you will not have to pay the principal. For a subsidized Stafford loan, you won't have to pay principal or interest during a defer-ment. See salliemae.com for more information.

3. Forbearance

Forbearance means that your loan payments will be temporarily postponed or reduced for up to one year. During the forbearance, the interest on your loan continues to accrue, but you don't have to pay it. You can get forbearance for various reasons, including certain kinds of medical internships, AmeriCorps participation, or active military service. The disadvantage to getting forbearance is that it results in higher costs for you in the long run as the interest is accruing. Go to salliemae.com for more information.

Note: If you have a Perkins Loan, you apply for a deferment or forbearance directly from your college.

How Can I Lower My Interest Rate?

Many lenders will lower your interest rate if you have your loan payments automatically deducted from your bank account or if you pay on time each month for a specified amount of time. Don't automatically assume that interest rates will be lower if you do these things. Call your lender to make sure.

DEFAULTING ON YOUR STUDENT LOANS

What happens if you're pretty broke and feel like you cannot make payments on your student loans? Or, what happens if you've already missed a bunch of payments? Whichever category you fall into, this section can help. But first you need to understand just how permanent student loan debt really is.

'Til Death Do Us Part

Student loans stick with you until you pay them off. Even if you declare bankruptcy, you still have to pay them back, which isn't true of most other bills and loans. If you don't pay back your student loans, the lender can take money out of your paycheck, sue you, or take your tax returns, among various other scary actions. Plus, it messes up your FICO score.

If you haven't made any payments in nine months, you are in default on your loans. Try to prevent that. If you feel like you might default, apply for a deferment or forbearance, change your repayment plan so that you'll come closer to being able to afford your payments, try consolidating your loans, or call your lender and see what you can work out.

Rehab for Your Loans

When you default on your loans, a collection agency will start hounding you. They'll ask you to pay them the entire balance in one lump sum. Don't do it (as if you could, anyway—you can't even make the monthly payments). There's a better way: the federal rehabilitation program. If you are in default on a federal student loan, this is the route to take.

Call the Federal Student Aid office at 1-800-4-FED-AID and ask about your repayment options on your defaulted federal loan. They will work with you to set up a repayment plan. If you make a series of on-time payments, default will be erased from your credit report. This is a great deal, one that your lovely credit card company certainly doesn't subscribe to, since they'd never just erase your little mishaps from your credit report. Once you do that, your loan will have been rehabilitated, which means the government is once again insuring that loan.

Once you've rehabbed your loan, you will get nine years to repay the loan. You can apply for rehabilitation only once, so this time be careful. (This plan isn't like the Promises rehab center or the Betty Ford Clinic— it's a one-shot deal.) For more information on rehabilitation, visit the Students section on ed.gov.

You should remember that the interest payments on your student loans might be tax deductible. To see if you can get this deduction, visit irs.gov and look into student loans.

The journey through school may be over for you—though the late nights out in the city with your sorority sisters certainly have a way of taking you back—but the journey through paying off that school debt is probably not. This chapter should have helped you tackle those student loan issues to make your journey a smooth one. Some of the main points to keep in mind: Make your repayment options work for your financial situation, know when to consolidate, understand and use a deferment or forbearance if needed, get your loans forgiven if you can, and by all means, if your loan is in big trouble, get it some rehab—quick! Finally, it is important to remember that paying off student loan debt is quite similar to paying off any other debt: Prioritize highest-interest debt first but always pay the minimum due on all debts. And remember to put your student loan debt into the bigger debt picture as we discussed on page 81.

Before we move on to auto loans, let me just say, "Cheers to you." Cheers to surviving college more than just intact—to surviving it smarter, savvier, and better equipped to take on the world. And with all those skills, you can definitely handle your student loan debt, and all the other debt we will address. See, ladies, college is already paying off.

CHAPTER 7

Car(b) Control
How to Pick and Pay for Your Ride

W hen I turned sixteen, I begged, pleaded, cried, and pleaded some more for my dad to please, please, please buy me a brand-new black BMW convertible. Ha! What I actually got was black, but new and a BMW? Not so much. My dad gave me his hunting truck: a black Ford Bronco with 200,000 miles on it, a gun rack, and KC lights (and if you don't know what those awful things are, don't bother traumatizing yourself by looking them up). You had to put it in drive before you could put it in reverse, and it almost never started when the temperature dipped below thirty degrees. The whole thing was beyond awful. Instead of being grateful to have a car at all, especially one that I didn't even have to buy, my bratty teenage self spent the next two years mortified by the car I did have, and then the next six years dreaming of finally having the "right" car.

So I get it. You see the advertisements for that shiny new Mercedes, you see the low monthly lease payments, and you just know you can totally afford it. Screw the used Honda. But I'm going to try to talk you down from that cliff. Believe me, the girly girl who drove the beat-up hunting truck totally understands wanting a brand-new Mercedes. But wanting something and truly being able to afford it are two different things.

This chapter will discuss what kind of car you can afford, whether to buy or lease it, and whether it should be a new or used car. This chapter will also provide guidelines for how to get the best deal on the car you buy, how to get the most money when selling your car, and how to understand your lease.

HOW MUCH CAN I AFFORD?

Bankrate.com, Edmunds.com, and cars.com have online calculators that can help you in this area. You'll need to take into consideration the down payment, monthly payments, dealer fees and other expenses, gas, maintenance, insurance, and any possible repairs in order to understand how much it will cost to own a car. Then you'll need to put this into the perspective of your entire financial situation. Will you be able to afford the monthly payments and down payment? Look at your budget, monthly spending, and debt-to-income ratio to determine this. Can you realistically cut enough spending so that you can afford these payments? Will this auto loan mean you are taking on too much debt? What does buying this car now mean for your other financial goals? I can't hold your hand through this process, as I have no psychic ability to know your exact financial situation, but go back to the Debt Diet introduction on page 80 and your budget on page 66 to determine if you can afford the monthly payments. Redo your budget to see what it will be able to accommodate.

WHY IT'S USUALLY BETTER TO BUY—AND BUY USED—THAN TO LEASE

The number-one reason it usually makes more financial sense to buy is that *you* own the car when you buy it. When you lease the car, the dealer owns the car. You're only borrowing it, so it's not yours. When your lease ends, you have nothing to show for all the money you've spent each month. (There are cases where it makes sense to lease, such as if you use the leased car for business and can deduct a significant portion of its costs on your taxes, but for the most part, leasing is not a financially savvy move.)

Not only should you almost always buy rather than lease, you should almost always buy used. Check out the Top Five Reasons to Buy Used box to see why it makes sense to buy used.

Top Five Reasons to Buy Used

Unless you're swimming in extra money, you should buy used. Here are the top five reasons you don't (you really, really don't) need that shiny new Mazda Miada convertible.

1. A new car loses 20 to 30 percent of its value within the first year, according to Edmunds.com. That's quite a loss in value! After the first year, the car will continue to decrease in value, but not at such a rapid rate. Let someone else pay for the luxury of having a brand-new car. A one- to three-year-old car is likely still in great condition.

2. Insurance on a used car is usually cheaper than on a new one.

3. There are a lot of good deals on previously leased cars. Because leases have strict mileage and wear and tear rules, owners of leased cars are often pretty careful with the car.

4. Used cars are more reliable today than ever before. Some used cars still have factory warranties. Many dealerships sell certified used cars, which include warranties.

5. You can check up on the car's history at carfax.com to make sure you're not getting a lemon. To do this, you'll need the VIN number of the car, usually found on the windshield. It costs $24.99, which isn't cheap, but checking your car's personal history could save you thousands in the future.

But buying can be expensive, so for those of you who cannot come up with a down payment for an auto loan, leasing may be your only option if you need a car. But beware—leases have strict terms such as mileage limits (you can't go over a certain number of miles per year) and wear and tear guidelines (you can have only a certain amount of wear and tear on the car). We'll review these conditions on pages 114–15. If you break these terms (for example, if you go over your allotted mileage or have excessive wear on your car), you'll usually be hit with hefty fees.

Bankrate.com has a handy calculator that can help you determine whether you can afford to buy the car. Remember that it's usually better to buy the car since you end up owning it in the end, but if you can't afford the monthly payments on an auto loan and you really need the car, leasing may be your only option. However, before you lease, please read the Guide to Leasing Your Car section to find the best lease you can get.

TRADE IN YOUR OLD CAR OR SELL IT?

Most of the time, it's better to sell it on your own. Car dealers are notorious for giving you a raw deal when you trade in your old car for another one. (The stereotype of the sleazy used car salesman isn't always far from the truth.) But if you really want to trade in your car, don't let the dealer know it until after you've already negotiated the best price on the car you're trading your old one in for. We'll talk on page 113 about how to negotiate this. Know the value of your old car (look it up on Kelly Blue Book at kbb.com) so you don't get low-balled by the dealer.

A GUIDE TO BUYING A CAR

After my poor little sister inherited the Ford Bronco — complete with more miles, a far shakier suspension, and a series of scratches that I had not-so-successfully tried to hide with a touch-up pen — I went with my dad to buy his next car so I could learn the ropes before buying my own. I, like many other girls I know, was a bit daunted by the entire process and barely said a word during the sale, assuming that my dad must know how to negotiate car deals better than me. That was a mistake that I feel many women make. Even if my dad did know better, I could have done my homework and at the very least asked questions when I did not understand the terms of the deal. Well, you know what they say: Hindsight's 20/20, and now I realize how silly that mentality was.

Here's what I've learned, ladies: We're just as smart, if not smarter, than those car dealers. We just need to understand their lingo and not be afraid to ask questions, negotiate, and walk away from a deal if it's not up to our standards. Sure, the dealer might be disappointed that he spent an hour answering a million questions and no deal came of it, but who cares? First of all, you don't even know the guy and probably will never see him again (and if you do, you can feel confident in the fact that you beat him at his own game). And second of all, better his disappointment than you paying way too much for a car, and thus putting your goals even further out of reach. So let's dive into the process of buying a car at a great price.

Step 1: Know What You Can Truly Afford, and Stick Within Those Price Parameters

Before you buy, understand the true cost of ownership. See pages 113–14.

Step 2: Do Your Homework

You need to know what the car is worth, as well as what all the car lingo means, so you can get a fair price.

Homework for buying a new car

Research the dealer invoice price, which is the price the dealer paid to the manufacturer for the car. The price you pay for the car should be close to the dealer invoice price, *not* to the MSRP, or Manufacturer's Suggested Retail Price. The MSRP is the sticker price on the car, and it's inflated. Ideally, you should pay no more than 3 to 5 percent over the dealer invoice price. To look up the dealer invoice price for the car you want, visit Edmunds.com.

Sometimes you can buy a car at or below the dealer invoice price. Here's why: Dealers sometimes have many unsold vehicles on hand, so the manufacturer will jump in to help them sell these cars—the more cars the dealer sells, the more they buy from the manufacturer. To help dealers sell cars, the manufacturer will offer incentives to consumers such as low-interest loans, employee prices, rebates (money back when you buy the car), or special lease deals. Web sites such as carsdirect.com or Edmunds.com will give you information on these incentives and whether or not they are available for the car you want.

Homework for buying a used car

If you are buying a used car (which I highly recommend over buying a new car; see page 110), visit kbb.com and look up the value of the used car. Try to get a price close to and preferably lower than that value. Remember that the Kelly Blue Book is not the be-all-end-all of car values. Consider resale value (if gas prices are rising, it might not be the best time to buy an SUV), repair costs (sometimes exotic cars can cost an arm and a leg to repair), insurance, and other relevant factors.

When buying a used car, you need to know the car's background. Once you've selected the car you want, get the VIN number and run a background check on it. See page 110 for details. It's also often a good idea to have an independent mechanic check out the car before you buy. If you are buying from a dealer, have him give you the car's inspection history. Consider a certified pre-owned car (CPO), which comes with a warranty—just make sure the warranty is from the manufacturer, not the dealer.

Step 3: Shop Around for an Auto Loan before Going to The Dealership

Yes, the dealership will offer financing, but you want to know what's out there before you go. Visit Bankrate.com to find out competitive auto loan rates in your area. You should shop around at local banks or credit unions as well as eLoan.com. When you find a great interest rate—and remember, the higher your FICO score, the better your interest rate offers will be—get pre-approved at that lender before you start negotiating with dealers. When you do go through with an auto loan, you should choose the one with the lowest interest rate. Try to pick the shortest loan term that you can afford (so if it's a choice between a three-year and a five-year term, choose the three-year if you can afford to).

Step 4: Negotiate to Get the Best Deal You Can

Use the knowledge you've gained to get the price you want.

When you are negotiating with a dealer, make sure you settle on the total price of the car before you discuss financing or monthly payments. Here's why: The dealer will often ask you what you can afford in monthly payments and then structure a deal to get you to those payments by extending the length of the loan/lease, or some other tricky plan. This is usually a bad financial deal for you because you'll pay way more in interest than you should. Instead, negotiate the price of the car first. Remember that when you are buying a new car you should ideally pay no more than 3 to 5 percent over the dealer invoice price (as discussed earlier), and you should pay close to and preferably lower than the Kelly Blue Book value (while also considering other relevant factors) when buying a used car.

During the entire negotiation, keep chanting silently to yourself, "sleazy car dealer, sleazy car dealer." Yes, it's rude, but he or she can't hear you and it'll keep you focused on getting yourself an awesome car deal instead of feeling like you should be nice to the dealer.

Know what's included in the sticker price and negotiate those items. These are:

* **Destination and delivery charges.** You can get these from Edmunds. com. The dealer should not make a profit on these, so what you see on edmunds.com is what you should pay.
* **Add-ons.** These are additional services like rust proofing, and for the most part, you don't need them. Review all the add-ons and do your homework as to which you'll actually need.

- **ADM: Additional dealer markup.** Don't pay it. It's just profit for the dealer with no gain for you.

Keep a watchful eye out through the entire negotiation.
From start to finish, make sure you understand every term and condition. Check to see that the items you have verbally agreed on end up in the contract. When you get to the contract stage, make sure the dealer doesn't add any unwanted charges into your loan or lease. (And remember the chant: "sleazy car dealer, sleazy car dealer.") To avoid inadvertently accepting any underhanded last-minute changes, calculate your own monthly payments first.

For more car-buying tips, check out carbuyingtips.com, carinfo.com, and Edmunds.com.

A GUIDE TO LEASING A CAR

I know, the "buy a used car" tidbit is difficult to digest. Why shouldn't you have a brand-new car every few years? You've told yourself that you look so much hipper in that shiny new VW Jetta than you ever did in your old Honda, and now cannot get it out of your head. You're a leaser through and through. Well, if you're going to do it (against your better judgment and my advice), you need to understand the terms of your lease. Alternatively, if you're (smartly) not obsessed with shiny new toys like the Jetta but need a car despite being unable to afford a down payment, you're going to need this same advice. So, here's your leasing lingo lowdown.

- **Manufacturer's suggested retail price (MSRP).** (Key word: "suggested." As in, you really need to take responsibility for negotiating this.) This is the sticker price, or the asking price, for the car. It does not include taxes, registration, and other miscellaneous fees.
- **Capitalized cost.** This is the total price of the car. Capitalized cost = vehicle price + fees + taxes.

  Negotiate to get this as low as possible so that you can lower your monthly payments. Do your homework before you go into the dealership so that you understand what you should be paying.
- **Residual value.** This is the value of the car at the end of the lease term. You don't have any control over this number. What you can do is choose to lease a car with a high residual value. Generally, the higher the residual value, the lower your monthly lease payments. To figure out the residual value of the car you want to lease, visit

cars.com. The best cars to lease are those whose twenty-four-month residuals are at least 50 percent of their original MSRP value.

* **Interest rate/money factor.** Your lease interest rate is expressed as a money factor, sometimes called lease factor, lease rate, or simply a factor. This money factor is expressed as a small decimal number. The dealer is not legally required to tell you the money factor, but you need to ask him or her to tell you.

  Once you know the money factor, here's how you calculate the annual percentage rate:

  Interest rate = Money Factor × 2400. So if you have a money factor of .00297, you will multiply .00297 by 2400. This gives you a 7.13 percent annual percentage rate, which means your interest rate is 7.13 percent each year. You want to get as low of an APR as possible. Note: Some dealerships might quote a value like 2.97 instead of 0.00297. If they quote the money factor this way, then just multiply the money factor by 2.4.

* **Term of lease.** The amount of time you'll lease the car—usually two to four years.

* **Upfront money.** The money you owe upfront on the car.

* **Number of miles.** You are allowed only a certain number of miles on the car. If you go over it, the dealer will hit you with major fees (usually a per-mile cost).

* **Insurance.** You are usually required to get comprehensive insurance on the car. See Chapter 12 for details on auto insurance.

* **Residual price.** At the end of the lease, you'll be offered the option to buy the car at a certain price, called the residual price. This is generally *not* a good deal.

* **Excessive wear.** You are only allowed a certain amount of wear and tear on the vehicle. If you go over it, you'll be hit with fees. Deep scratches, major dents, large upholstery stains, among many other items might be considered excessive wear.

Visit LeaseGuide.com for more information on leasing. Visit Bankrate.com for terrific calculators that will help you determine your monthly payments and other useful information.

A GUIDE TO SELLING YOUR CAR

Obviously you want to get as much money for your car as you can. The more money you get for your car, the more you can save (and, if you get a really great deal, you could always buy that patent leather YSL tote, if it's now in your budget). Here are the top five tips for getting the most money you can for your car.

1. *Figure out what the car is worth, and set the price accordingly.*
   Visit Kelly Blue Book at kbb.com to determine what your car is worth. Also, check through your local paper to see what cars in your area are selling for. And use your intuition—just because Kelly Blue Book says it's worth a certain amount of money doesn't mean that it is. Remember that if you have a popular car, you might be able to get more for it. When you set the price, it's usually best to ask a little more than you're willing to accept.

2. *Clean and fix it up.*
   Waxing, washing, detailing, and minor repairs can increase the amount potential buyers are willing to pay. Remember, looks matter (as if I have to tell you that).

3. *Advertise the car for sale.*
   Where you put the ads is up to you, but you have many choices: local publications like the newspaper; online sites like Edmunds.com, Used Vehicle Locator, and Craigslist; bulletin boards in the area; word of mouth; a sign in the window of the car. Sometimes placing an ad, such as in your local newspaper, can be expensive, so it might be worth trying out free advertising options before you pay for advertising space.

4. *Don't be afraid of negotiating.*
   First, know the lowest price you're willing to accept. Sometimes when you're in the middle of a negotiation with a buyer, you get a little miffed and end up accepting a lower offer than you really want. Before a buyer even sees your car, know the lowest offer you're willing to accept. Don't let yourself go below it. Second, don't just take the first offer the potential buyer throws out there (unless he's offering exactly the amount you asked or more). Try asking him or her for more money.

5. *Transfer the title and get your money.*
   Once you have the money from the sale (preferably cash, cashier's check, or a money order; beware of personal checks as they might bounce), transfer the title to the new buyer's name. To find out how to do this, contact the Department of Motor Vehicles in your state. If your DMV offers a Release of Liability form, fill it out.

   If you still owe money on the car and the bank is holding the title, you should probably conclude the sale at the bank where the title is held. Call the bank ahead of time so that they'll have the title ready, then go there with the buyer. The buyer will bring the money, which will pay off the balance of the loan, and then the bank will sign the title over to the buyer.

I know I've mentioned this issue in passing, but it's an important one, so I want to dive into it one last time. Whether buying, leasing, or selling a car, many women I know get intimidated by car-related transactions. They are afraid that they don't know enough about cars, that they'll sound like idiots if they ask a bunch of questions, or that someone won't like them if they try to haggle over a price. Ladies, this is ridiculous. You are a smart, together woman—remember? You're a smart, together woman with the entire Internet and this entire chapter at her fingertips. So don't feel like you are some uninformed bumpkin. You aren't, as long as you do your homework and ask questions. If you don't know, ask or look it up. And if you feel like you are getting bullied by a buyer or dealer, you probably are. Don't be afraid to take charge of the negotiation or walk away from the deal if need be. Stop constantly putting other people first. During a negotiation, so many women I know worry about whether the other person—a person they will probably never see again no less—likes them or not. This is not helping your bottom line. It's far more important that *you* like you and where your life is going than that some random person does.

Keeping that in mind, it's also important to remember these key points from this chapter: It's usually better to buy, and buy used, than to lease. When you do buy, you need to understand what you can truly afford (the total cost of the loan, not just the monthly payments). Do your homework on the car, compare auto loans before you even get into the dealership, and negotiate the best deal you can by knowing the terms and conditions that make sense for you. When you lease, many of these same rules apply, such as understanding what you can truly afford as well as the terms and conditions of your lease. Finally, when selling your car, do your homework on pricing, clean up the car, advertise smartly, and don't be afraid to negotiate. And as with every step in the Debt Diet, put your auto loans into the big debt picture like we discussed on page 81. Pay as much as you can on the highest interest loans while always paying the minimum amount owed on all loans.

And voilà, that concludes the Debt Diet. Ladies, look how far you've come. You've polished your (spending) style, put yourself on a (debt) diet, and now you have only one more thing to do before you are fully on the path to financial freedom: Get (financially) fit. And that's exactly what Part IV will do for you—buff up your bottom line, *big time.*

PART IV:

(Financial) Fitness

AN INTRODUCTION TO FINANCIAL FITNESS (AND HOW IT WILL BEEF UP YOUR BOTTOM LINE ONCE AND FOR ALL)

Even you, the girl whose workout tapes are covered in a thick layer of dust, whose running shoes are still sparkly white, who thinks walking to her car every morning constitutes a workout—even you can get fit. I, of course, mean financially fit, because I am sure that addressing your relationship with the treadmill requires a completely separate book.

But first things, first: What does it mean to be financially fit? It means you're making smart financial decisions that will set you up for a rich—in every meaning of the word—life down the road. Cue up those goals from Chapter 2 here, ladies. This is the part where they come true. Just remember that your financial fitness is built upon your success in managing your spending (as we discussed in Part II) and taking care of your existing debt, and of the debt you might take on in the future, responsibly (as outlined in Part III). After all, no matter how (financially) fit you may be, if it's thwarted by an ugly (spending) style and a derailed (debt) diet, it's not going to make as much of an impact. Keeping that in mind, here's what your financial fitness routine is going to require.

- **Making savvy choices about your career.** Corner office here you come.
- **Investing smartly for retirement.** You'll never, ever, (ever!) have to look at your boss's ugly mug on a Monday morning again.
- **Building up savings for emergencies and other goals.** You'll finally have the cash to traipse around Venice with your new beau.
- **Fully insuring yourself and your stuff.** Here's where that vintage handbag collection—and many other things that are important to you—gets all the protection it deserves.

- **Buying a home (for most of you).** You're moving on up—to floor-to-ceiling windows and to-die-for city views or at least to a place you can call your own.
- **Handling your taxes well.** Here's where the snarly IRS starts working—for you.
- **. . . And if you're with somebody special, getting your joint finances in tip-top shape.** Cheers to a happy and rich life—together!

Whew, I realize that seemed like quite a lot to digest, but not to worry. This part breaks it out in manageable steps. Look at it like going to the gym. If you want to tone your entire body, you'll need several different machines. The equipment that tones your abs is not the same as the equipment that tones your tush. Getting financially fit is no different—it takes several different mechanisms to make it happen.

Financial fitness doesn't have to be overwhelming. Break it up just like you'd do with your workout. At the gym, you spend a certain amount of energy on squats, a certain amount on crunches, a certain amount on push-ups. You'll do the same thing with your financial fitness—a certain amount of energy on retirement savings, a certain amount on buying a home, etc. Likewise, the amount of energy and time you devote to each body part, depends on how much work it needs. If you already own a home and are paying it off in full and on time, you can turn more of your energy to other items.

Still need a bit more encouragement? I'm on it. You can do this! I mean, you survived college, didn't you? Think of when you were a freshman and it seemed so daunting—four whole years and so much to do: Pick a major, select a sorority, deal with roommates, figure out who to date, learn how to drag yourself to class after closing down the bars the night before. . . . But you know what? You got through it. Sure, there were some slip-ups, but you survived, and with a degree no less. It's the same thing here—a series of smart decisions in the coming years will make your goals a reality. Stay focused and don't get yourself down if and when setbacks, like not saving enough one month or losing a job, happen. Ladies, if you can survive the epic embarrassment that certain college experiences always contain, then I assure you, you can get past money setbacks. And guess what, getting financially fit is the *final* step in your money makeover. By the end of it, you'll be in the best financial shape of your life.

CHAPTER 8

Climb the Career Ladder
How to Navigate Your Way to Your Dream Job and a Pretty Paycheck

L ook, I know it's not exactly your dream to be fetching coffee for your type-A psycho boss for the rest of your life. The fact that you literally fell asleep under your desk today—despite having, for once, an early night—doesn't bode well for your job satisfaction. Or those briefs . . . well, let's just say that you might officially lose it if you see another one. Plus, you'd like to be able to eventually afford a home and a nice vacation, so you really, really need a raise (and not the crappy 3 percent that your boss insists is generous).

Trust me, I've been there. My first job may have been on Madison Avenue, but old Mad Ave sure doesn't pay what it used to. I know many of you are so broke working an entry-level, low-income job that it's impossible to save much money. That's where this chapter comes in. It will help you navigate your career so that you'll eventually be able to get your financial life together. You'll learn how to evaluate whether your current job is right for you, how to land your dream job or figure out what in the world you want to do, and how to advance your career. Corner office, here you come!

EVALUATING YOUR JOB

First things first. You need to evaluate your current job or the job for which you're being considered to determine whether it's the right move in your career trajectory. And this is *not* just about money. Gasp! It's true—right now, it's actually more important that this job will move you up the career ladder than whether it currently pays you well. Here are the questions to ask yourself when evaluating a job.

#1: Will This Job Get Me Where I Want to Go?

This is the *most important question* you can ask yourself when evaluating a job—even more important than salary and benefits. Think about the contacts you are making and the experience you are gaining—will those land you a better job in the future? Maybe you don't get paid much now, maybe you don't love your job now, but if this job will lead to the career you want, you should keep plugging away. Being in a company that promotes from within and that offers on-the-job training that will help you advance your career is also important.

But how do you figure out if this job will get you where you want to be? First, determine your specific dream job. For example, you want to be Editor-in-Chief of *Elle Decor*. (I know that some of you have no idea what you want to do—that is totally okay; see the What to Do When You Have No Idea What You Want to Do section for some tips on seeking out your dream career). Then, make a career ladder. This is a specific list of jobs that you are willing to take to progressively move up to the job that you want.

Take my friend Lindsay, for example. She knows she wants to be a publisher for a major magazine, and despite being only twenty-six years old, she's well on her way. How does she already make well over six figures in a job that's right in line with the job of her dreams? Because every job she's taken has moved her closer to her goal of publisher. Her career ladder looks like this: She began as a media buyer at a major New York City ad agency, then leveraged this media-buying experience to get a job as an account manager at a small magazine. She used that job to land her current position as an account manager at a larger magazine. Next up on her career ladder: account director, group director, associate publisher, and finally she'll end up the publisher of a major magazine.

You can make your own career ladder in just the same way by listing every job, in chronological order, that will culminate in your dream job. It often helps to make your career ladder pretty specific by adding in details about companies or types of companies that you'll want to work for. It's great to choose companies that will promote you from within so that you won't have the hassle of lacking specific experience on your résumé to move up in a job.

Before you can build your career ladder, you need to figure out how people in the job you want ended up there. What jobs did they take as they climbed the career ladder? Did they go back to school? I suggest joining a professional network in your area so that you can meet people in your field. Ask questions and do research to figure this out—remember that Google, as always, is your BFF.

#2: Is the Salary Fair and Can I Get Paid More?

To find out what others in your field with a level of experience similar to your own earn, do some research. Visit salary.com, careerbuilder.com, and payscale.com, all of which will give you a basic salary analysis for free. For the purposes of this exercise, there's no need to pay the extra money for their in-depth salary analysis. This is not the be-all-end-all when it comes to your salary, but it's a good place to get a sense of whether or not you're paid what you should be.

In answer to the Can I get paid more? question, see below. It almost never hurts to ask for a raise as long as you have put sufficient time and effort into the company.

#3: Are the Benefits Fair?

Again, it's not just about the money. Yes, your salary is important, but you should also look at the benefits offered by your job. Benefits can include retirement plans like 401(k)s; insurance like health, life, and disability; tuition reimbursement; stock options; bonus plans; vacation and holidays; sick days; and more.

Health insurance, tuition, and other benefits are expensive if you have to buy them on your own, so make sure you consider this when you're evaluating a job.

This is an individual assessment—I can't tell you what benefits are better for you than others except to say the following: If your employer offers a 401(k) with matching funds, participate (more on this in Chapter 9). Most of the time, it's much less expensive to take advantage of employer-sponsored health plans rather than to pay for health care on your own, so think about that when evaluating your benefits package (more on this in Chapter 12). As for the other benefits, maybe it's important to you to have more vacation time, so you should look at that when deciding whether you are getting what you want out of your job. Or maybe you want to go back to school at night, so the tuition reimbursement is more important than the number of vacation days. It's hard to quantify some of these benefits, but it's important that you consider them when evaluating your job.

#4: Do I Like This Job?

What do I look like, your shrink? I can't tell you whether you like it or not. You just have to evaluate this on your own. Here's what I can tell you, and it's not going to answer the question of eternal happiness, but if you wake up and think, "Dear God, if I have to look at my desk for another day, I might just [fill in the blank with whatever dramatic insanity you feel]," then, well, you might just need a career change. Look into your heart and decide if this is what you want to do with your life. Yes, money is important. But what's money if you aren't happy? It's easy to think that a gorgeous downtown loft will erase your job complaints, but let me tell you, it won't. I know a lot of very rich, very unhappy girls, and while they have nicer drapes and sofas than most of us, they aren't very satisfied with their lives.

Take my friend Ingrid, who—let me preface this story by saying—I adore. But frankly, I'm not sure how, since I simply never see her anymore. She's got that life you think you want. A beautiful apartment in the West Village that would make even the snootiest Upper East Side princess consider a downtown move, a high-powered job in a big law firm, and a closet that even Angelina Jolie wouldn't scoff at. But it's what I call the on-paper-perfect life, because that's all it is—perfect on paper, not so in reality. Ingrid puts in roughly seventy-hour work weeks, sleeps with her BlackBerry not more than three feet from her head, and often has to pop a Xanex so she can turn the office off. And you know what, she doesn't even love it. To be honest, I really don't even think she likes it. What's worse: It's affecting her life. Dates? Not too many anymore. "Who has time?" she deflects, when we ask about the boy situation. Friends? Well, it's starting to annoy a few of them that she always has to cancel plans because she's "stuck at the office." Family? Alone time (other than sleep)? Workouts? Hobbies? All suffering. And all suffering for something she doesn't love. So is the chicly furnished pad, the rows of buttery soft handbags, the sexy job—is it all worth it? Well, it's her life and her choice, so I can't answer for her. But if her life sounds something like yours, think about it. Maybe you could take a little less money—and cut your spending to compensate—so you could have the life you really want. Ferragamo may be beautiful, but it doesn't laugh with you over drinks or keep you company when you're old and wrinkly.

WHAT TO DO WHEN YOU HAVE NO IDEA WHAT YOU WANT TO DO

There are a variety of tools out there to help you decide what career might be right for you. Check with the career counseling services at your university or a university nearby. They probably have a career counselor who can help you, or career tests they can administer to match your skills and interests with a career. There are also a series of quizzes on CareerBuilder.com that may help pinpoint a good career for you. That's a good place to start, as it will at least give you ideas about possible jobs; however, a career counselor is a trained professional so he or she will be able to provide even more targeted advice. There are also a series of books on the subject of finding the right career, such as *How to Find the Work You Love* by Laurence Boldt.

HOW DO I FIND JOBS?

Well, there are the sites you probably already know about: CareerBuilder.com, Monster.com, and Hotjobs.com. I can almost hear your groans, as I know many of you have probably already sent plenty of resumes to job postings on those sites without ever receiving a response. It is, after all, difficult to get a response from the companies who post jobs on these large sites, as they often receive thousands upon thousands of résumés in response to their listings. So what else can you do?

1. Network

    Talk to friends, family, peers, and former colleagues to see if they know of available jobs. Talk to your university and see what they can do. Join groups for people in the profession you'd like to enter.

2. Consider a headhunter

    A headhunter will match you with a company that is looking for employees—she makes a commission when she fills the job. Try headhuntersdirectory.com to find a headhunter in your area.

3. If you are having trouble finding a job because you don't have the right qualifications, consider doing an internship or part-time assignment in that field.

I know, you don't have the money for this, right? I mean, you need a full-time gig. But if this part-time job will help you land the career you want, it might be worth it. Yes, you may have to accumulate a little credit card debt—yes, I just said that—but you *will* pay it off with that better job. And you *will* be careful about how much you spend on the card. If this is the only route to getting your career on track, you may just have to do it.

HOW TO ADVANCE YOUR CAREER

Smart, savvy planning will show you what jobs you need to land to move up your career ladder; a smart, savvy work ethic will help you land these jobs by helping you get promoted from within, make the right contacts in the workplace, and more. These five tips are your ticket right on up your career ladder.

1. **Arrive before your boss and leave after her (and don't let her catch you slacking).**

   Believe me, ladies, hard work is rewarded. I know that when the clock hits six you are so ready for a giant glass of Pinot and some chitchat with chicks who don't bore you to death, but if you want to advance in your career, you need to prove that you are willing to give it your all. And P.S., learn to angle your computer screen so your boss doesn't catch your G-Chatting with your friends.

2. **Get your work done correctly and as best as you can.**

   This seems simple: Do a good job. But I can't tell you the number of women who turn in work late and try to make excuses for it, or ladies that don't check over their work before submitting it to the boss. A little attention to detail can make a big difference, so put in the effort.

3. **Work your charm.**

   Network, network, network. If your colleagues and boss adore you, you'll reap the benefits. They'll help you when you need it and they'll be way more forgiving when you screw something up. And join professional organizations so that you can network with people in your field. This will make it so much easier to get a new job.

4. **Make yourself indispensable to your superiors.**

   Anticipate what your boss will want you to do and start doing it before she asks. She'll love that you took initiative. Learn skills that no one else in the office has.

5. **Go above and beyond the call of duty.**

   Volunteer to work on additional projects that will help the company out. Make smart suggestions for improving processes and projects.

NEGOTIATING A RAISE

She makes *what*?! But she has the same job as me! You've all probably experienced this moment of truth. The moment you realize your coworker or someone you know—a woman or man who holds a job quite similar to your own—makes more than you.

You might have gone through the seven stages of grief upon this realization—shock ("There's no way she makes more than me! She leaves at 6 p.m. every day!"); anger (admit it, you hid that stapler from her); sadness ("Do I really do such a bad job?"), et cetera. Let's hope you're now at the "hope" stage. Hope that you can make as much as she does or at least get a significant bump in pay. And if you play your cards right, you probably can. Here's how.

Prepare for the Salary Negotiations

1. **Assess your job performance.**

   Take a 360° evaluation of your job performance from the quality of your work to the quality of your relationships with colleagues. Some criteria to think about: job knowledge, productivity, dependability, attendance, adaptability to change, organization skills, problem solving, decision making, communication, relationships with others, leadership, and teamwork. Be honest with yourself.

   If you feel that you do a good or great job in most of these areas, you're ready to proceed to the following steps. If you could work on many of these areas, you should make a concerted effort to shape up—or risk not getting that raise.

2. **Put together a portfolio of your best work.**

   It's easy for your boss to forget how valuable you are—especially when she's faced with having to give you more money. So be prepared with a portfolio of the great work you've done. It will help convince her that not only are you a valuable employee, but you're also very serious about getting this raise.

3. **Know the salary range for your position.**

   There are many free tools available on the Internet to show you what people in your position make. Salary.com is a great resource, giving you the basic salary range of thousands of jobs for free. If you are at the lower range of this bell curve, you will have a good argument for your boss.

4. **Make an appointment with your boss (don't just grab her in the hallway).**

Make sure your boss knows you have something important to discuss—and you want her undivided attention when discussing this issue. Set aside adequate time to discuss all the elements you want to go through—the last thing you want is to have two minutes to make the case for your raise.

5. **Prepare what you'll say in the salary negotiation.**
Rehearse the points you want to get across in the salary negotiations: Know how much of a raise you want and the specific reasons you deserve it. Prepare what you'll say if your boss says no. You want to be calm and collected at this meeting, so reviewing the meeting beforehand in your mind should help prepare you.

During the Salary Negotiation

1. **Make your desire for a raise specific and clear and make a compelling case for why you deserve it.**
Let your boss know why you called the meeting right away and present her with compelling evidence for why you deserve a raise. Show her your portfolio, list your stellar skills and accomplishments, and inform her that you're at the low end of the salary range. Give her whatever information will convince her that you're worth the raise. This is not the time to be shy about how great you are—if you want this raise, show your boss that you deserve it.

2. **Be the first to throw out the number.**
Make sure your request for a raise is specific (and reasonable)—and state the amount of the raise before your boss does. You want to be the first to suggest the number, as this number is usually the anchor of the negotiations from then on.

3. **Ask for more than you think you'll get.**
Ask for a larger raise (within acceptable limits) than what you'll accept. For example, if you will accept a $5,000 raise, try asking for an $8,000 raise. (Don't go pie-in-the-sky here—use good judgment without underestimating yourself.) Your employer will probably try to negotiate downwards, so if you are willing to accept less than you asked for, this will likely work in your favor.

4. **Do not let the negotiations become emotional or hostile.**
Keep the tone fair and calm. Even if your boss says no, do not become angry. Keep in mind that the goal of this negotiation is a win-win situation—you feel good about your raise, and your employer feels that they're keeping you happy so you won't leave the company.

5. **Ask for an explanation for the refusal and request an opportunity for another evaluation.**
If your boss says no, ask her why—and listen carefully to her reply. Make sure you understand what it will take in the future for you to get a raise. If the climate seems right, you might want to ask your employer if there is anything else they can do to reward your hard work (another week of vacation, for example). Finally, let your boss know that you will enact her feedback, and thus would like the opportunity for another evaluation in six months or so, at her convenience.

Now, ladies, before you go charging into the world, ready to bust into the corner office, remember that these things often take time. And time, of course, means patience. So don't expect to climb the career ladder overnight or to immediately get a raise just because you asked. It may take some trial and error; it may take some waiting. But remember, you can do it. Repeat after me: no more fetching coffee, no more changing ink cartridges, no more working for a moron. Repeat it and insert your own career gripes in there. Get good and annoyed—lord, your boss is a pain in the butt!—and thus good and ready for your dreams to come true. Now start making plans for your career ladder, your raise, your new career path, whatever it is that you want. You'll get there. You just need to motivate and plan.

Why is this all so important to your financial fitness? Because your career is a key part of your financial fitness, as it is often your primary source of income. And without money, of course, the other financial fitness items are much harder to enact. You can't very well save for retirement or any other goals without the money to actually put into savings. So if you skimmed over this chapter, go back through it more thoroughly. For most of you, your career is the financial engine for the rest of your financial goals. Maximize its potential to ensure a secure financial future. Once you've gotten your career in line, you're ready to begin building a "fit" financial future, a primary part of which is saving smartly for retirement. The next two chapters will show you how to do that.

CHAPTER 9

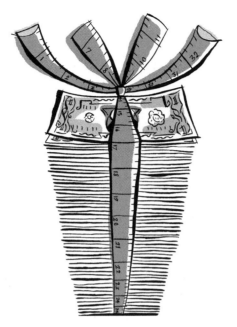

Race Toward Retirement

How to Retire Well Before You're Ancient

L adies, this is the no-more-boss-ever part of the book, otherwise known as retirement, which is when you get to stop working, forever. That means no more memos, no more conference calls, no more defective copiers, no slacker colleagues. Retirement means that all you have to worry about is you and whatever it is that you want to do, whether it's padding around in your pj's eating bonbons, or lounging on a tropical beach, with a piña colada in one hand, and a hot young man keeping you company. You'll have the freedom to do whatever you want, but you'll also need the money to do it.

You may be telling yourself that you won't need to worry—your husband will take care of you or you'll save for retirement later when you make more money. Again, and I can't stress this enough, Prince Charming may very well arrive to help you out, but the odds are not in your favor. And the broke musician/artist/hipster is often a lot more fun than the stuffy (but rich) investment banker who seems to want to talk only about his "fabulous pad." Right, buddy. Seriously, you can't help who you fall in love with, and you definitely can't guarantee that he or she will fund your retirement.

And waiting to save for retirement is just a bad idea. The sooner you start saving, the more time your money has to grow. Refer to the chart on page 7 to show you just how dramatic a difference an early investment can make. This chart assumes an 8 percent return on investment (this is pretty standard for smartly invested retirement fund returns over the long term). If you put $300 per month into your retirement account starting at age twenty-five, you'll be a millionaire at age sixty-five. If you wait until you're thirty-five to start contributing $300 per month, you'll have only $440,445. That's less than half the money you'd have if you'd started saving a decade earlier! In case you need more evidence of the importance of starting to save early, see page 7 for an example. If the thirty-five-year-old in this situation wants to become a millionaire, she will have to almost double her monthly contributions (from $300 to $600 *every single month*) until the age of sixty-five. The lesson: It doesn't take that much to become a millionaire if you start saving early in life, but it takes a lot to become a millionaire if you start late.

This chapter will help you start planning for your dream retirement by giving you an overview of the different types of retirement plans and which one is right for you. So conjure up those fantasies of the piña coladas and the younger man, of the bonbons and the pj's, or whatever it is you dream of for retirement, and let's get started.

HOW MUCH WILL I NEED TO SAVE FOR A COMFORTABLE RETIREMENT?

For the answer to this question, I am going to direct you to the retirement calculator in the Money section on AARP.org. There are also a series of retirement calculators on Bankrate.com. As a general rule, you should be putting away 13 percent of your gross income (your income before taxes) into saving for retirement, though this may not be enough. Use the calculators to get an estimate more specific to your personal financial situation. Also, I think it's a good idea to assume that your retirement will cost even more than you think. Better to have too much saved than not enough.

You need to determine the amount of money you'll need for retirement so that you can determine how much you'll need to save each month. Remember that the average American woman will live to be eighty years old. So if you want to retire at age sixty-five, you're going to need enough money to live on for at least fifteen years, and to be safe, you'll probably want to save more. And I wouldn't count on Social Security. Have you heard the news lately . . .?! At the rate we're going, it looks like the Social Security fund will be dried up before we'll ever see those benefits.

If you read no further in this chapter, you should at least heed this retirement-planning advice: When you are young, you should contribute to your 401(k) up to what your employer matches and max out your Roth IRA if you are eligible, at the minimum.

WHAT ARE THE DIFFERENT OPTIONS FOR SAVING FOR RETIREMENT?

There are two main types of retirement plans.

- Employer-sponsored plans (i.e., 401[k]s).

    This is a retirement plan set up by your employer. Employees contribute pre-tax money to this plan, meaning that you do not have to pay taxes on the money you contribute until you withdraw it from the account (and hopefully that's many, many years down the road). So the money grows, tax deferred, for a long time. If you work for a public school, charity, or religious organization, you might be offered a 403(b), which is quite similar to a 401(k). For the purpose of this book, I'll refer to the 403(b) as a 401(k).

- Individual retirement accounts (i.e. IRAs).

    These are not set up by your employer. Instead they are private retirement accounts set up by brokers, banks, and mutual fund companies. There are two main types: traditional IRAs and Roth IRAs.

    Note: There are many other options for saving for retirement, such as pensions, SIMPLE IRAs, and SEP IRAs, which will be discussed briefly at the end of this chapter.

401(K)S

This is a retirement plan that your employer sets up. Here are all the facts you'll need to know to understand your 401(k).

How Does a 401(k) Work?

The money you contribute to your 401(k) is pre-tax money, meaning that you don't pay taxes on the money you contribute until you withdraw it from your 401(k) account (which, as I said before, should be a time far in the future). If you make $35,000 per year and contribute $2,000 to your 401(k), you will be taxed as if you made only $33,000 that year. You also delay paying taxes on the interest you make on your 401(k) until you withdraw that money.

401(k) Lingo Lowdown

These are the terms you need to understand to comprehend your 401(k).

Matching funds

Your employer will match a certain amount of money that you put into the plan. This is literally free money—a pretty awesome offer! Make sure you contribute to your 401(k) up to what your employer will match.

Vesting

Naturally, with an offer as good as free money, there are often strings attached. In this case the string is called vesting. Vesting is the amount of time until those matching funds are actually yours. Your employer doesn't want to give you free money and then have you quit your job, so they protect themselves with vesting. But the money you personally contribute to your 401(k) is yours, no strings attached, no matter how short your employment is.

Contribution limits

In 2009, you can contribute $16,500 to your 401(k) as long as this doesn't exceed 100 percent of your earnings that year.

Questions to Ask HR about Your 401(k)

If you don't know whether your company offers a retirement plan, you need to ask your HR department. Then you'll want to find out the details. Ask the following questions about your retirement plan:

1. When can I enroll?
2. How do I enroll?
3. What is the maximum amount of money that I can contribute to the plan each year?
4. Does the employer offer matching contributions, and if so, how much?
5. How long is the vesting period?

Other 401(k) Questions and Issues

How do I sign up for a 401(k)?

To sign up for the plan, simply fill out the paperwork provided to you by your HR department or another company official. Now, of course, this is easier said than done because you have to make decisions about where to invest this money. I will discuss your options in the next chapter.

How is the money taken out of my paycheck?

Your employer withdraws the money automatically, which is perfect. There is no way you can spend it because you literally never touch it. (Now if they'd only do that with the cookies they leave in the break room . . .)

What happens when I switch jobs?

You have three options when you switch jobs.

1. If you have more than $5,000 in your 401(k) when you change jobs, you can leave the money in your employer's 401(k) plan.

   If you are happy with your current 401(k) plan or if your new employer's 401(k) requires new employees to work for the company for a certain length of time before allowing them to participate, then it might be a good idea to leave the funds where they are for now. If you aren't in love with your current plan, you might want to roll over the money into a new plan. If you have less than $5,000 in the plan, many employers will require you to move the money. In that case, you will need to roll the money over into a new account (see below).

2. Roll your balance into your new employer's plan.

   This means that contributions and the matching funds that are fully vested will be moved into your new employer's plan. Contact the HR department to do this. They will have all the forms that you'll need to fill out.

3. Roll your balance into an IRA.

   This just means that contributions (again, the matching funds will need to be fully vested) will be moved into an IRA of your choice. It's often a good idea to do this because 401(k) plans can be limited (we'll talk about this more later). To roll over your balance, you'll want to call the company—brokerage firm, mutual fund company, et cetera—where you'll be setting up the IRA and it will walk you through the process.

You cannot directly move your 401(k) into a Roth IRA, which is an individual retirement account in which you contribute money that you've already paid taxes on. You have to move the funds into a rollover IRA, which is just a traditional IRA. Once it's in the traditional IRA, you can convert that into a Roth IRA if you want. But you will have to pay the taxes owed on that money once it goes into the Roth. Why? Because your IRA was funded with pre-tax money whereas the Roth IRA is funded with after-tax money. More on IRAs later.

Notice how none of these options involves cashing out your 401(k). That's because there is almost no good reason to do this, and it's actually costly—you'll have to pay the taxes in addition to an early withdrawal penalty fee.

The lowdown on loans against your 401(k)
Sometimes your 401(k) plan allows you to take out a loan against it. You can usually borrow half of your vested balance as long as this amount is not more than $50,000. Note that this is a L-O-A-N. The loan usually has to be paid back within five years. What's enticing about this loan is that the interest rates are usually low, and you are paying the interest to yourself since it's your 401(k). But it's a little too good to be true. Here are three reasons you want to think twice before taking a 401(k) loan.

- When you put money into your 401(k), you contributed with before-tax money. When you pay back the loan, you are using after-tax money. This is a costly proposition.
- For the period during which you took out the loan, the money was not sitting in your 401(k) earning interest. Instead, it was buying whatever it was that you needed that loan for.
- If you leave your job, you will be required to pay back that loan upon your departure. And "upon your departure" does not mean years later. It means very soon after you leave, sometimes as soon as sixty days from termination of employment. So you better *love* that job if you are going to take out a 401(k) loan.

In short, try *not* to take out a 401(k) loan (you *do not* need it just to take a vacation or buy something fabulous, trust me). For a down payment on your house or for some other important use, it might make sense. But be very careful about this loan. You may be stuck with your crappy boss for a *long* time while you pay back that loan, so consider the toll that would take on your mental health.

Rules of the 401(k)
1. If you withdraw money before age 59½, the IRS will zap you with a 10 percent penalty. Plus, you'll have to pay those income taxes on the money you withdraw.
2. You are required to begin withdrawing the money after you turn 70½.
3. There are certain situations in which you can take out money before age 59½ without incurring the 10 percent penalty. Look at your plan to see how it defines these hardships, but they are usually really high medical expenses or permanent disability. You will still have to pay income taxes.

IRAS
IRAs are private retirement accounts set up by brokers, banks, and mutual fund companies. There are many types of IRAs: traditional IRAs, SEP IRAs, Roth IRAs, SIMPLE IRAs, and more. For the purposes of this section, I'll focus on the main two: the traditional IRA and the Roth IRA. If your employer doesn't offer you a retirement plan (and even if they do), you should probably also open an IRA.

Advantages of IRAs
The main advantage an IRA has over a 401(k) is that an IRA usually has more flexible investment options. However, remember that if your employer matches your contributions to your 401(k), do not forgo doing this—that's free money! F-R-E-E: a four-letter word that's actually awesome.

Two Main Types of IRAs
Traditional IRAs
These are a lot like 401(k)s—you contribute before-tax money and defer paying taxes on the money and its earnings until you withdraw it from the account. The money grows, tax-deferred, until you take it out upon retirement. If you withdraw your money before age 59½ (exceptions apply

for home purchases and college funding; see Investopedia.com), you will have to pay a 10 percent penalty plus income tax.

Here's an example to illustrate this: Let's say you withdraw $10,000 form your IRA before age 59½ and your income means this withdrawal gets taxed at a 25 percent average rate. You will owe $2,500 in federal income taxes. Then you'll owe $1,000 for the penalty fee. So you'll end up with only $6,500. And this number might be even lower if you owe state and local taxes from this early withdrawal as well.

Roth IRAs

With a Roth IRA, on the other hand, you contribute money on which you've already paid taxes. Once the money is in the account, you won't have to pay taxes on it or its earnings when you take it out upon retirement. You can withdraw your contributions (but not the earnings) at any time with no penalty or taxes to pay.

Which type of IRA should I choose?

Because you are young, I (along with Suze Orman, David Bach, and many other financial advisors) recommend the Roth IRA for the majority of you. Since you will most likely be in a higher tax bracket later in life, it's better to pay the taxes now rather than when you withdraw the money. But remember, if your employer matches your 401(k) contributions, you should contribute up to what they match and then contribute to your Roth IRA.

Can I have a 401(k) and a Roth IRA?

Yes, and you probably should! Ideally, you would max out your 401(k) and your Roth IRA. Realistically, it's probably not going to happen unless you are really disciplined. So the closest-to-ideal scenario would be that you max out your Roth IRA and put as much money in your 401(k) as you can—at least as much as your employer will match. Do not miss the 401(k) match.

Can I contribute to both a traditional and Roth IRA?

Yes, but you cannot contribute the yearly maximum toward each of the IRAs separately. In 2009, the max on the Roth and the traditional IRA was $5,000. So you could *not* contribute $5,000 to each account. It's $5,000 total combined balance in the accounts.

How do I open an IRA?

If you feel confident in your abilities to make your own decisions about what financial products to select for your portfolio (and after reading this book, you should), I recommend using a discount brokerage firm or no-load mutual fund company such as Vanguard (vanguard.com), TD Ameritrade (tdameritrade.com), or Fidelity (fidelity.com). You can also get an IRA from your bank or from credit unions, but often these offer more limited investment options. Sometimes they also only allow you to invest in CDs and cash, so it's not always the best option. If you feel that you still need a financial advisor, see page 157.

Rules of the Roth IRA

In 2009, the maximum you could contribute to your Roth IRA in a given year was $5,000 or up to 100 percent of your income, whichever was less. In 2010 and beyond, max Roth contributions may be increased to keep pace with inflation. But not just anyone is allowed to contribute to a Roth. To be eligible, you must have a modified AGI within certain limits.

How to Calculate Your Modified AGI

To determine your modified AGI you will first need to figure out your AGI (adjusted gross income), which I go over in detail in Chapter 14. Visit page 207 and calculate your AGI using that information. To get your AGI from last year as well as get an idea of how it was calculated, check our your tax forms: In 2008 the AGI was listed on line 37 if you filed Form 1040, and line 21 if you filed Form 1040A. Once you know your AGI, you can calculate your modified AGI, or MAGI. Here's how to get your MAGI.

Subtract the following from your AGI:
Income from Roth IRA conversions (this is when you converted a traditional IRA into a Roth IRA)

Add the following to your AGI:
Traditional IRA deduction
Student loan interest deduction
Tuition and fees deduction

Domestic production activities deduction
Foreign earned income exclusion
Foreign housing exclusion or deduction
Exclusion of qualified bond interest shown on Form 8815
Exclusion of employer-provided adoption benefits shown on Form
8839

Does this all seem a bit overwhelming to you? Visit irs.gov and look up IRS Publication 590. It goes through all the Roth IRA information in detail.

Here's a chart to help you determine whether you are eligible for the Roth IRA:

2009 Roth IRA Contribution Limits

TAX FILING STATUS	MAGI	CONTRIBUTION LIMITS
Single, head of household, or married filing separately (and you did not live with your spouse during the year)	Up to $105,000	Full (In 2009, you can contribute up to $5,000 or 100 percent of your income, whichever was less.)
	At least $105,000 but less than $120,000	Partial: You can contribute, but not the full $5,000.
	$120,000 or more	You cannot contribute.
Married filing jointly	Up to $166,000	Full
	At least $166,000 but less than $176,000	Partial
	$176,000 or more	You cannot contribute.
Married filing separately (and you lived with your spouse for at least part of the year)	Up to $10,000	Partial
	$10,000 or more	You cannot contribute.

To determine how much a partial contribution would be, visit irs.gov and look up Publication 590.

The Rules of the Traditional IRA

Anyone can contribute to an IRA, but depending on your income, you might not be able to fully deduct your contributions from your income taxes. Whether you can deduct contributions depends on your tax filing status (single, married filing jointly, etc.), whether you contribute to an employer-sponsored plan, and your modified AGI (adjusted gross income). You have until your taxes are due (usually April 15) to fund your IRA for the year, but it's better to start contributing to it as early as possible so your money has more time to accrue interest.

2009 IRA Deduction Chart for Those Who Are Covered by an Employer Retirement Plan

TAX FILING STATUS	MAGI	DEDUCTION AMOUNT
Single, head of household, or married filing separately (and you did not live with your spouse during the year)	$55,000 or less	Full deduction up to contribution limit. (In 2009, the contribution limit was $5,000 or 100 percent of your income, whichever was less.)
	More than $55,000 but less than $65,0000	Partial deduction up to contribution limit
	$65,000 or more	No deduction
Married filing jointly	$89,000 or less	Full
	More than $89,000 but less than $109,000	Partial
	$109,000 or more	No deduction
Married filing separately (and you lived with your spouse for at least part of the year)	Up to $10,000	Partial
	$10,000 or more	No deduction

2009 IRA Deduction Chart for Those Who Are *Not* Covered by an Employer Retirement Plan

TAX FILING STATUS	MAGI	DEDUCTION AMOUNT
Single, head of household, or married filing separately (and you did not live with your spouse during the year), married filing jointly or separately with a spouse who is *not* covered by an employer-sponsored retirement plan	Any amount	Full deduction up to contribution limit (In 2009, the contribution limit was $5,000 or 100 percent of your income, whichever was less.)
Married filing jointly with a spouse who is covered by an employer-sponsored retirement plan	$166,000 or less	Full
	More than $166,000 but less than $176,000	Partial deduction up to contribution limit
	$176,000 or more	No deduction
Married filing separately with a spouse who *is* covered by an employer-sponsored retirement plan	Up to $10,000	Partial
	$10,000 or more	No deduction

Let's go through an example to make these charts a bit clearer. Let's say you are single and have a MAGI of $50,000 per year. You contribute $5,000 to your IRA in 2009, which makes you eligible for the full deduction. Thus, when you do your taxes, the IRS will tax you as if you made only $45,000. This will be explained in more detail in Chapter 14. If you are in the partially deductible category, the IRS determines the exact amount you can deduct. Visit irs.gov and look up Publication 590.

ROTH 401(K)

A Roth 401(k) or Roth 403(b) is basically a Roth IRA account that your employer sets up. You invest after-tax dollars and pay no tax when you withdraw the money upon retirement. The big advantages of the Roth 401(k) are that you can contribute more of your income to it than you can to a Roth IRA—$16,500 in 2009 (versus a mere $5,000 for the Roth IRA)—and that there are no income restrictions. I'd recommend using this option over a traditional 401(k) if your employer offers it, assuming that you think you will be in a higher tax bracket upon retirement (and since most of you are young, it's probably a safe bet).

OTHER RETIREMENT PLANS

There are many other types of retirement plans. I recommend starting with investopedia.com to get a sense of the differences between retirement plans. Here is a brief description of some of the most common other retirement plans offered by small businesses.

* SIMPLE IRA plan: Savings Incentive Match Plan for Employees
  Operates similarly to a 401(k) with pre-tax contributions. You can contribute up to $11,500 per year as of 2009 and your employer must match 100 percent of your contributions up to 3 percent of your compensation, or contribute 2 percent of eligible employees' salary into the plan.
* SEP-IRA: Simplified Employee Pension IRA
  This plan is usually set up by business owners without employees. The contribution limit is up to 25 percent of your compensation, up to a max $49,000 in 2009. See sepira.com for details.
* Solo 401(k)
  This option is only for a one-person or family-only businesses. It works like a traditional 401(k) but is less expensive to administer. Good for you to open if you are a freelancer or do contract work. You can contribute up to 25 percent of your compensation.

Pensions, or defined benefit plans, are worth mentioning, though you may never be offered one because they are expensive for employers to maintain. Pensions are retirement plans mostly or fully funded by the employer, providing post-retirement benefits that are usually based on duration of employment and on salary.

Let's do a quick recap of this chapter, since the next chapter builds on this one.

* There are two main types of retirement plans:
  1. Plans set up by your employer such as 401(k)s and 403(b)s.
     You contribute pre-tax money to these plans.
  2. Individual retirement accounts
     These are private retirement accounts that are set up by brokers, banks, and mutual fund companies. They include traditional IRAs, in which you contribute pre-tax money and Roth IRAs, in which you contribute money you have already paid taxes on.
* If your employer offers the match on your 401(k), you should take it.

- When you switch jobs, do not cash out your 401(k).
  Instead, roll it over to another retirement account or leave it where it is.
- Try to avoid taking out a loan against your 401(k).
- IRAs tend to have advantages over 401(k)s because they usually have more flexible investment options.
- For many of you, the Roth IRA is the way to go.
  If your employer offers you a 401(k), use it up to what they match, then max out your Roth IRA.

Deep breath—I know that might have seemed like a lot to digest. Just remember, understanding all this is your ticket to no more boss, copiers, strange coworkers, briefs, proposals, and on and on. But to make it happen, you need to start planning smartly for your retirement right now. You now know the basics, but you still need to learn about which investment choices are right for your retirement plans. The next chapter will walk you through this.

CHAPTER 10

Work Out Your Worth
How to Invest Your Retirement Savings

I can't think of a better way to illustrate this chapter than by writing about my girlfriend Serena. Her take on smart investments for life after work: "Investing for retirement? Um, well, I'd rather invest in something I really know about. Besides, the economy is total crap right now," she confided in me. Now ladies, her statement makes complete sense on the surface. I'm sure many of you have told yourselves the same thing. But let me break it down for you. The investing "in something I really know about," in Serena's case, is surely code for her "investment" in that exquisite vintage wardrobe of hers. And I'll give it to her, the brown suede Gucci doctor's bag from the '60s is pretty enviable. So is that collection of silk Pucci scarves. But the bags, shoes, gowns, scarves, and jewelry are simply not going to fund Serena's retirement—not even close. Unless she (and you) really knows about stocks, bonds, mutual funds, index funds, and more, she's probably not setting herself up for a secure retirement. And yes, the economy may be crap right now, but that is no reason for young women like us to stop saving for retirement. In fact, no financial advisor worth their salt would tell you to stop saving for retirement just because the economy isn't raging right now.

I think Serena's just intimidated by investing, and I imagine many of you are as well. And you know what? I've been in that same position. You're probably thinking: "Okay, sure, credit cards, auto loans, I can grasp that, but investing—way too complicated." And yeah, investing can be scary—that is, until you know how to do it. But it's like almost anything: Do your homework, apply yourself to learning about it, and you will get it. And this chapter is going to show you all the basics of investing so you can get started. So no more thinking you'll score that one-of-a-kind Gucci piece that will set you up for life, no more blaming the economy for your lack of investments, and certainly no more waiting around before you start investing in your future. Need I remind you: Retirement means never, ever having to answer to your crotchety old boss; never, ever having to sit on an endless conference call listening to the mindless droning of your brownnosing coworkers; never, ever having to meet your numbers, revise that presentation, develop an ROI analysis, or any of the other things that you sometimes think may be driving you into an early grave. And the earlier you start, the sooner you can retire. So, good lord, let's get started!

First, let's learn the lingo. I'm going to give you the major definitions you'll need to know to get started (and probably impress a date. Can't you just hear yourself? "Yesterday, I was examining the expense ratios of the Vanguard Index Fund versus the Fidelity Index Fund . . ."). From there, you'll learn how to smartly invest your retirement savings.

LINGO LOWDOWN

Here are the terms that will start you on the path to becoming an investment whiz, while simultaneously wowing that sexy banker you're dating.

Asset Allocation

This is a fancy term for the mix of different types of assets such as mutual funds and bonds that you'll choose for your retirement portfolio.

Stocks

A stock is a share of ownership in a company. When a company needs money, it often sells shares of itself as stock in order to raise the money it needs. When you own stock in a company, you are a part—if only a very, very small part—owner in the company, aka a shareholder.

Stocks are generally categorized in these ways: by company size (called market capitalization, or market cap), by sector, and by growth patterns. Company sizes range from small companies (small-cap), medium-sized companies (mid-cap), or large companies (large-cap). Large companies are considered more established and less risky, small companies the most risky. Stocks may also be categorized by the sector into which a company falls, such as technology or health care. Stock growth patterns tend to fall into two main categories: growth and value. Growth stocks are shares of companies that investors think will grow quickly. Value stocks are shares of companies that investors think are undervalued.

Stocks are considered fairly risky investments. But with risk comes reward. For example, according to CNN Money, from 1926 to 2008, the S&P 500 returned an average annual gain of more than 9 percent. Standard & Poor's reported similar findings: From 1970 to 2008, the average annual compounded rate of return for the S&P 500, including reinvestment of dividends, was approximately 9.7 percent.

Why You Shouldn't Swear off the Stock Market

Now, ladies, I realize that in the current economic climate many of you want to swear off stocks altogether—you've seen your retirement fund dip, listened to your parents complaining about how the stock market will never let them retire, or heard some talking head on the news freak out about this being the Great Depression all over again. But let me assure you, staying away from the stock market when you're our age—not smart. Here are the reasons:

Since you're young and saving for a long-term goal, these market fluctuations are not the end of the world for you.

It's extremely likely that the market will recover. Sure, it may take a few years, but since we're talking about long-term investing here, you have years and years before you will withdraw the funds for retirement. So try not to panic over market fluctuations, which

will likely make you do something irrational with your retirement investments. If you are practicing the dollar cost average method of investing (see page 153), I recommend you keep at it.

Despite downturns, average returns over the long term still tend to be high.

Let me preface this by saying that history is not a guarantee of future success, but still, it can't hurt to point out that bad times have hit us before. And yet, solid, regular investors (like those who use the dollar cost averaging method on page 153, or something similar), have come out on top over the last sixty years even through those rough patches. Look at the above example of 9 percent returns.

People who try to time the markets usually end up losing out financially.

Ladies, if you think you'll just time the markets to where you get out when it's bad and go back in when it's good, I recommend you think long and hard about this. It's a huge risk because when you're out of the market you might miss a huge rally, which would be very hard to recover from financially. Here's a bit of research to make my case: A study by Ned Davis Research found that missing just ten of the best days out of the more than six thousand trading days in the past twenty-five years (the study concluded on October 31, 2008) could reduce your investment by nearly 50 percent.

When the markets are down and out, you can get great deals on stocks.

And great deals today, can make you a very rich lady in the future.

Dividends and Retained Earnings

Let's say you own stock in the Catey Corporation. If Catey earns a profit, it will do one of two things with that profit: a) reinvest it in the business (this is called retained earnings), or b) pay it to the shareholders as a dividend. Usually, dividends are paid out in cash, but they can also be paid out in stock. You can often opt to reinvest your dividends, which means that your dividends will not be paid out to you directly and instead will be used to automatically purchase you additional shares of the stock.

Bonds

Basically, a bond is an IOU—with interest. It is one of the ways the government and corporations borrow money. When someone buys a bond, the government and/or corporation agrees to pay that person the principal, which is the amount the person paid for the bond, plus interest, by a certain date, called the maturity date.

Bonds are considered safer investments than stocks, but the rewards over the long term are historically less than they are with stocks—only about 3 to 4 percent. So why do people choose bonds if stocks have traditionally done better? First, because of their relative safety, people use bonds as a safer storage vehicle for their money. Second, since bonds pay interest at fixed intervals, they use bonds as a source of income, and third, they can save money on their taxes with certain bonds. For example, the interest earned on many municipal bonds is exempt from taxes. One of the main problems with bonds is that inflation often erodes the value of the interest payments. Thus, the higher gains we've traditionally seen with stocks have a better chance of outpacing inflation.

Bonds are often analyzed based on the amount of risk they carry. A risky bond carries a fairly high probability of default, which is when the issuer cannot repay the bond. U.S. Treasury bonds, which are bonds backed by the U.S. government, are considered the safest bonds, followed by municipal bonds, which fund local government, and corporate bonds, which fund corporations. Junk bonds and unrated bonds carry a much higher risk. Of course, it generally works out that higher risk bonds pay more interest, which makes sense since you have to compensate people for taking a risk in some way.

To find out the risk level of a bond, check out Moody's Investor Service or Standard & Poor's, both of which rate how safe bonds are using a credit rating system starting with AAA (S&P's) or Aaa (Moody's) as the lowest long-term risk and moving down the scale into C's and D's as the bonds get riskier. See bondsonline.com for the bond rating system for these agencies. Investment grade bonds are the safest and have an S&P's rating of AAA, AA, A, or BBB, or Moody's rating of Aaa, Aa, A, or Baa. Junk bonds are one of the least safe and have an S&P's rating below BBB or a Moody's rating below Baa.

It is also common to characterize bonds in terms of their maturity—short, intermediate, and long term. To learn more about different types of bonds and investing in bonds, visit investinginbonds.com.

Capital Gains or Losses

A capital gain is a profit that results from the sale or trade of stocks, bonds, real estate, or other financial assets. So if you sell your stock for more than you bought it for, that's a capital gain. Capital loss is just the opposite—you buy the asset at a higher price than you sell it for, resulting in a loss. Capital gains are often taxed.

Annuities

This is a tax-deferred investment (like a traditional IRA or your 401[k]) offered by an insurance company. You put money into the annuity, and it will pay you a series of payments for a fixed amount of time. The downside: Annuities are not tax deductible, so this investment is better suited to someone who has already maxed their other retirement options such as their IRA or 401(k). There are two types of annuities: fixed and variable. The fixed annuity gives you a fixed interest rate on your investment over a set time period. The variable annuity operates similarly to a mutual fund in that the interest rate varies. Ladies, there's very little chance that an annuity is good for you. Most of the time, it's better to invest in low-cost index funds (see page 150).

Mutual Funds

This is an investment vehicle that pools the money of many people and puts it into a variety of stocks, bonds, and other investments. It may start to sound weird, but bear with me here. A good mutual fund is like a fabulous handbag: It holds everything you need in one chic, accessible place. So it's basically a big purse for a bunch of different assets. When you buy a mutual fund, you are buying shares of the mutual fund. Shareholders own the mutual fund.

Some mutual funds are closed-end funds, which means there are a limited number of shares and if you want to buy into the fund, you have to buy an existing share. Most mutual funds are open-end funds and have an unlimited number of shares, which means that the fund simply creates a new share for each new buyer.

Net Asset Value

The price at which you can buy and sell a share in the fund is the net asset value (NAV).

Diversification

Mutual funds are great because they give you the benefit of diversification. This means that you aren't putting all your eggs in one basket, so to speak; you are spreading your money out across a variety of different investments. And this is a good thing because it lowers your risk. Because a mutual fund is invested in many different types of stocks, your risk is much lower than if you invested in single stocks.

How mutual funds invest

With mutual funds the money is placed in different kinds of stocks, bonds, and other investments. Here's how it works: The fund pools the money from many investors and then uses this money to buy the assets that will go into the fund. The pooling of this money is good for the small investor because it gives you instant diversification at a lower price and less hassle than you could get by buying each individual stock or bond.

Here are a few categories of mutual funds based on the types of investments they hold: stock-based, which invest in stocks; bond-based, which invest in bonds and other debt instruments; money market funds, which invest only in high-quality, short-term investments issued by the U.S. government and corporations (we will discuss MMFs in Chapter 11); and balanced funds, which invest in both stocks and bonds.

Stock-based mutual funds are often subdivided into categories based on the types of stocks in which they invest (see page 148 for an explanation of what these types of stocks mean). For example, there are funds that focus on company size such as large-cap funds, mid-cap funds, and small-cap funds, and funds that focus on a certain sector, such as energy or biotechnology. There are also growth funds, which own shares of companies that investors think will grow quickly; value funds, which own shares of companies that investors think are undervalued; and blend funds, which own both growth and value stocks. There are many other types of mutual funds, such as income funds, which invest in stocks that pay regular dividends; international funds, which invest in international stocks; index funds, which buy stocks in a particular index (we will discuss these more shortly); and exchange-traded funds (ETFs), which behave like mutual funds but can be traded like stocks (see page 152).

Bond-based funds are also sometimes subdivided into categories based on the types of bonds in the fund—such as U.S. government bond funds, municipal bond funds, and corporate bond funds (see page 147 for these details). Note that bond funds are invested in a variety of bonds, and thus do not have a set maturity date or fixed interest rate, which means your interest rate may fluctuate. Since bond funds vary widely in the types of bonds they will invest in (some can invest in junk bonds, for example), the amount of risk they expose investors to varies from fund to fund. It's certainly possible that you will not get back all that you invested. If you own bond funds, make sure their holdings are in line with your bond-based investment needs.

Balanced funds invest in bonds and stocks, as do growth-and-income funds and equity-income funds. The overall goal of these funds is to grow the principal, while also generating some income. Each of these three types of funds has slightly different ratios of stocks to bonds, and thus satisfies different investment goals. If you own one of these funds, make sure to check that its asset allocation is in line with your investment needs.

Active vs. passive management

Mutual funds are either actively managed or unmanaged. And while unmanaged may sound bad—I mean, imagine what happens to your hair when you don't manage it—it's actually not. A managed mutual fund has a professional portfolio/money manager making decisions on where to invest the money. You've probably learned from your time on the job that some managers are good and some aren't. An unmanaged fund—typically called an index fund—has no portfolio manager, so while it doesn't have the benefit of a professional managing the funds, it also doesn't run the risk of a bad manager making less skillful decisions.

Index Funds

An index fund is an unmanaged mutual fund that tracks a certain index, meaning that there is no portfolio/money manager making investment decisions. The index fund buys and sells stocks within its market index. The goal: to keep pace with the market index (that expression may sound a little foreign, but I'll explain). So while the portfolio manager of an actively traded mutual fund is trying to beat the market, the index fund is merely trying to keep pace with it.

Market Index

What the heck is a market index? You probably already know that the Dow Jones Industrial Average is a market index, another is the NASDAQ, and yet another is the Standard & Poor's 500 Stock Index (you've probably heard it called simply the S&P or the S&P 500). Basically, the market index figures out how all the stocks in its arena performed and puts that into one number. The Dow Jones is made up of thirty stocks of the most prestigious companies in America. When those stocks gain and lose value, the Dow moves up and down. The S&P 500 is made up of five hundred stocks of mostly large, established companies. If you own an index fund that tracks with the S&P 500, then it will have to own all five hundred stocks. The NASDAQ composite is made up of more than five thousand stocks with companies of all sizes.

Okay, blah blah, how does this matter when it comes to you? Well, most of the financial gurus agree that for inexperienced investors, index mutual funds are the way to go for long-term investing. Why? Because actively managed funds generally charge investors higher fees, while index funds charge less in fees. And less expensive fees generally mean greater returns for investors. Plus, just because someone has a fancy title like portfolio manager, it does not mean that he or she knows what they're are doing. Case in point: Index funds over the course of history have done better than actively managed funds.

Expense Ratios

The expense ratio is the annual fees a fund charges to cover operating costs. The lower the expense ratio, the better. All funds have an expense ratio. Actively managed funds are typically more expensive to own, charging about 1.5 percent annually, while index funds generally charge less, usually about .25 percent annually. And that's the secret to the index funds' success—lower fees!

Loads

This same secret applies to loads: The lower the cost (no load is best), the better. A load is a sales commission paid to the broker, financial advisor, or whoever sold you the fund. Not all funds have a load. Here are a few different kinds of loads:

- Front-end loads
  You pay these fees when you buy the fund. Here's how it works. Say you have a 5 percent front-end load. That means you pay 5 percent of every dollar you invest in the fund to the salesperson. The rest is invested in the fund. These funds are also called A-share funds, and have an A at the end of their name.
- Back-end load or deferred sales charge
  You pay the fee when you sell the fund. These are also called B-share funds and have B at the end of their name. Often these funds have high expense ratios.
- Level-load
  You pay the fee over a certain number of years.

Since lower fees usually mean bigger profits to you, opt for a no-load mutual fund, which does not pay commission to the person who sold the fund.

ETFs—Exchange Traded Funds

This is a mutual fund that trades like a stock, not like a mutual fund. Here's what that means: When you want to sell a mutual fund, you have to wait until the market closes to do so. With an ETF, you can sell at any time. Most ETFs track an index like the S&P 500, which means they are similar to index funds. When buying an ETF, look for the same qualities you'd look for in an index fund—low cost. A popular ETF is the iShares 500 index. It doesn't hurt to have ETFs in your portfolio since they are essentially index funds, but for long-term investing, you generally don't need to be able to trade on a whim. That's why they call it long-term investing. If you opt for ETFs, look for a low expense ratio. It is important to note that unlike with a no-load mutual fund, when you buy and sell ETFs, you will pay a commission.

Ladies, if you have any questions about these terms or want to learn more, investopedia.com and the glossary in the personal investing section on raymondjames.com are great resources. CNN Money and Bankrate. com also provide easy-to-understand investing resources.

THE TEN BEST THINGS YOU CAN DO TO MAXIMIZE YOUR RETIREMENT SAVINGS

1. **Start early.** Remember the example on page 7. The earlier you start, the longer your money has to grow.

2. **Get the match.** If your employer matches the funds in your 401(k), you *must* participate. (The only exception is that if you have a long vesting period and know that you'll leave the company before you get the match). See page 132.

3. **Choose the right plan.** For most of you—because you are young and will likely be in a higher tax bracket later in life—you'll want to max out your Roth IRA and contribute at least up to what your employer matches into your 401(k). Ideally, you want to max both your Roth and your 401(k).

4. **Use the dollar cost averaging method.** All this means is that you invest fixed amounts of money at regular intervals into your retirement account. For example, you put a certain amount of money (say $250) out of each paycheck or a certain percentage of your paycheck into your retirement account at regular time periods. Just keep making these regular deposits, *even when the market looks bad.* Yes, I know there have been many freak-outs in the past few years over the market—but here's the thing, you are investing for the long-term. So while investments may lose value in the next few years, in the long run, you'll most likely see gains. Don't forgo saving for retirement because the market is having a rough year. Obviously, as you make more money through the years, you'll want to increase the amount you contribute to the retirement account.

5. **Make it automatic.** Have the money automatically deducted from your paycheck or bank account and transferred into your retirement account. This way you never touch the money, so you'll never be able to spend it. I know those hot little greenbacks in your hand can easily translate into hot little heels on your feet, so your best bet is to keep the moola out of your wallet entirely.

6. **Invest in index funds with low expense ratios.** Vanguard, Fidelity, Charles Schwab, and T. Rowe Price all have low expense ratio index funds from which you can purchase shares. To find out the expense ratio, ask for a copy of the prospectus, a fancy word for the paperwork that describes the details of the fund. At the time of the writing of this book, I found fees as low as .09 percent, though the average is usually about .25 percent. Shop around.

7. **Allocate your assets smartly between low-cost stock-based index funds and bonds or bond-based index funds.** Please see page 150 for details.

8. **Diversify.** Diversification means that you have a variety of different investments—you aren't putting all your eggs in one basket. If one of these investments tanks, it won't totally ruin you. Mutual funds offer instant diversification because they invest in a basket of different stocks and bonds. Here are two tips for diversification:

   ● Choose an index fund that tracks the entire market.
   Index funds that track the entire market, usually called Total Market Index Funds or Extended Market Index Funds, offer a lot of diversity. The Vanguard Total Stock Market Fund (VTSMX), Fidelity Spartan Total Market Index Fund (FSTMX) and the Vanguard Total Stock Market ETF (VTI) are examples of total stock market funds or ETFs with fairly low expense ratios; the Vanguard Total Bond Market Index Fund (VBMFX) and T-Rowe Price U.S. Bond Index (PBDIX) are examples of total bond market funds. Many of the index funds offered by Dimensional Fund Advisors (DFA) also do the same thing. If you don't want to go the index fund/ETF route, make sure you choose a mutual fund that offers many different kinds of stocks—large, mid, and small cap, as well as growth and value stocks.

   ● Get some exposure in both domestic and international investments.
   Take the total amount you'll be investing in stock-based mutual funds and put about 70 to 85 percent of that into a domestic stock fund or funds, and 15 to 30 percent in an international stock fund(s). You can get total market domestic and international funds from companies like Vanguard, Fidelity, and T. Rowe Price.

   A sample retirement plan (I'll use Vanguard funds in this example) might include investing your stock-based allocation as follows:

   70 to 85 percent in a domestic stock fund like Vanguard Total Stock Market Index Fund (VTSMX).

   15 to 30 percent of your stock-based index fund money into an international stock fund like Vanguard Total International Stock Index Fund (VGTSX).

9. **Avoid buying funds with a load.** As we discussed above, a load is a sales commission paid to whoever sold you the fund. There's almost no need to ever buy a mutual fund with a load attached to it. (See

page 152 to review the examples of different types of loads.) Note that a commission-based financial advisor—and many of the advisors at full-service brokerage firms work on commission—probably won't sell you a no-load fund because he or she'd make no money off it. To avoid buying a fund with a load, review the fund's prospectus.

10. **Review and rebalance your portfolio every six months.** You'll want to review your investments every six months or so. Just because you originally invested 90 percent in stocks and 10 percent in bonds six months earlier does not mean that your portfolio still reflects this 90/10 allocation. If the stock market had a bad few months, your stocks could have lost their value and now represent only 70 percent of your portfolio. Ideally, you'll want to buy more shares of a stock-based mutual fund to get back to that 90/10 allocation.

There are a number of funds, often called lifecycle funds, which will automatically rebalance your portfolio to a target allocation for you so that you don't have to worry about it. One option is the Vanguard Target Retirement Fund, which invests mostly in Vanguard index funds. There are of course other lifecycle funds that do this—just make sure they invest mostly in index funds and have low expense ratios. Also, remember that as you get older, you'll want to put more and more of your investments into bonds.

Now, ladies, I know that many of you have IRAs in a bunch of different locations. This makes rebalancing a little harder because you have to do it for all the different accounts. You might want to consider consolidating your accounts. Find a low-cost brokerage or mutual fund firm with the investment choices you want and put all the money there. You'll find that rebalancing one account is far easier than dealing with a bunch of them.

WHERE TO PUT YOUR MONEY

These are broad guidelines to help the beginning investor figure out where to put her retirement savings.

* Early to mid-twenties:
    You should invest about 85 to 90 percent of your retirement fund in stock-based index funds and the other 10 to 15 percent in bonds or bond-based index funds.

* Late twenties and early thirties:
    You should invest about 80 to 85 percent of your retirement fund in stock-based index funds and the other 15 to 20 percent in bonds or bond-based index funds.

- As you get older:
  Adjust your portfolio to reflect more bonds or bond-based index fund products the older you get, as these are less risky. When you are young you can and should take risks with your retirement portfolio.

Another broad guideline for asset allocation for the beginning investor is this: the percentage of stock-based index funds in your portfolio should equal 110 minus your age. So if you are twenty years old, 90 percent of your portfolio should consist of stock-based index funds (110 - 20 = 90). The rest should be bonds or bond-based index funds.

It is important to remember why you're choosing stock index funds instead of selecting individual stocks. First, index funds, like other mutual funds, offer instant diversification, which will better protect your investments. For example, if one stock in the fund has a rough go at it, it doesn't ruin your entire portfolio. Second, since an index fund is unmanaged (no portfolio manager), it generally offers lower fees than other mutual funds. These low fees generally mean higher returns for you.

It is important to understand why I am saying bonds or bond-based index funds. Shouldn't I be all about index funds? Well, certain kinds of bonds are safer than bond-based funds (as discussed on page 150), and with the market the way it is, it doesn't seem like a bad idea to opt for these. Try Treasuries or CDs, which we will discuss in Chapter 11. And because interest rates are relatively low now, you might want to go for shorter-term bonds, just in case interest rates rise in the future. You don't want to be locked into a low rate. But look, if the hassle of buying individual bonds is annoying, I completely understand. The bond-based index fund, assuming you choose one smartly, is a fine investment.

There are other factors to consider when deciding how to allocate your retirement savings, such as the state of your health and any potential major life changes that might affect how soon you'll need the money and how much you'll need. If you visit smartinvestingbook.com and click on the Allocation tab, you can take a quiz that will give you a very thorough assessment of how you personally should allocate your retirement savings.

WHAT TO DO WHEN YOUR 401(K) DOESN'T OFFER GOOD OPTIONS

Many 401(k)s simply don't offer the options they should—for example, many do not offer low-cost index funds. But you are going to have to pick from the options they give you if you want to participate. The keys to a great 401(k) retirement mix are the same as those listed earlier: proper asset allocation, diversification, index funds (if possible), et cetera. When your options are less than ideal, here's what to do: If you don't have any index funds offered, invest your stock-based allocation in roughly this way: 20-30 percent large-cap value fund, 20-30 percent large-cap growth fund, 15-25 percent mid-cap fund, 15-30 percent international fund, and 10-20 percent small-cap fund. This mixture gives you a good amount of diversification, but should be tweaked according to your specific needs. Look for low expense ratios. The prospectus will tell you what types of funds each option has. Put your bond allocation in a low-cost bond-based fund that invests in the type of bonds your portfolio requires (see pages 147–48).

Answers to Top Investing Questions

Should I invest in company stock?
It's most likely not a good idea to invest in company stock. Remember, single stocks offer no diversification, so they are very risky.

How do I track the performance of my fund?
Enter the fund's ticker—made up of five letters and ending in an X—or the fund's full name into finance.google.com. In the example above, the Vanguard Total Stock Market Index Fund has a ticker symbol of VTSMX. The Google Finance site will show you a chart of the fund's performance.

HOW DO I FIND A COMPETENT, LOW-COST FINANCIAL ADVISOR?

If these investing options are thoroughly confusing to you, or if you have some extra money and would just rather have an expert deal with them, you'll want to find yourself a competent financial advisor. A financial advisor will look at your entire financial picture and determine the best course of action for a secure financial future. FYI: The title "financial advisor" is often used interchangeably with "financial planner." Just because someone holds this title does not mean that they are competent enough to handle your finances. If you don't have a recommendation for a financial advisor from someone you trust, it might be a good idea to look for a certified financial planner (CFP) or a chartered financial consultant (ChFC), both of whom are financial advisors that have received national certification after taking extensive coursework and passing a series of exams. When dealing with investment companies, here are a few more certified financial professionals: chartered financial analysts (CFAs), chartered investment counselors (CIC), and certified investment management analysts (CIMAs). To find a financial advisor/planner, you can visit napfa. org and click on the Consumer Information tab. Also ask around and get advice from peers and friends.

Here are some tips for finding a competent and reputable financial planner.

1. **Look for a fee-only advisor.** These advisors do *not* work on commission, so they won't push investments on you that don't make sense for you. You pay them a flat fee — usually by the hour. Shop around for the best rates.

2. **Interview the advisor thoroughly.** Visit napfa.org for a great questionnaire that you can ask potential advisors. You will want to ask them about the following:

    ◉ Credentials. Such things as whether they are a CFP, ChFC, etc.

    ◉ Experience. Includes time on the job and number of clients.

    ◉ Compensation requirements. Includes commissions, fees, and whether the advisor or a member of his or her firm gets compensation from recommending certain investments or financial products.

    ◉ Whether they are a registered investment advisor (ask to see documentation of this, which in many cases will be Form ADV, see #3 below)

    ◉ Services. Make sure that the services the advisor offers are the same services that you need and whether she will personally deal with you or whether an associate will.

3. **Ask to see the advisor's Form ADV.** Form ADV is the form used to register as an investment advisor with the Securities and Exchange Commission (SEC). This form can tell you if they've had problems, lawsuits, or complaints against them in the past, which should be a warning sign to you.

4. **Go with your gut.** Sure, all these questions and documents are important, but even if the advisor passes your tests with flying colors, this does not mean he or she is right for you. Remember how much

you hated the good-on-paper guy once you got to know him? Same situation here. Ask yourself whether you trust this person and think they will do a good job. If there's doubt, move on.

5. **Consider asking the advisor you decide to hire to sign a fiduciary oath.** A fiduciary oath is a document that lays out ground rules for advisor behavior, including a promise to act in the best interest of the client—you. A sample of this oath can be found in the Comprehensive Advisor Diagnostic manual on the National Association of Personal Financial Advisors' Web site at napfa.org.

Once you've found the right advisor, it is important that you don't blindly trust him or her. After all, you read this chapter; you know that your advisor should be recommending low-cost index funds, ETFs, or passively managed funds for your retirement investments. You are smart, successful, and savvy, so don't doubt your ability to do this on your own, and don't stop yourself from telling your advisor that you simply don't understand her rationale if something seems unclear.

Okay, ladies, let's recap those ten steps to successful retirement investing because they are really, really important to that no-boss-ever-again plan of yours. So here goes:

1. The earlier you start saving for retirement, the better off you are.
2. If your employer matches your retirement contributions, you should participate.
3. Choose the right retirement plan(s), which for those of you who qualify, will probably be the Roth IRA in addition to your 401(k) at least up to what your employer matches.
4. Use the dollar cost averaging method to invest your retirement savings.
5. Automatically have contributions to your retirement savings withdrawn from your paycheck or account so you can never spend them.
6. Invest in index funds with low expense ratios.
7. Based on your age, allocate your assets smartly between low-cost stock-based index funds and bonds or bond-based index funds.
8. Make sure your retirement fund is diversified with index funds that track the entire market and some international exposure.
9. Avoid buying mutual funds that have a load.
10. Review and rebalance your portfolio every six months.

Well, there you have it—the basics of investing. You are now armed with enough financial know-how to start investing smartly, *in something other than vintage Pucci*. Remember what I told you in the beginning of this chapter? Conquering investing is like conquering all those other things you've conquered in life: Do your homework, apply yourself to learning about the topic, and you will get it. And in the moments of frustration, just picture your perfect retirement, whether it's living in a clapboard house with a wraparound porch on a white sandy beach, traipsing around the globe with the man of the moment, or whatever else you can imagine. Those pictures alone, I can promise you, will get you through the tough times. It's all about perspective!

Now, I know it's hard to motivate yourself since retirement seems so far away. Come on, Catey, where's my little interim treat, you might be asking. Where's my next vacay, where's my new house? My answer: They're coming right up. The next chapter is all about how to save for your short-term goals.

CHAPTER 11

Sweat Your Savings
How to Buffer Yourself from Life's Little Challenges

You know how life works: Just when everything is sailing along smoothly, *bam!*—something happens. You're kicking butt at your job, putting in some serious overtime and making great connections, and then, *bam!*—massive layoffs at your company. Or, you and your BFF move in together, are getting along great, and then, *bam!*—things go sour (I mean, really! She thought it was okay to borrow your cream cashmere wrap, dump wine on it, and then return it without even offering to pay for dry cleaning?) and you are stuck with having to move. You need to prepare for bumps in your life—they'll happen, and you'll need accessible money to get yourself through them. That's what your emergency fund is for. Or as I like to call it: the in-case-I-get-fired, -sick, -screwed-over, or -otherwise-set-back fund.

You will need an emergency fund in addition to funds for those short-term financial goals (savings goals you want to achieve in the next five years) that you wrote down on pages 22–23. Goals like: saving for a down payment on a home, saving for a week of zipping down the slopes in Aspen with your adorable new beau, saving for a car, saving for the leather and rabbit fur–lined jacket that calls to you when you pass Bendel's. These are your short-term—and by short-term I mean within the next five years—savings goals, and you'll need money to make those happen as well.

Of course, it's also important to save for retirement and other long-term goals, but this chapter is devoted to short-term savings.

THE EMERGENCY FUND

The emergency fund is just what it sounds like: money that you save in case of an emergency. You should have enough money in this fund to be able to live for six months without an income.

THE SHORT-TERM GOALS FUND

For goals that you want to achieve in five years or less—for example, putting a down payment on a house or taking a trip—you'll need a savings nest. The amount of money you'll need to have in this fund depends on how much the goal will cost you. So if you want to go on a vacation next year, do your homework to determine how much the goal will cost (and this includes everything, so don't lie and pledge that you won't buy a few treats while on vacay—you know yourself better than that). That's how much you'll need to save.

WHERE SHOULD I PUT MY EMERGENCY FUND AND SHORT-TERM GOALS FUND?

Your emergency-fund money should be relatively safe, easy to withdraw, and, ideally, earning interest, though the ease of withdrawal and amount of risk will depend on the goal. I suggest the following options:

Certificates of Deposit (CDs)

When you buy a CD from a bank or credit union, it will pay you a fixed interest rate on your money when you keep it in that bank or financial institution for a certain amount of time. The longer you leave your money in the bank, the higher the interest rate becomes. Word of warning: If you try to withdraw your money before that set amount of time is up, you may have to give up some of the interest. CDs are FDIC insured.

CDs are great for your short-term goals fund because you can choose the maturity date based on when you'll need the money—so if you want to go on the vacation next year, you'll choose a maturity date of one year. CDs are not as good for your emergency fund, because there is often a penalty for early withdrawal.

Here are the major types of CDs, courtesy of Bankrate.com.

Traditional
Deposit a fixed amount of money for a fixed amount of time and receive a fixed amount of interest. Note that you will be penalized for early withdrawal of your funds.

Variable
This is like a traditional CD, except that the interest rate may change over the term of the CD.

Bump-up
If you think that interest rates will rise over the term of your CD, this may be a smart option for you. The bump-up CD allows you to take advantage of higher interest rates if they occur. The downside is that your initial interest rate is usually lower than with a traditional CD.

Liquid
In this case, you can withdraw money from the CD without penalty, although you may have to maintain a minimum balance in the account. The interest rate is usually lower than for a traditional CD. Make sure you know how long you have to hold the CD before you can withdraw the money without penalty and the number of withdrawals allowed.

Zero-coupon
These CDs are sold at a huge discount, but you get the full value of the CD upon its maturity. You do not receive any interest payments over the CD term and instead get the entire value of the CD upon its maturity. There are possible tax disadvantages to these CDs, so do your homework before buying.

Callable
The bank can "call" the CD away from you after a certain period of time. So if you bought a CD at 6 percent interest and rates fell to 5 percent, the

bank would likely call your CD so they didn't have to pay you the higher interest rate. Then they'll reissue your CD at the 5 percent rate. You will receive the full interest and principal earned up until the recall, but from then on, you will be earning the new, lower, interest rate. The advantage to the consumer is that banks may pay more in interest on a callable CD than they would on a CD without the call feature. Bonds can also be callable.

Brokerage

A brokerage CD is simply a CD sold through a brokerage. These CDs often pay higher interest rates than CDs from your bank. They are also more liquid than bank CDs because they can be traded on the secondary market, which means that you can buy and sell them just like a bond.

Money Market Mutual Funds (MMFs)

An MMF is a mutual fund that invests in low-risk, short-term securities (a security is basically just an investment instrument like a stock or bond), such as CDs and Treasury bills. Short-term, in this case, usually refers to securities with a maturity date of under one year. It is considered a fairly safe investment vehicle. This account is not FDIC-insured.

Money Market Accounts (MMAs)

This is a type of savings account that usually pays a little bit more interest than a traditional savings account, *but* there are limits to how many checks you can write out of this account and there is often a fee if you go over. This account is FDIC insured. This option allows you to withdraw your money and interest at any time without penalty, *but* interest rates are typically lower than with a CD.

High-Interest Savings Accounts

This is a savings account that offers higher-than-usual interest rates. As of the writing of this book, the interest rates on these accounts were about 2 percent.

Treasury Bills or Treasury Notes

Treasuries are issued by the U.S. government and are considered some of the safest investments out there. A treasury bill, commonly called a T-Bill, has a maturity of less than a year. You buy the bill at a discount and then are paid the full amount, which includes the interest you have earned, upon maturity. Treasury notes, or T-Notes, have a maturity of two to ten years, and you earn interest every six months until maturity. You can learn more about these items at treasurydirect.gov. The downside of T-Bills and T-Notes is that you often get better interest rates with other investments.

Bonds with a Short Maturity

See Chapter 10 for an explanation of bonds. For your short-term savings, you will need a bond that matures within the amount of time in which you'll need the money and pays the highest interest relative to the amount of risk you are willing to take.

Depending on your savings goals, look into I-Bonds, considered safe investments as they are backed by the U.S. government. I-Bonds are savings bonds that earn interest while also protecting you from the risk of inflation. You can learn more about them at treasurydirect.gov. It is important to note that you have to hold an I-Bond for at least a year, and you will pay a penalty of three months' earnings if you redeem the bond before owning it for five years. However, this penalty might be worth it, depending on your savings goals.

Go to Bankrate.com to shop for CDs and MMAs. T. Rowe Price and TIAA-CREF both offer MMFs that let you open the account for little money. ING, HSBC Direct, and E-Trade all offer high-interest savings accounts. For T-Bills, T-Notes, and I-Bonds, visit TreasuryDirect.gov.

As for which option to choose for your savings, I'd let interest rate and the amount of flexibility you need be your guide. For example, if the account is for your emergency fund, choose an account with a high interest rate—like an MMA, MMF—or a high-interest savings account that will let you withdraw the money without penalty. It is also important to consider the risk inherent in an account. For example, some bonds are risky and thus are not appropriate for your emergency fund. Look at which option offers you the highest interest rate relative to the amount of risk you are willing to take. If you cannot stand to lose your money, you should pick an account that is FDIC-insured or an option like a treasury that is backed by the government, and then from those, choose the one that will pay you the highest interest rate and offers the flexibility you need. Remember that corporate bonds may not be all that safe, so do not park your emergency fund there. However, your short-term goals fund might benefit from a bit more risk, assuming that risk could provide you higher yields.

OTHER QUESTIONS

Do I Save or Pay off My Debt First?

This depends on your interest rate. If you have a 17 percent APR on your credit card but will earn only 5 percent on your savings, then you should be paying off your credit card. If the interest rate on your debt is more than the interest you'd earn on savings, then pay off that debt.

Since Many of These Accounts are Considered Safe, Why Not Put All of My Retirement Savings in Them, Too?

Because the amount of money you yield in savings accounts is likely to be much lower over the long term than if you invest it in the retirement products like index funds, which we discussed in previous chapters. Think about it—savings yield might be around 4 percent but the historical returns from the stock market over the long term are much higher than that. Plus, inflation might eat into your savings.

Should I Save for Retirement or Build up My Emergency Fund First?

If you have an employer who matches your 401(k), then you must participate in that. After that, you should build up at least half of your emergency fund before funding your retirement. Why? Because if something does happen to you, you don't want to have to pay for it on your high-interest credit cards or from your retirement savings. When you tap into your retirement accounts, you will probably be hit with a penalty for early withdrawal, not to mention other possible penalties (see Chapter 10). So it's better to go ahead and build up a good portion of your emergency fund so that you can avoid credit card debt or having to tap your retirement fund early.

What is the Annual Percentage Yield (APY)?

The APY is the interest you'll earn over the course of a year. It's useful because you can use it to compare savings products like CDs and MMAs even if they calculate interest differently (i.e., one compounds interest monthly and one compounds it annually). For example, a 4.0 percent interest rate would have an APY of 4.0 percent if interest was compounded annually, but the APY would be 4.06 percent if interest were compounded quarterly. Why? Because of how compounding works (see page 6). So the APY can be a very useful tool when comparing different products. Do not confuse the APY with the APR. The APR is most often not as helpful (see page 194 for an explanation of APR).

I've Heard Inflation Can Eat into My Savings. What Does This Mean?

In basic terms, inflation is the rise in prices of goods and services. For example, if an apple costs you a dollar today and the inflation rate is 3 percent, that same apple will cost you $1.03 in a year. So you can imagine what this does to your savings. If you have $100 in a high-interest savings account with an APY of 3 percent, you will have $103 a year from now. However, because the inflation rate in this example is also 3 percent per year, in effect, you net out even—inflation has eroded the value of your earnings on the savings account. This is one of the main reasons that you'll put a lot of your retirement investments in stock-based index funds—those returns have historically been much higher than the rate of inflation.

After reading this chapter, when the *bam!* moments happen, you'll be prepared. You can fix that oil leak in your car, ride out a job loss, replace your roof, be prepared for whatever life throws at you—all without going into debt. No dumping it all on your credit card, no taking out a loan. Nope— smart, savvy you will pull it out of your savings. Just remember that it usually takes cutting your spending (refer back to Part II) to properly fund your accounts. After all, when you spend all your money at Jimmy Choo, there's really nothing you can put into your savings account. Sure, shoes are great, but they simply will not pay to fix whatever emergency comes your way.

CHAPTER 12

Step Toward Security

*How to Get the Best Insurance to Protect You
and Your Assets*

My friend Sarah is shoe obsessed, a phenomenon I am sure many of you—and your closets—are intimately familiar with. And by obsessed I don't mean that she has fifty pairs of shoes—we're talking hundreds. They are stored under her bed, in her closet, even in the oven. She has flats, stilettos, wedges, and boots in every conceivable color and fabric: chocolate, black, red, and white; suede, leather, patent leather, even feathered. Well, I was chatting with her at work one day and she commented, "I don't have renter's insurance on my place. What if someone stole my shoes?! I mean, to steal the Queen of the Stilettos' one true love?! Not to mention all the other things in there—my grandmother's jewelry, my TV. What would I do?!"

And it made me think, lord, there must be a million women who don't have the insurance they need. It's not just about shoes, it's about everything you love—your health, your home, and so much more. Without insurance, you can lose it all. I mean, how could you ever even come close to replacing those things?

So that's the big secret of this chapter: that you can be a lot more confident when someone (besides your malfunctioning alarm system and yippy Pomeranian) will protect your fabulous vintage handbag collection, the jewelry your grandmother gave you, those snazzy new wheels you just bought, and anything else you hold close to your heart. That someone is your insurance company. Insurance protects the important things in your life such as your health, car, home, belongings, and more.

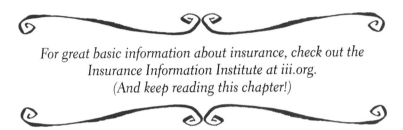

For great basic information about insurance, check out the Insurance Information Institute at iii.org. (And keep reading this chapter!)

LINGO LOWDOWN

These are the terms that you will need to know in order to understand your insurance policies.

Premium

This is what the insurance company charges you for the insurance. Usually the premium is collected in monthly or semiyearly installments. It is usually determined by how much of a risk the insurance company deems you to be—the more likely they think you are to make claims, the higher your premiums will be.

Deductible

This is the amount of money you have to pay out of your own pocket *before* the insurance company will start paying your claim. So if you have a $200 deductible, you will have to pay $200 out of your own pocket before the insurance company pays anything.

Coinsurance

This is the percentage of the claim that you must pay. For example, if you have a $1,000 claim and a 10 percent coinsurance charge, you will pay

$100 (or 10 percent of the $1,000) and the insurance company will pay the remaining $900. This assumes you have already met your deductible.

Co-payment (co-pay)
This is the flat dollar amount that you will have to pay for a claim.

TOP INSURANCE TIPS

- The higher the deductible, the lower the premium. So to reduce your premium, increase your deductible. But only do this if you can afford to cover the deductible, if it comes to that.
- What insurance do I really need?

STATUS	THE INSURANCE YOU MOST LIKELY NEED
Single with no dependents	Health, auto, homeowner's or renter's, disability
Married no kids	Same as above *and* possibly life insurance if your spouse would have a hard time supporting himself without your income
Married with children	All of the above *plus* life insurance

- What insurance do I probably *not* need?
  Flight insurance, credit life insurance, and life insurance for your children. If you are strapped for cash and have had or anticipate having few dental procedures, you might also be able to forgo dental insurance (unless your employer pays for it) temporarily, as the policies are often expensive and the coverage limited. Ladies, if you can afford dental insurance, it's a good idea to have it, though.

HEALTH INSURANCE
If you get health insurance through your employer (or your spouse's employer), thank your lucky stars. For the rest of you, you should try to get covered under COBRA—we'll talk about that later—or an individual plan. You *need* health insurance. If something happens to you and you do not have health insurance, it can literally bankrupt you.

No matter whether you have an employer plan or your own individual policy, you probably have many choices. The main types you'll see are: HMOs, PPOs, PSOs, fee-for-service plans, HDHPs.

Fee-for-service (Indemnity) Plan

You can go to any doctor you choose (no networks, no referrals). This is the most flexible plan, but it is often the most expensive. Often you have to pay up front and then are reimbursed.

Because they are expensive for employers to administer, these plans are becoming less common. If you have this plan, remember to look at the benefits schedule so you will know what it covers and doesn't cover.

Health Maintenance Organizations (HMOs)

An HMO is a group of health care professionals and medical facilities that sell health care services for a fixed price. You have a primary care physician, and he or she must refer you to all the other doctors or specialists you may need to see. The advantages of an HMO are lower out-of-pocket costs and no claims forms. The disadvantage is that if you see a specialist outside of your network, you will likely not be reimbursed. If your network is small, you'll have very limited choices.

Preferred Provider Organizations (PPOs)

This is like a combination of the indemnity plans and HMOs. You still have a network of doctors, and when you use them, the insurance company covers much of that cost. But you can also be reimbursed for doctors who are outside of your network; you just won't get as much reimbursement as you would with an in-network doctor.

Point of Service (POS)

This is a combination of an HMO and a PPO. Like an HMO, you pay no deductible and usually only a minimal co-pay when you use a health care provider within your network. Your primary care physician makes all referrals. If you choose to go outside the network for health care, POS coverage functions more like a PPO. You will likely be subject to a deductible and a co-pay.

High Deductible Health Plan (HDHP)

This plan has very low premiums but a very high deductible (about $1,050 for an individual and $2,100 for a family). It is used in conjunction with a Health Savings Account (HSA), which is an account that you can use to save money for medical expenses. You fund the account with pre-tax money out of your paycheck. You contribute pre-tax money into your HSA, which you can then use to pay your medical costs. Withdrawals for qualified medical expenses are not taxed, but withdrawals for non-medical expenses are taxed and you'll pay a penalty. The idea is that your HSA will help you pay your deductible. The funds from your HSA roll over year after year, so you can end up saving a lot of money in that account if you never touch the funds. For more information on HSAs, visit ustreas.gov/offices/public-affairs/hsa.

Additional Health Insurance Terms

Out-of-pocket maximum
Most insurance policies cap the amount that you will have to pay out of pocket each year. Once you have paid this amount, you will likely not have to pay any more (as long as your medical bills are legit to the insurance company).

Flexible Spending Account (FSA)
A Flexible Spending Account lets you put pre-tax money into an account to help pay for medical or other qualified expenses as defined by your health plan. Depending on the specifics of your FSA, vision care items like contact lenses and solution, dental care items like toothpaste, and over-the-counter drugs like aspirin may be covered. Like an HSA, if you withdraw the money for qualified medical expenses, you do not have to pay taxes on it. However, FSA funds are "use it or lose it," meaning that you have to use all of the funds within a specified amount of time (usually a year) or you'll lose the money. Not all health plans offer an FSA option.

Health Reimbursement Accounts (HRAs)
With an HRA, your employer sets up an account for you designed to help you pay for qualified medical expenses. So, the point of an HRA is to reimburse you for certain medical expenses such as co-payments, coinsurance, deductibles, and services that are not covered by the company's selected standard insurance plan. You will not have to pay taxes on qualified reimbursements. You do not have to pay your employer for the right to participate in an HRA. The expenses that are reimbursed vary from plan to plan, so talk to your HR department.

Consolidated Omnibus Budget Reconciliation Act (COBRA)
This plan allows employees who lose their health insurance for certain reasons (see below) to buy health insurance for themselves and their dependents at the group rate for a certain amount of time.

EVENT	BENEFICIARY (The person who receives the payment)	COVERAGE PERIOD
Job termination (other than for reasons of gross misconduct)	Employee, spouse	18 months
Reduced hours	Dependent child	18 months
Employee can get Medicare	Spouse, dependent child	36 months
Divorce or separation	Spouse, dependent child	36 months
Death of employee	Spouse, dependent child	36 months
Loss of dependent child status	Dependent child	36 months

❋ *How do I apply for COBRA?*

You have to notify the plan's administrator, usually someone in your HR department, when you are affected by one of the events listed in the above table. The plan administrator has two weeks to let you know, in writing, what your rights are under COBRA. You have sixty days from the date of the event to decide whether you want to continue coverage under your employer's plan. Once you choose to continue the coverage, you will pay premiums retroactive to the date of the event, so you will have no gaps in your health coverage. The COBRA cost is the employer's actual cost *plus* a 2 percent administrative fee. You will have a grace period, usually thirty days, to pay the premium. If you don't pay it, coverage will be terminated. Coverage automatically ends at the end of the coverage period. Coverage will also be terminated if your former employer stops offering health insurance, if you get coverage from your new employer, or if you become entitled to Medicare (you probably won't, but you can check at medicare.gov).

❋ *Should I choose COBRA?*

You should always have health insurance. Unless you can find health insurance at a better cost through an individual policy, you will want to elect to do COBRA.

For those of you with serious health problems, you might want to opt for COBRA while you wait to pick up coverage from your new employer, because the law says that an insurance company cannot limit your coverage based on a preexisting condition if you've been continuously covered by insurance for a year straight. Also, when you lose coverage, ask your employer (or your spouse's employer) to give you a written notice stating that you were continuously covered by insurance for twelve months so that you can prove this to the new insurance company.

Make the Most of Your Insurance Plan

If your company has a flexible benefits plan (aka a flex plan or cafeteria plan), reap the benefits.

On a flex plan, you can choose benefits that make the most sense for you. Talk to your HR department to discuss your options.

Use your FSA (Flexible Spending Account) to your advantage.

An FSA allows employees to set aside pre-tax income for routine medical expenses.

Look for a policy that does not cap lifetime benefits at a rate that is too low. You want a policy that has lifetime benefits of at least $1 million.

For those of you whose employer does not provide health insurance, you can go online to ehealthinsurance.com and digitalinsurance.com to get quotes for individual health insurance. Also, your state's insurance department Web site will have useful information. For more health insurance information, visit healthinsurance.org.

AUTO INSURANCE

If you have a car, you are required to have auto insurance, though the requirements vary from state to state. Here are the different major types of auto insurance coverage.

TYPE OF AUTO INSURANCE	WHAT IT COVERS
Bodily injury liability*	Protects you if someone is injured in an accident that you caused
Property damage liability*	Covers damage to other cars and property
Collision	Covers damage to your car
Comprehensive	Protects you from theft or weird stuff that could happen to your car, such as fire
Uninsured/underinsured motorist	Covers your medical expenses and lost income if an uninsured motorist hits you
Personal injury	Covers medical bills and lost wages no matter who is at fault in the accident

*Note: Liability protects you from being held responsible for *someone else's* injuries/damages.

What Do I Really Need?

If you don't have much in terms of savings or investments and you don't own a home, you should get at least $100,000 in bodily injury coverage per person, $300,000 in bodily injury insurance per accident, and $100,000 in property damage liability. If you have significant assets like a home and many investments, you'll want to get more coverage. Everyone should get about $100,000 in uninsured/underinsured motorists coverage. As for collision and comprehensive insurance, whether you need them depends on the value of your car. If you have an older car, they might be worth dropping because what you'll pay in deductible and annual premiums may be more than what the insurance company would give you for your car. Look up the value of your car in the Kelley Blue Book or at kbb.com and subtract that cost from your deductible and annual premiums. If your deductible plus your annual premiums are more than the value of your car, drop your collision and comprehensive coverage. If you already have separate health, disability, and life (if you needed it) insurance, you probably don't need personal injury insurance. Visit SmartMoney.com's auto insurance section for calculators and more information to determine the exact amount of auto insurance you will need.

To save money on auto insurance, first of all, drive safely (naturally). Buy a car that won't require higher-cost insurance—sports cars and cars that are more likely to be stolen have higher insurance rates than other cars (check with your insurance company before buying to get their recommendations on cars). Ask your insurance company if they will reduce your rates if you do something like install a security system on your car, and shop around for the best rates. Finally, don't file too many claims—if you have a small dent, just let it be or pay out of pocket, because filing a claim for it will increase your rates.

DISABILITY INSURANCE

Disability insurance protects you if you are injured and cannot work by providing you with income until you can work again. A typical plan would pay you about 60 percent of your current salary for a specified amount of time. There are two types of disability insurance: short-term, which pays you an income for a short period of time—usually six weeks to two years—and long-term, which pays you income for a few years up until age sixty-five. Disability insurance has an elimination period—this is the amount of time between when you were injured and when the insurance company will start paying you. The shorter the elimination period, the longer the amount of time you'll get the benefits, and the higher the premium will be.

Here's what to look for in disability insurance:

- Try to find a policy that defines disability as your inability to perform *your own* job. Some policies define disability as your inability to perform any other job. In that case, if you couldn't do your job, but you could work as a garbage collector or some other job you *don't want*, they would not pay you. And, ladies, I'm pretty sure your perfectly put-together office wardrobe would be kind of useless amid the waist-high piles of smelly Hefty bags.
- Non-cancelable and guaranteed renewable policies (see below).
- A provision that adjusts your benefits based on cost of living. This ensures that payments will keep up with inflation.

Three Types of Disability Insurance

1. Non-cancelable and guaranteed renewable: The insurance company can't drop you and they will let you renew the policy for as long as you want with the same premiums and the same benefits.
2. Guaranteed renewable: They can't drop you but they can raise your rates.
3. Conditionally renewable: They *can* drop you *and* raise rates. Avoid this type of policy.

You should buy residual disability benefits, which will give you partial benefits if you aren't totally disabled but can only work part-time.

Check to see if your employer offers disability insurance. If so, read the fine print. You may need to supplement their policy by buying an additional policy on your own if your employer's coverage won't adequately protect you. Shop around for the best rates. Disability insurance usually runs you about 1 to 3 percent of your annual pre-tax income, but this, of course, depends on your risk level. Ideally, you would have both short- and long-term disability insurance. However, if you have enough in savings to cover your lifestyle until a long-term disability plan would kick in and you need cash freed up (cash that you would be spending on short-term disability), you could forgo getting short-term disability.

How to save money on disability insurance: Choose a longer elimination period, if you can afford to.

HOMEOWNERS INSURANCE

Homeowners insurance reimburses you if your house and any other structures on your property are damaged, destroyed, or stolen. It covers the actual structure of the house, as well as what's inside (this can even mean your fabulous collection of vintage handbags). It also protects you from having to pay medical bills if someone is hurt on your property. If you own a home, you need this insurance.

What Should I Look for in My Homeowners Insurance?

- Guaranteed replacement or extended value: Guaranteed replacement ensures that no matter what it costs to rebuild your home, the insurance company will pay, whereas extended value covers about 20 to 25 percent for overruns in the cost of rebuilding your home. Because guaranteed replacement is more expensive than extended value, you should think about whether or not you really need it. Those of you who do not live in an area prone to disasters and keep your policy up-to-date with current market conditions probably do not need guaranteed replacement coverage. If you opt for actual cash value coverage, know that the insurance company will pay only for the value of your stuff *minus* depreciation—this will make it very hard to replace your items.
- Replacement cost guarantee: This ensures that the insurance company will reimburse you for your belongings (furniture, clothes—whatever's inside the house) at today's prices. Otherwise, they would give you much less than what you'd need to actually replace the items in your home; in other words, they would factor in depreciation.
- At least enough liability coverage to cover the total dollar amount of all your financial assets (your financial assets include your home, retirement funds, investments—anything that's worth money), and you probably should have enough to cover double the amount of your financial assets.
- Coverage against natural disasters like floods and earthquakes, if you are in an area prone to them. Most homeowners policies already protect against fires.
- You might also need to add more coverage for certain valuable items in your home, like artwork or jewelry. Check your policy to see what it covers. If these items are not covered, you will need to add a scheduled personal property provision to your policy to make sure you will be reimbursed.

Make sure that you write down all of the valuable items in your house and take pictures and/or save receipts. This will help you if you ever need to make a claim. Nationwide Mutual, Allstate, Erie Insurance, and Liberty

Mutual all sell homeowners insurance. Prepare to pay roughly $35 per month per every $100,000 of home value.

To save money on homeowners insurance, see if you can get a package deal—different types of insurance, like auto and homeowners, from the same company—for a discount. It's also worth talking to the company to see if things like installing a security system or deadbolt locks or paying electronically will lower your monthly fees. You also probably do not need to insure the sales price of your home; just the cost of rebuilding it.

PRIVATE MORTGAGE INSURANCE (PMI)

When the down payment on your house is less than 20 percent of the purchase price, the lender is going to make you get private mortgage insurance (PMI). This insurance protects the lender in case you default or stop making payments on your loan. PMI is not one of those optional things like life insurance—those greedy lenders will require it to keep people from defaulting on their mortgages. PMI will cost about $55 per month per $100,000 loaned.

PMI can be canceled once you own 20 percent of your house outright. If that sounded like a foreign language, here's an example: If you bought a $100,000 house and put down $15,000, you would own 15 percent of your home. The lender's term for this is equity: the percentage of your home that you own outright. The remaining $85,000 is the amount of your home that the lender/bank owns. And remember, you'll be paying the bank much more than $85,000 because you pay interest, too. Please note that the bank calculates this percentage of ownership based on the current market value of the home and not on what you paid for the home.

Should I Roll PMI into My Mortgage Payment?

Your PMI will be a separate monthly bill unless you roll it into your mortgage payment. Rolling your PMI into your mortgage payments will lower your monthly costs as it will allow you to pay off your PMI over thirty years. Also, since the PMI is rolled into your mortgage payments, it becomes tax deductible. Plus, you'll have only one bill to deal with instead of two. The downside is that it will typically cost you about 1 percent of your mortgage amount to do this. To decide whether it's right for you to roll your PMI into your monthly mortgage payment, ask your lender to break your monthly payments into two parts: one part with PMI rolled into your mortgage, and one with PMI and mortgage payments made separately. Don't just assume that your lender will automatically cancel your PMI when you get to 20 percent—they have a way of "forgetting" to do that.

RENTERS INSURANCE

If you rent, you need it. Your landlord's insurance does not protect your belongings. If you or your guests damage his property, you will have to pay him. (And he is probably not going to be amused with your adorable little excuses as to why you can't pay. I mean, look at what he does when the rent is late.) Plus, if someone is injured in your apartment, you are responsible. Renters insurance helps you out with all of these things.

Try to get a policy that gives you replacement cost coverage. If your policy gives you actual value coverage, the insurance company is going to factor in depreciation, which means that they think your belongings lose value over time, so you probably will not get enough money back to replace the cost of your belongings. Make sure you write down all the valuable items in your house and take pictures. This will help you if you ever have to make a claim.

Go to insurancequote.com and click on the Renters tab to get a quote.

LIFE INSURANCE

If you are single with no dependents, you probably do not need life insurance. If you are married with no dependents and your hubby could easily support himself if you died, you probably don't need life insurance. But if you have dependents, it's a good idea to get life insurance—it provides those dependents with financial support if you die. The sole purpose of life insurance is to replace your income in case you die, so that your dependents can maintain their current lifestyle. It's generally recommended that you purchase life insurance worth five to eight times your annual salary, but it's more important to think about what your beneficiaries' financial needs will be and purchase life insurance accordingly.

Term life insurance, the least expensive type of life insurance, is the right choice for people in their twenties and thirties. Choose the term based on how many years you expect your dependents to rely on you. There are a bunch of other types of life insurance—the main ones are cash value/whole life and universal, which are both life insurance policies and savings vehicles, though you can likely do better by saving your money elsewhere. These other types are generally more expensive, and young people are almost always better off choosing a term life policy. Make sure you get a guaranteed renewable policy, meaning that you can continue your coverage even after the term ends without proof of medical eligibility. To get the best value on insurance, ask the agent where the break points are. Break points in the premium structure indicate where you get the best value. For example, getting $140,000 of coverage may cost you the same or more as getting $150,000 in coverage, so you might as well get the $150,000 in coverage.

To learn more about life insurance, visit CNN Money's (money.cnn. com) Money 101 section under the personal finance tab. There is a life insurance section in this area.

UMBRELLA POLICIES

An umbrella policy offers you additional liability protection. Remember that liability insurance protects you from being held responsible for other people's injuries. Insurance companies will typically offer auto and homeowners insurance up to around $500,000 for liability, which is usually enough to cover most claims. But if you are in a serious auto accident or someone is badly injured in your home, your homeowners and auto insurance may not offer enough liability protection. That's where an umbrella policy comes in. Do you need it? If you don't have significant assets, you probably do not. However, it depends on your personal situation. For example, if your home has a pool or some other feature that may be dangerous, it's worth considering.

HOW DO I BUY INSURANCE?

I recommend visiting Insurancequotes.com or the Bankrate.com Insurance section, which will give you quotes on a variety of different kinds of insurance. You can also call insurance companies such as Allstate, State Farm, or Liberty Mutual directly. But when you call these places, remember that their agents work on commission, so they are motivated to try to sell you whatever makes them the most money. Ask the agents whether they offer a discount if you purchase many kinds of insurance with their company. Also, use Google, and call around to get the best rates. Visit ambest.com to see how your insurance company stacks up. Also, organizations like Standard & Poor's, Weis Research, and Moody's rate insurance companies. Go to your local library and look up the directories that these organizations publish.

Money-Saving Tips on Insurance
1. Shop around for the best rates.
2. If you can afford it, go for a higher deductible and more coverage.
3. Don't file claims on every little thing that goes wrong. This will raise your premiums.
4. Read your policies carefully. Do you pay too much for coverage that you really don't need?
5. Ask the company what you can do to lower the cost of insurance.

Insurance is crucial. Your perfect life can turn on a whim, and insurance is the best way to protect yourself from whatever mishaps might befall you. You could be robbed, fall ill, crash your car . . . there are plenty of worst-case scenarios out there ranging from full-on catastrophe to everyday bad luck. Without insurance, even little mishaps can bankrupt you. Now if you could find a way to insure your perfect relationship with Mr. Right. . . .

CHAPTER 13

Push for a Pad

How to Buy a Home (or at Least Become a Savvy Renter)

The American Dream: gorgeous spouse, gorgeous home, and two gorgeous little kids. Sounds nice, right? And you know what? It's totally achievable . . . well, at least the home part. No, I can't land you a gorgeous hubby or get you started on that perfect family, but at least this advice can help you get your very own pad. Whether you dream of a sun-drenched downtown loft or a Victorian clapboard with a white picket fence, this chapter will help you figure out how to get there, or at the very least, how to get a place that you can truly afford and call home. So let's get started.

ARE YOU READY TO BUY?

Again, your favorite answer: It depends. This table will show you the advantages and disadvantages of each.

	ADVANTAGES	DISADVANTAGES
Buy	You own the place once you pay if off.

It traditionally has been a good investment, in spite of all the recent bad news about home prices and subprime mortgages.

Tax advantages | Often more expensive than renting: If you can't see yourself in that place for several years or more, it may make more sense to continue renting. Why? Because with all the out-the-door costs of buying (and we'll go over these soon), you might end up spending a lot more than you originally anticipated.

If the real estate market is unfavorable (i.e., home prices in your area or interest rates are inflated), it might not make sense to buy.

If you have a great deal on a rental, you might be better suited to put the money you've saved into your retirement plan or another high-yield investment.

More responsibility: You will be responsible for maintenance, upkeep, and repairs. |
| *Rent* | Can be cheaper than buying

Less responsibility: Often you do not have to pay for repairs, maintenance, and upkeep | You do not own the place.

No tax advantages |

Now I realize that you're probably thinking, "Well, that's great, but what about my specific situation?" I can't pop over to your house and figure that out for you, but I do have the next best thing: a rent vs. buy calculator so you can see for yourself. On Bankrate.com, there is a "Rent or Buy?" calculator under the mortgage tab. Remember that when you own a home, you'll have to pay your mortgage payment (principal and interest); homeowners insurance to protect your home and its contents; property taxes; repairs and maintenance; bills such as sewer, water, gas, and electric; landscaping, condo, or co-op fees; appliances; furniture; and more. You should consider all of this before deciding to buy.

I'M READY TO BUY, NOW WHAT?

So, you've considered all of this, and now you're saying, "All right, so it makes sense for me to buy. Now what?" First you need to understand how much house you can afford and what it really costs to buy and own a home.

Step 1: Figure out What You Can Afford

Expect to spend no more than 28 percent of your pre-tax monthly income on your housing costs, which include mortgage payments, both principal and interest; property taxes; and insurance. Plus, you'll need to consider the amount of debt you already have. All of your debt combined—mortgage payments, student loans, auto loans, credit cards, et cetera—should not exceed 36 percent of your pre-tax monthly income.

That may have looked like a bunch of mathematical gobbledygook, so here's a really easy way to see what you can afford. Visit bankrate.com, click on the Mortgage tab, then click on the How Much House Can I Afford? link. Or visit money.cnn.com, click on the Personal Finance tab, then visit the Real Estate section. Fill in the blanks and voilà, you'll be able to figure out if you can truly afford your dream pad (or, as the case may be, your not-too-dreamy-but-it-will-do-for-right-now pad). Now this may take some research on the property tax rates in your area, but never fear, your BFF Google is there to help you.

And remember, as much as you may love the sunlight streaming through the floor-to-ceiling windows in your perfect loft, if you have to sacrifice a lot of the things that you love—going out to dinner, new shoes, decent quality eyeliner—for many years just to keep that house, it may not be worth it. So think about what your life will really be like financially once you buy. And remember that there are more costs to owning a home than mortgage, taxes, and insurance. Consider repairs, home improvements, and any other expenses associated with upkeep. Ladies, at the time of the writing of this book, the economic outlook is not looking pretty, so it is important that you do not try to buy something that you cannot really afford.

Step 2: Start Saving for the Down Payment and Other Closing Costs if You Haven't Already

We'll talk more about this later, but you will need money up front to buy a house, so start saving now.

Step 3: Get Yourself in the Best Financial Position to Get the Loan

In the current mortgage arena, it's harder than it's been in a long time to get a loan. But hard does not mean impossible. Let's look at how the lenders will judge you, so that you can improve in these areas if you need to.

- Your FICO score (if you've been reading this book, you already know this!)
- Your ability to come up with a down payment—the amount of money you can put toward the house up front (usually 3 to 20 percent of the purchase price)
- Your income

    The general rule is that you can't afford to spend more than 28 percent of your pre-tax monthly income on your housing costs, which include mortgage payments, principal and interest; property taxes; and insurance.

    However, if you have a stellar FICO score or a huge down payment ready, the lender may bend this rule a bit.
- How much debt you have

    Lenders want a debt-to-income ratio that doesn't exceed 36 percent. We calculated your debt-to-income ratio in Part III.
- Job history

    If you've worked in the same industry for a least two years, lenders consider that a good sign.
- How long you've been at your current address

    Lenders like people who don't move around too much, even if you have a good reason for each move.
- Background

    Lenders may check for criminal and civil convictions and warrants out for your arrest. No, your little run-in with the po-po in college isn't just going to disappear.

Step 4: Get Pre-approved for a Mortgage Loan

A mortgage loan is a loan for the cost of your home minus your down payment. It's a good idea to get pre-qualified or pre-approved for one, meaning that the lender has approved you for a specific loan amount before you begin the home-buying process. To do this, you'll need to provide the mortgage lender with a bunch of paperwork including your W-2s and tax returns from the past two years, income documentation, list of debts, bank statements, proof of assets (investments, cars, property, etc.), and proof of mortgage or rent payments. We'll talk more about loans—where to get one, how to apply—later in the chapter.

Step 5: Start Shopping

● Find a real estate agent.

If you are a first-time home buyer, it's smart to get a real estate agent you like and trust. They are well versed in the legal and financial factors that come with buying a home. Plus, they can hold your hand throughout the process. However, a real estate broker works on commission, so the more you spend, the more they make. Do not let them talk you into spending more than you want to.

To find a real estate agent, do a Google search for "real estate agent" and the name of the city or town where you live. Your local chamber of commerce or the local board of real estate agents may have some recommendations, and you can ask friends, family, peers, and coworkers. Shop around.

Now vet your agent candidates like you'd vet a date: look for the right background, right personality, and long-term potential. Ask about his or her experience and for the names of clients you could contact to do a background check. Think of it like this: If you could have talked to your ex's ex-girlfriend, imagine how much heartache you could have avoided. It's also important to consider how well the two of you communicate—you'll be spending a lot of time with this person as you home-shop, so it's a good idea to be discriminating.

● Consider the neighborhood.

Check it out thoroughly before buying. Go back at different times throughout the day. Is it safe at night? Does the train roar by? Are there good schools nearby? (And even if your throat closed up at the thought of having kids, you never know when it will happen; plus, it can improve the resale value when your house is in a desirable school district.) Do you think this neighborhood will be a good investment? (Is it an up-and-coming neighborhood; if not, will it at least retain its property values?) What is the property tax situation?

● Consider the condition and possible resale value of the home.

Think about whether this particular home will make a good investment for the future. Maybe you love that ultra-modern look, but will you be able to sell it down the road? If you are considering a fixer-upper, make sure you can truly afford all the renovations you'll want to do. Before you buy, you'll need to have the house inspected, but for now, try to assess whether it will be a good investment based on your own judgment.

- Do your research.

  A well-informed buyer will be better off on all counts. What are homes in the area selling for? Knowing this can help you reign in an inflated home price. What is the direction the real estate market is taking—will you pay a lot for this house now only to see its value drop significantly in the future? This requires a bit of Googling and talking to friends and family, but it's worth it to understand the current market conditions before buying. Trulia.com is a good start for researching home prices in your area. Also, check local real estate listings online and in newspapers. For the real estate market conditions, keep abreast of the news. Your real estate agent can also help you with this process.

I'VE FOUND THE HOUSE I LOVE. HOW DO I BUY IT?

Once you find the house you love, you'll make an offer. This is a legally binding, written document stating the amount you are willing to pay for the house and the time frame for the purchase. You'll have to put down an "earnest money deposit" on the house, which is usually around $1,000, and usually credited to the sale price of the house if the sale goes through. In most cases, you will get the money back if the sale doesn't go through.

When the seller accepts your offer, you will notify your mortgage company. They will perform an appraisal to make sure the home is worth what you offered. Once they approve the sale, you can sign the Purchase and Sale Agreement. In today's market, mortgage contingencies in these agreements are becoming increasingly popular for the buyer, as they can help protect him or her. The mortgage contingency clause states that you are obligated to the sale only if you are able to get a mortgage. Thus, you don't risk losing your deposit should the credit market or another factor prevent you from getting a mortgage. An inspection contingency is an important part of this agreement to ensure that you are not obligated to follow through with the sale should an inspection find something wrong with the house (depending on the clause, the seller may have the opportunity to then repair what's wrong). Go over the wording of the entire agreement and all the clauses with your real estate agent so you understand the exact terms.

To close the deal, you will have to show proof of homeowners insurance, and the bank will have to give final approval on the loan. Right before closing, you'll walk through the house to inspect it, most likely with a professional inspector. If all is in order, you'll meet with the seller, realtor, and closing attorneys to transfer the property to you. Your real estate agent can walk you through the nitty-gritty details of the offer and closing.

Costs Associated with Buying a Home

⊛ Down payment

This is the amount of money you give the lender up front. Lenders love a down payment of 20 percent of the purchase price, but they'll usually settle for less (unless you're one of those lucky girls who is going for a co-op in Manhattan that won't let you in without a spotless background *and* 20 percent down). Remember that if you put down less than 20 percent, you'll have to purchase Private Mortgage Insurance (PMI).

⊛ Closing costs

Closing costs are all the fees that the lender charges you to close the mortgage loan deal. Closing costs will usually run you about 2 to 3 percent of the cost of your mortgage. That means that if you have a $250,000 mortgage, your closing costs may run $7,500. You will have to bring this money to the closing to make the deal happen. Closing costs consist of fees for things like processing, taxes, appraisal, attorneys, postage, points (see below), and more. Your lender is required to give you an estimate for closing costs when you apply for the loan.

⊛ Points

Part of your closing costs may come from points. One point is equal to 1 percent of the loan amount. Points are basically prepaid interest. For each point you buy, the lender will lower your interest rate (to find out the exact amount that they'll lower the interest rate by, you should contact the lender). If you want to know whether it's better for you personally to buy points, go to Bankrate.com, click on the Mortgage tab, then on the mortgage points calculator. It will tell you whether buying points is a good idea in your situation. As a general rule, if you don't plan to live in your home for an extended amount of time, it's probably not such a good idea to buy points. Points are usually tax-deductible in the year that you paid for them (see Chapter 14).

⊛ Private Mortgage Insurance (PMI)

See page 179.

⊛ Homeowners insurance

See page 177.

- Mortgage payments

  Your mortgage payments consist of the principal, which is the amount you borrowed from the lender, and the interest, the fee the bank charges you for the mortgage loan.
- Property taxes

  Taxes paid to the town, city, or county. Ask your real estate agent to give you tax rates in the areas in which you are looking to buy.
- Co-op, condo fees, homeowner association fees, where applicable

  These are fees associated with living in a co-op or condo building. These fees usually cover things like maintenance and upkeep of common areas.
- Upkeep and repairs

  You're now your own landlord, so you get to deal with all of the costs of upkeep and repairs—unless the damage that needs repairing is covered by your homeowners insurance.
- Title insurance

  This ensures the lender that the title is legit.

Closing Costs

The closing is when you and the lender sign the papers on your mortgage loan. Upon signing, you are agreeing to pay the mortgage loan and the lender is agreeing to fund the loan. You will see all of these papers before the closing. You should ask your lender to explain the costs to you beforehand. Understand how much these fees will cost you. Usually you will be asked to bring a certified check to the closing, which covers your down payment and closing costs, if they weren't already rolled into your loan. The lender will specify the exact amount of the check(s).

What are closing costs comprised of?

1. Points (see page 189)
2. Loan fee

   A fee that the lender may charge you to administer the loan. Not tax deductible.
3. Credit check

   You pay the fee for having your credit report checked.
4. Taxes

   You may have to pay pro-rated property taxes.
5. Appraisal

   You pay for the independent appraiser who determines the value of your property.

6. PMI
   See page 179.
7. Prepaid interest
   Depending on when you move in, you may have to pre-pay some interest.
8. Homeowners insurance
   You will have to prepay one year's worth of homeowners insurance.
9. Title insurance
   This protects the lender in case there are problems with the validity of the title.
10. Transfer fees
    Some government agencies charge fees for transferring deeds.
11. Recording fees
    Some government agencies charge fees for filing titles.
12. Survey
    A survey determines the boundaries of a property.
13. Condo, co-op, homeowner association fees
14. Other fees include: escrow account fee, commitment fee, document preparation, underwriting, wire transfer, flood certification, pest and other inspections, postage, and more.

Ask your lender to explain what all of the fees are. You have the right to understand where your money is going and why.

LOAN OPTIONS?

There are three main types of loans: fixed, adjustable, and hybrid.

1. Fixed-rate mortgage
   The interest rate never changes, so your monthly payments never change. There are two main types of fixed-rate mortgages: the thirty-year and the fifteen-year. With the thirty-year, you have thirty years to pay off the entire mortgage. With the fifteen-year, you have fifteen years to do so. If you get a shorter fixed rate, your monthly payments are much higher, but you pay way less over the long term.

For example, on a $200,000 mortgage at a 6 percent interest rate, the fifteen-year option will save you a total of $127,888! Here's how these two options compare for a $200,000 mortgage at a 6 percent interest rate.

	15-YEAR	30-YEAR
Interest rate	6 percent	6 percent
Monthly payment	$1,687	$1,199
Total interest paid	$103,788	$231,676
Total paid	$303,788	$431,676

Assuming you can lock in a good interest rate (and as of early 2009, interest rates were at a historically low 5 to 6 percent), this is probably the best option for you if you plan on staying in the house for at least the next ten years. You'll never have to worry about interest rates skyrocketing.

2. Adjustable-rate mortgage (ARM)

The interest rate changes depending on the general direction of interest rates in the overall economy, plus the lender usually adds a little margin into that rate as well (as if they aren't making enough money as it is!). The initial interest rate on an ARM is usually lower than on a fixed-rate mortgage but then changes. Usually the rule is that the rate can go up or down only by 2 percentage points in a year, with a max of six points over the life of the loan.

How does this work? Your rate adjusts at time periods specified in the terms of the loan. There are two main types of ARMs: the rate cap and the payment cap. The rate cap puts a limit on how high your loan's interest rate can go both over the adjustment period—called a periodic rate cap—and the life of the loan —called a lifetime rate cap. The rate cap ARM is the better kind of ARM to get. A payment cap limits how much your payment can go up during an adjustment period. This can be a bad situation, because when interest rates are rising but your payment cap doesn't allow you to pay enough interest to cover the interest owed, you are accruing interest on your interest, which means that you'll owe even more money.

This can be a scary mortgage to enter into because of the adjustable rates. Interest isn't cheap, after all. What if your interest rates jump? Will you be able to afford the payments? But it can make sense for you if you don't plan to own the house for very long—you'll take advantage of the initial low rates and then sell the home before rates go up. However, will you really be able to sell your home? At the time of the writing of this book, the real estate market had seen better days, so beware of taking this kind of risk. Or if you know you'll make a lot more money in the future and can take the higher payments (and you really, really need to be honest with yourself here, taking into account the current economy and your true likelihood of climbing that career ladder), an ARM can work for you. An ARM does not make sense if there is not much difference between its initial rates and fixed rates, or if you plan on staying in the home for a while and fixed interest rates are reasonable.

3. Hybrid mortgage
A mix of a fixed-rate and an adjustable-rate mortgage. The initial interest rate cannot change for a specified period of time (two to ten years, depending on loan terms) and after that period the rate can change. For some hybrid loans, your rate will change just once after the initial period and for others, your loan will become like an ARM after the initial period.

Two common hybrid mortgages are the 5/25 (your initial interest rate is locked in for 5 years and the adjustable rate kicks in for the following 25 years) and the 7/23 (your initial interest rate is locked in for 7 years and the adjustable rate kicks in for the following 23 years).

Many people who plan to move in five years or less choose the five-year hybrid mortgage, which can be a good option, assuming you can actually sell your house (and at the present time, this is a big assumption). This mortgage will offer you an interest rate for the first five years that is well below the thirty-year fixed mortgage interest rate. But after that period, interest will jump, so if you end up being unable to sell your home, you're going to get hit with high payments. For those moving in ten years or less, consider a ten-year hybrid (or a seven-year hybrid or whatever works for you). It can work for the same reason: You want to pay that low interest at the start, and by the time interest increase kicks in, you'll have moved and will have a different mortgage. But this can be a gamble. What if you can't sell your house before the ARM part of the loan kicks in? Be smart about this option.

Other loans
In the current real estate climate, the economy is such that it is extremely unlikely that you will be offered either of these types of loans, as they are extraordinarily risky. However, it is important that you understand what they are and how they work, just in case you are offered such a loan.

- Interest-only loans

    You pay interest only on the loan for a fixed amount of time, usually three to five years. After this fixed time period is up, you begin to pay off the principal in addition to the interest. So for that fixed amount of time, you are building no equity—you are merely paying the interest.
- Balloon loans

    You pay an initially low interest rate for a fixed amount of time. Once this fixed amount of time is up, you owe the entire amount of the loan. If you are offered this type of loan, you need to make sure that you will be able to pay off that entire loan when the term is up.

Where Do I Find the Best Rates on a Mortgage?

To compare mortgage interest rates in your area, check out the Mortgage section at Bankrate.com. Choose the lender with the lowest rate. Other useful sites include Lendingtree.com, eLoan.com, and hsh.com. First-time homebuyers can often get good deals on mortgages from state and local housing agencies and the Federal Housing Authority (FHA). Visit hud.gov/local.html to check for deals as well. Make sure you look into these options if you are a first-time homebuyer.

Many mortgage loans are quoted using an APR, or annual percentage rate. The difference between the APR and the interest rate is that the APR includes both the interest rate *and* its associated fees and expenses, whereas the interest rate does not—it's simply the interest rate. Which should you use? It's often better to use the interest rate when evaluating your mortgage loan. Why? Because with an APR, fees like closing costs are averaged out over the course of the loan. Let's say you want a thirty-year loan but plan to sell the house in ten years. You don't want to know those fees as they look averaged out over thirty years. You want to see them itemized up front. So use the interest rate instead of the APR when comparing rates.

How Do I Pay Back My Mortgage Loan?

Each month you'll be required to send the lender your mortgage payment, which is the principal plus the interest, and sometimes insurance and taxes as well. Look at the amortization schedule, which is a schedule of your payments owed to the lender over the course of the loan. It will break out the payments each month into interest payments, principal payments, and the remaining balance owed. I recommend that you set up online bill pay so that your payment is automatically deducted from your account—you'll never have a late payment again. During the early years of a mortgage loan, you typically pay way more in interest than you do on the principal of the loan.

Make sure you know whether or not your mortgage payment includes insurance and taxes. If it doesn't, you will need to pay these on your own. If it does include them, your lender will typically set up an escrow account. When you pay your mortgage payment every month, part of this money will go into an escrow account to cover the tax and insurance bills when they are due. The lender will pay these for you from your escrow account.

If you are offered the option to do biweekly payments, it's worth looking into. If you are paid every two weeks, which is the norm at many companies, you can just have your mortgage payment automatically deducted from each paycheck. On a traditional mortgage, you pay every month, twelve payments a year. With biweekly payments, you pay every fourteen days. You'll pay off your loan more quickly this way, which will save you money—a thirty-year mortgage can be paid off in about twenty-three years and a fifteen-year mortgage in about fourteen years. Ask your lender if they offer this option, but make sure they do not charge a big fee for the biweekly payments. And ask for the amortization schedule. Can you really afford this type of payment system?

Should I Pay off My Mortgage as Quickly as I Can?

Probably, as this results in you paying less in interest in the long run. However, think about this in terms of your entire debt load. Remember that you want to pay the highest interest debts off as quickly as you can while always paying off the minimum owed on all debts. So if you owe credit card debt at 18 percent interest, and your mortgage loan at 6.5 percent interest, work on paying that credit card off quickly, then work on paying off more on your mortgage loan (though you should always pay the minimum each time it's due). Make sure you tell the lender to apply the extra payment to the principal (write this on your check). And make sure you know whether your lender has a prepayment penalty, and if so, what it is.

Should I Refinance My Mortgage Loan?

First off, what is refinancing? It's when you replace your old loan with a new one that has a lower rate or a different term. It can be a good idea to refinance when interest rates have fallen at least 1.5 percent below what you are currently paying *and* you plan on staying in the house for more than a few more years. But beware: There are fees associated with refinancing, so it doesn't always pay to do it. That's where the staying-in-the-house-for-a-few-years part comes in. If the amount you will save on interest is less than the fees associated with refinancing, this is not a good deal. It *may* be a good idea to refinance if your ARM is about to adjust, thus jacking up your interest rates. Or you can refinance and take advantage of those lower interest rates to shorten the term of your loan (but make sure you can truly afford this), saving you tons in the long run.

You may be able to refinance for more than the value of your current mortgage if you've built up a lot of equity in your home. This is called cash-out refinancing, and you will get cash along with a new mortgage loan. Remember, this is not free cash. You pay interest on it just like you do with the rest of the loan. This kind of loan can be useful when you need to do home renovations.

Ask the lender to run you an analysis on refinancing options that includes an interest rate on the new loan and all the associated fees and/or closing costs. If you are thinking about refinancing, check out Bankrate.com's refinancing calculator.

How Much Will I Save in Taxes by Owning a Home?

Because you can deduct mortgage interest, real estate taxes, and, in certain cases, points that you pay at closing on your income taxes, owning a home can have great tax advantages. To see how much you'll save each year in taxes by buying a home, check out freddiemac.com, which has a home ownership tax savings calculator.

What if I Missed a Payment?

So life didn't exactly turn out as you had planned, and you're now going to miss a mortgage payment. What should you do? Contact your lender if you think you're going to miss a payment, explain your situation, and try to work out a payment schedule with them that you can follow. Look into refinancing, extending the term of the loan, or asking friends or family for money. Do what you can to avoid missing the payments, as this will hurt your FICO score.

If you do not make your mortgage payments for ninety days, you are in default on your loan and your lender will probably start foreclosure proceedings. (Ladies, you're not alone. CNN reports that there were more than 3.1 million foreclosure filings issued in 2008 alone.) This means that the lender can seize your house and sell it to recoup their money. This is not good for your FICO, not to mention that you lose your home. You can help protect your credit in this case by holding a pre-foreclosure sale at which you sell the house to pay back the lender. You can also get a deed in lieu of foreclosure. Ask your lender about this option.

What Are Home Equity Lines of Credit and Home Equity Loans?

A home equity line of credit (HELOC) is a secondary loan on your home, based on the equity you have built up in it. The great part about a HELOC is that you owe interest only on the part that you've used, so you can use only what you need and let the rest sit there in case of an emergency without having to pay interest on it. The HELOC interest rate is variable, so be careful. A home equity loan is also a secondary loan on your home, based on the equity you have built up in your home. But you receive the entire amount of the loan up front and thus owe interest on the entire amount. The interest rates are fixed. Whether you want a HELOC or home equity loan depends on what you need it for. If you need the whole amount ASAP and want a fixed interest rate, then go with the home equity loan. If you want to make a series of payments drawn out over a period of time, the HELOC might make more sense. But remember, failing to pay back these loans can mean that you lose your home.

RENTING 101

So the elusive dream of home ownership is not in your cards—a white picket fence of your own just isn't happening yet. And, ladies, this isn't a strike against you. Maybe you can't afford your own place yet, maybe you love to hop around from city to city and don't want to settle down. Whatever the reason, you're probably going to need a place to live, and that will likely mean renting an apartment. This section is your guide to getting the most out of rental apartments.

How Much Rent Can I Afford?

You should expect to spend no more than 30 percent of your pre-tax income on your rent. And definitely try to spend less than that so you can work on paying off your debt and saving.

Where Do I Find an Apartment?

Craigslist, word of mouth, community bulletin boards, ads in local media, local real estate offices, and just cruising the neighborhood looking for

For Rent signs can help you find an apartment. It also might be worth checking out apartments.com, apartmentguide.com, and other online apartment listing sites. There are a variety of ways to find out about apartments for rent. If you end up using a real estate broker to help you find a place, it is likely you will pay some kind of fee for their services. Just weigh whether the fees are worth what you will ultimately get out of the deal.

Make sure you understand the costs associated with renting an apartment so you can save accordingly. These are some key costs you'll want to take note of.

- Credit check or apartment application fee (often a landlord charges you for the cost of running your credit report when checking you out for the apartment)
- Security deposit
- Monthly rent
- Other fees paid to the landlord (for example, a landlord may ask you to pay the last month's rent up front)
- Late rent payment fees
- Utility bills, deposits, hookup fees (gas, electric, TV, Internet, water, phone, heat, etc.)
- Furniture
- Renters insurance
- Agent/broker fees (if you used a real estate agent in your apartment hunt)
- Moving fees (for example, renting a U-Haul to move your stuff)

When you move into a new city, you often have to pay an excise tax on your car when you register it. This can be hundreds of dollars, so look into it with that city clerk's office before you move. Note that your auto insurance rates may also change when you move to a new city. Also, it's worth looking into the cost of living in a new place so you can have an idea what you'll be spending on basic things such as food. You can check this out online, using a cost-of-living calculator like bestplaces.net/col.

Not all of these costs are set in stone, though, and here are a few ways to save money.

- Shop around

    You may be able to get lower rates on some of the costs above like renters insurance (see page 180), phone, TV, Internet, et cetera, so shop around. When shopping for furniture, consider Goodwill or other secondhand shops, Craigslist and other local Web sites, and asking your parents or others to give you their old furniture. I know Crate & Barrel is adorable, but can you really afford it?

- Pay your rent on time to avoid late payment fees. If it's a possibility, have your rent automatically deducted from your bank account via online bill pay so that you don't miss payments.
- Keep the apartment in good condition to avoid the landlord taking your security deposit.
- Some moving expenses are tax deductible, so that's worth looking into. Check irs.gov for more information.

Understanding Your Lease

The lease spells out the terms of your occupancy in the apartment, everything from the amount of time you can live there, to the amount you owe in rent, and the nitty-gritty rules of day-to-day existence. A normal lease contains many provisions to protect your landlord, along with a few things to protect you, which are required by law to be included. So first of all you need to actually *read* the lease. R-E-A-D. Make sure you understand all of the terms, which may include the rent, the security deposit, and other up-front money owed (sometimes the landlord will require first and last month's rent and a security deposit immediately after you sign the lease), and where to pay them. Pay attention to what the lease has to say about rent payment late fees, responsibility for payment of utilities, whether pets are allowed and if there is a deposit for pets, number of people allowed in the apartment, rules for painting and decorating, wear-and-tear provisions, penalty for breaking the lease, et cetera. Do you have to give written notice of your intent to stay or leave when the lease is coming to a close? You'll also want to know who to call when you have issues—a leaky roof, broken appliance, et cetera. If you don't understand the lease terms, ask the landlord to explain them and look them up online if you can. If you do agree on a change to the lease, make sure the change is in writing.

If you sign a month-to-month lease, your landlord can raise the rent at the end of every month, or kick you out anytime. But you are obligated to live there for only one month, so this can work out for you if you plan to move soon. However, you may still have to give written notice of your intent to leave at the end of a given month. If you need to break the lease, most landlords will charge you a fee, though you may be able to sublet the place to another tenant with your landlord's written permission.

Security Deposit

This is a fixed amount of money you owe the landlord when you sign the lease. The landlord will hold on to this money until you move out. If, after you leave, the landlord has to fix items you broke, clean the place, or deal with other provisions in the lease that cost him money, he will use the money in your security deposit to take care of this. Each state has different laws on how landlords must handle the security deposit (for example, whether they owe you interest accrued on the deposit), which you can find out about at rentlaw.com.

To make sure you get your security deposit back, first get a receipt from your landlord when you hand over the deposit and keep the canceled check. This is proof that you paid the security deposit. Then go through your entire apartment as soon as you move in and take pictures of everything that is broken, dirty, or damaged in any way. Keep these photos in a safe place. Make a list of all the broken, dirty, and damaged items and send them to your landlord. Keep a copy of this list for yourself as well. Before you move out, clean the apartment thoroughly and repair any damage. Photograph the entire place upon your departure. Remove all of your belongings from the apartment. Give the keys directly to the landlord and leave him your forwarding address so that he can mail the security deposit check to you.

Treat a pet deposit in the same way. Make sure you repair any stains or damage caused by your pets. Make sure the odor of your pet is gone from the apartment before you move out.

Deposits for Utilities

Many utilities—water, cable, electric, gas, et cetera—require a deposit from you when you move into the new place before they will start your service. Sometimes these can be avoided. Call your utility company (if it will be the same as in the new apartment) and tell them that you are moving. Ask if they can transfer your service to the new place and waive your deposit in the new place. Even if you don't have the same utility company, it's worth calling before you move to see how you can get the deposit or hook-up fee waived. Sometimes they will waive a hook-up fee if they don't have to come to the place and turn on the utility. In that case, call ahead to have the bill transferred from the old tenant's account to your name, starting on the first day of your new lease. When you move out, make sure to request your deposit back from the utility company. Also, make sure to call the utility companies to tell them when you are moving out. You do not want to inadvertently owe money for the new tenant's utilities.

RENTING WITH ROOMMATES

Let me begin by saying that I have seen too many roommate issues, even between BFFs. You may think you love your roommate and that she'd never screw you over, but you never know. Two of my good friends no longer speak to each other because of a security deposit, and you know what? They're both normal, sweet girls. The whole issue was just a giant misunderstanding. It happens, so read on.

Roommate Rule #1: Find Roommates Who Are Responsible and Trustworthy.

Who hasn't been there, and made the wrong decision? Living with the cool party girl seemed brilliant until she "borrowed" your gorgeous Victorian coat and ran off with her boyfriend for a month, only to return coatless. Or how about the girl you sort of knew from your English class who you assumed would be a sweetheart, until she let her dog loose in the house and you ended up with a ripped couch and three chewed pairs of shoes that she refused to refund you for. Lesson: If you need to live with someone you don't know well, ask around about them. Ask them to provide references from their old roommates and landlords if need be. I know this sounds psycho, or, at the very least, excessive, but it can save you a lot of heartache down the road. It's also important to be on board with your roommates on things like cleanliness, noise and parties, and guests.

Roommate Rule #2: Decide How You'll Deal with Signing the Lease.

There are two basic ways that you can set up the lease and pay the rent.

* All roommates sign the lease, and all are all liable for rent and damages.

    If one person does not pay her share, everyone is liable for it. So let's say you move in with Jane and Katie. If you and Jane pay your share of the rent but Katie does not, the landlord can evict all three of you.

* One person signs the lease, and she is solely responsible for paying the rent.

    She sublets the rooms to other people, collects rent from them, and pays it to the landlord. Some apartments do not allow subletting, so you'll have to check to make sure it's okay. Subletting is complicated and puts an immense responsibility on the sublessor to make sure that everyone pays in full and on time. The sublessor is solely responsible for paying the rent, as she is the only person on the lease. On the upside, she can kick out a non-paying roommate. Assuming she received a security deposit from this person, she'll use it to pay the rent, and then find someone to replace the deadbeat roommate.

If you are the sublessor in this instance, you'll want to create a contract between yourself and your subletter outlining her responsibility for the rent, security deposit, utilities, damages, duration of sublet term, and anything else. Even with this agreement, you as the sublessor are still solely responsible for the rent payment to the landlord. Both Tufts University and the University of Pennsylvania offer a good template for this contract. Visit their Web sites to get copies of these agreements. Obviously it's better for a real legal professional to create this contract for you, but that can be expensive, so using these templates is better than nothing. Just make sure that you tweak the documents to fit your needs.

Roommate Rule #3: Put the House Rules and Obligations in Writing Before You Move In.

This may seem like too much, but I can't tell you how many fights I've had with roommates over stupid things. I mean, what an ex-college roommate who shall remain nameless thought was okay (having a party on the night before my last exam), was not cool with me. You and your roommates will create a written document that spells out your obligations to each other, such as how much each will pay for rent, utilities, security deposit, et cetera. Anything for which you want to lay ground rules—parties, guests, food shopping—should be written into this document. Make the provisions very specific so that everyone understands the rules.

This document does not absolve you from your responsibility to the landlord, but it's important. It establishes the rules before any conflicts arise, and when conflicts do arise, you'll be able to point to this document that you've all signed and agreed on to figure out a solution. Make sure you note the property (i.e., couches, beds, etc.) that is yours in this document so there is no dispute when you move out. You can find a sample contract available at youngconsumer.org.

Roommate Rule #4: Keep Receipts and Checks on Large Joint Purchases.

If you guys make large joint purchases together, you need to be able to prove that you paid for part of the item. Pay by check and make a note on the check, "Jointly owned television set" or pay by credit card. Just make sure your method of payment is traceable in case there is ever a dispute.

Roommate Rule #5: Get Renters Insurance (See Chapter 12).

Whether you rent or own, it is important that your pad is a place you can truly afford. If we've learned anything from the real estate crash of 2008, it's that taking out a giant loan on a home you can't afford is simply not worth it—I don't care how perfect that lawn was, how beautiful those floor-to-ceiling windows seemed. Ladies, believe me, I love real estate as much as the next girl (just ask my boyfriend whom I drag to open houses of multimillion-dollar Manhattan apartments that we know we'll never buy), but just because you have a keen appreciation for swanky digs does not mean that you need to move into a place you truly cannot afford.

CHAPTER 14

Tackle Your Taxes
How to Finesse Uncle Sam into Padding Your Pocketbook

et's take a little trip back to high school. Wait, wait, don't snap this book shut yet—I am not talking about that traumatic, pimply, cliquey version of high school that even years of therapy can't make you forget. Rather, I'm thinking about that high school history class—right at the moment when your sexy-yet-nerdy teacher chuckled knowingly and offered you this little nugget of wisdom from Ben Franklin: "Nothing is certain but death and taxes." Ladies, old Ben was onto something with that one, I can assure you. But for those of you who want to take a nap at the mere mention of a white-haired founding father, let me bring old Ben into the new millennium. You're about as likely to (legally) avoid paying taxes, as you are of living happily ever after with George Clooney, becoming a Victoria's Secret model, or managing to go a week without fighting with your mother. Taxes—unlike most men, your hair, and your singing career—are a sure thing. And since you can't escape them (taxes, that is), you better understand how to make them work in your favor as much possible.

That's exactly what this chapter will do: help you understand your taxes so you can work the good ol' IRS (legally, of course) just like you work your man—a few little tweaks, some much-need alterations, and voilá, going just the way you want it to. Ladies, doing your taxes correctly and on time can save you thousands of dollars. And you know those thousands of dollars are so much better off under your watchful little gaze than lining the pockets of the suits at the IRS. Don't wait to read this chapter until right before tax time—these are strategies you should be working on all year to save yourself money.

Since income tax is usually the largest tax bill people pay, this chapter will focus on understanding and lowering income taxes. Things like property, sales, and use taxes vary so much from state to state and locality that it's best to research this on your own, depending on where you live.

INCOME TAX

Your personal income tax consists of federal and sometimes state and local income taxes. Because state and local taxes vary according to where you live, I'm going to talk only about federal income tax: what it is and, more important, how you can reduce it. Note that state income taxes often closely parallel federal income taxes in terms of deductions and credits. To find out more about your state's income taxes, visit Bankrate. com's state tax calculator. This provides state income tax levels as well as links to the relevant tax sites in your state.

How Much Will I Pay in Federal Income Taxes?

Well, first of all, it depends on your income. Generally, the more you make, the more you pay in income taxes. But it's not quite as simple as that. It also depends on the adjustments, exemptions, credits, and deductions that you claim, and the tax brackets that you fall into.

Here are four steps to help you figure out what you'll pay in income tax:

Step 1: Determine how much income you'll be taxed on (i.e., Total Taxable Income).

Step 2: Find out what tax brackets you fall into and calculate the taxes owed.

Step 3: Subtract your tax credits from total taxes owed.

Step 4: Check to see if you are subject to the Alternative Minimum Tax.

Step 1: Determine How Much Income You'll Be Taxed on (i.e., Total Taxable Income)

The IRS definition of income is more than just your salary; it's a bunch of things that provide you with money. And there are certain items that may provide you with money that they don't consider income. So I've outlined what they call taxable income, which is income on which they'll make you pay taxes, and what they call nontaxable income, which is income on which you won't have to pay taxes (or on which you can defer paying taxes).

Just a note so that you can avoid confusion: Taxable income is not the same as Total Taxable Income. Total Taxable Income includes adjustments, deductions, and exemptions, whereas taxable income does not. You will use your Total Taxable Income to determine the exact amount of money you'll be taxed on.

Taxable income may include:
- Your salary (minus the money you have deducted for your employer-sponsored retirement plan)
- Interest earned on bank accounts and bonds
- Dividends on investments
- Bonuses
- Severance pay
- Sick pay
- Unemployment compensation
- Tips
- Capital gains on investments
- Gambling and lottery winnings
- Withdrawals from an IRA or annuity
- Alimony paid to you

Nontaxable income may include:
- Money contributed to tax-deferred retirement accounts like your IRA
- Disability income on benefits you paid for with after-tax money
- FSA funds
- Child support

But taxable income is not the entire picture. In fact, it's only the beginning, and this is a good thing. You need to get to Total Taxable Income, which is the amount of income that the IRS will use to calculate what you owe them. Total Taxable Income is affected by the adjustments, deductions, and exemptions you claim (defined below). These reduce the amount of income you'll have to pay taxes on. So the higher these are, the better off you are.

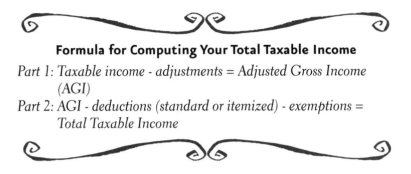

Formula for Computing Your Total Taxable Income

Part 1: Taxable income - adjustments = Adjusted Gross Income (AGI)

Part 2: AGI - deductions (standard or itemized) - exemptions = Total Taxable Income

Not so complicated, right? See below for definitions of the terms in the formula above.

Adjustments

Items you can subtract from your taxable income. These may include:

* Contributions to tax-deferred retirement accounts like IRAs
* Moving expenses
* Interest paid on student loans

Adjusted Gross Income (AGI)

Your taxable income *minus* adjustments. Check out your IRS Form 1040 for your AGI from last year. It is at the bottom of page 1 on Form 1040.

Deductions

Like adjustments, deductions lower the amount of income that you'll be taxed on. When you file your income tax return, you choose between taking the standard deduction, which is a flat amount that you subtract from your taxable income, or itemizing all of your deductions, which would mean listing out all your eligible deductions individually. If your total itemized deductions are greater than the standard deduction, you'll want to itemize (we'll discuss this more later).

These were the standard deduction amounts in 2009.

* Single or married filing separately—$5,700
* Married filing a joint return or qualifying widow/widower—$11,400
* Head of household—$8,350

These numbers change each year. Check out Form 1040 and 1040EZ on irs.gov for current numbers.

Deductions are things that you can itemize on your tax return, and they may include:

- Interest paid on your home mortgage or home equity loan
- Points you paid at the closing of the home you bought
- Real estate taxes
- Personal property taxes
- State and local income taxes
- Charitable donations
- Medical expenses
- Job-search expenses
- And many more. See Schedule A (included with the long version of IRS Form 1040) for a complete list of all the deductions you can itemize, or visit irs.gov for a copy of this form. You can also check out turbotax.intuit.com/tax-tools for an understanding of your deductions.

Exemptions

Like adjustments and deductions, exemptions reduce your taxable income. Most Americans get one exemption for themselves, and, if applicable, one for their spouse, as well as one for each of their kids. In 2009, each exemption was worth $3,650, meaning that with each exemption you could deduct $3,650 from your taxable income (with some exceptions).

For example, if you make $36,000 per year but you take a $3,650 exemption, your tax rate will be computed using $32,350 of income.

All right, ladies, once the IRS has determined your Total Taxable Income, they will then use this number to calculate how much you owe them. So on to Step 2.

Step 2: Find Out What Tax Brackets You Fall into and Calculate the Taxes Owed

Your Total Taxable Income is taxed based on tax brackets. Each bracket has a different tax rate. Here are the tax brackets for your federal income tax. Visit irs.gov for the latest figures.

2008 Federal Income Tax Brackets

FILING STATUS	10 %	15 %	25 %	28 %	33 %	35 %
Single	Not more than $8,025	$8,025–$32,550	$32,550–$78,850	$78,850–$164,550	$164,550–$357,700	More than $357,700
Married Filing Jointly	Not more than $16,500	$16,050–$65,100	$65,100–$131,450	$131,450–$200,300	$200,300–$357,700	More than $357,700
Married Filing Separately	Not more than $8,025	$8,025–$32,550	$32,550–$65,725	$65,725—$100,150	$100,150–$178,850	More than $178,850
Head of House-hold	Not more than $11,450	$11,450–$43,650	$43,650–$112,650	$112,650–$182,400	$182,400–$357,700	More than $357,700

But it's not as simple as "I'm single and my Total Taxable Income is $36,000, so I'm taxed at the 25 percent rate." The income that falls within each tax bracket is taxed at the rate within that bracket. Here's an example to clarify.

Let's say you are single and your Total Taxable Income is $36,000. Here's how you would be taxed:

* $8,025 of your income is taxed at the 10 percent rate.
    You owe $802.50 ($8,025 × 10 percent)
* $24,525 of your income is taxed at the 15 percent rate.
    ($24,525 is the difference between $32,550, which is the upper limit of the 15 percent tax bracket, and $8,025, the upper limit of the previous tax bracket)
    You owe $3,678.75 ($24,525 × 15 percent)
* $3,450 of your income is taxed at the 25 percent rate
    ($3,450 is the difference between your income of $36,000 and $32,550, the upper limit of the previous tax bracket)
    You owe $862.50 ($3,450 × 25 percent)

TOTAL FEDERAL INCOME TAXES OWED: $5,343.75
(This is the total of the taxes owed within each bracket—$802.50 + $3,678.75 + $862.50)

Step 3: Subtract Your Tax Credits from Total Taxes Owed

A tax credit is a dollar-for-dollar reduction in your taxes. So if you get a tax credit of $1,000, you will subtract $1,000 from the total taxes owed. In the example above, your $1,000 tax credit would mean that you pay only $4,343.75 in taxes ($5,343.75 - $1,000).

You can often get tax credits for the following (qualifications for credits are for 2008).

* Retirement savings contributions

  Credit of up to $1,000 (or $2,000 if filing jointly) for low- or modest-income individuals (this includes married individuals filing separately and singles with incomes up to $26,500; married couples filing jointly with incomes up to $53,000; and heads of household with incomes up to $39,750) who made eligible contributions to a qualified IRA, 401(k), and certain other retirement plans.

* Child and dependent care

  Credit of up to 35 percent of your qualifying expenses, depending on your income, if you paid for care for one of your dependent(s), such as a child under age thirteen or another qualifying person, so that you and/or your spouse could work or look for work.

* Education

  Hope Credit

  Credit of up to $1,800, depending on your income, for those who pay qualified higher education expenses. The Hope Credit is available only in the first two years of college, for students who are pursing an undergraduate degree or recognized education credential, and only for two years per eligible student.

  Lifetime Learning Credit

  Credit of up to $2,000, depending on your income, for those who pay qualified education expenses, which include college costs as well as job-training courses. Available for an unlimited number of years, and the student does not need to be pursuing a degree.

* Mortgage interest

  If you were issued a mortgage interest credit certificate by a state or local government, you may be able to deduct this interest from your federal income tax. The credit usually equals the interest paid multiplied by the mortgage interest credit certificate rate set by the certificate issuer.

* Low/moderate-income working families

  You may be eligible for the Earned Income Tax Credit (EITC), a credit designed to help out low- to moderate-income individuals and families, if your earned income and adjusted gross income (AGI) were each less than $38,646 (or $41,646 for married filing jointly) with two or more qualifying children; $33,995 (or $36,995 for married filing jointly) with one qualifying child; $12,880 (or $15,880 for married filing jointly) with no qualifying children.

* For a basic list of tax credits, go to irs.gov/taxtopics/tc600.html. You can also find a list of tax credits on Form 1040, and on the tax section at About.com.

For details on how to qualify for any of these credits, visit IRS.gov and use their search box to find the name of the credit you are interested in.

Do the Dirty Work for Me

There are a bunch of online calculators that can help you figure out how much you'll owe in taxes. A good one is the Tax Estimator calculator from TurboTax (turbotax.com). To get the correct data using this calculator, you're going to need to understand tax deductions, credits, and capital gains, which I will explain later.

What's the difference between a tax credit and a tax deduction/ exemption/adjustment?
While a tax deduction, exemption, or adjustment reduces the amount of income on which you are taxed, thereby reducing your total taxes owed, a tax credit is a dollar-for-dollar reduction in your taxes. So a tax credit is generally a much better thing to receive.

* If you get a tax deduction of $1,000 and your average tax rate is 25 percent, you'll get about $250 in tax savings ($1,000 x 25 percent = $250).
* But if you get a tax credit of $1,000, you will get $1,000 in tax savings.

Step 4: Check to See if You Are Subject to the Alternative Minimum Tax

The Alternative Minimum Tax might be the most confusing tax on earth. It's basically a different method for computing income tax, which is usu- ally less forgiving than the method I outlined above. It was designed to ensure that wealthy individuals, trusts, estates, and corporations paid at least some income tax despite all their deductions and exemptions, but now it doesn't just affect the wealthy and corporations.

Taxpayers must calculate their tax obligations through the regular tax system and through the AMT system, paying the greater of the two amounts. Visit irs.gov and look for the Alternative Minimum Tax (AMT) Assistant to determine if you owe the tax. The AMT is often triggered when an individual has numerous personal exemptions, many itemized deductions or medical expenses, or Incentive Stock Option (ISO) plans. When you use an online tax preparation software like TurboTax, it figures this out for you.

TOP TEN TAX TIPS THAT SAVE YOU MONEY (AKA: LESS MONEY TO THE IRS = MORE MONEY FOR YOU)

1. Don't Get an Income Tax Refund

Many of you probably have too much withheld from your paychecks. If you got a big refund last year, this is a sign you have too much withheld. Why is this bad? Because the money that the IRS is holding could be money in your pocket. You could be paying down your debt with that money or putting it into a high-interest savings account. Instead, they are holding it for you—and they aren't giving you interest on it—and they will return it to you when you get your refund. You'd be better off earning interest on the money or paying off high-interest debt with it. However, by not having them withhold the money for you, you might owe the IRS money at the end of the year. You'll need to stash away money to pay them. But again, you'll earn interest on this money that you've stashed away, so it's a good proposition, unless you absolutely cannot be trusted to do that.

So how can you change how much money is withheld from your paycheck? By changing your W-4. IRS Form W-4 determines how much federal income tax is taken out of your paycheck. It's that pesky form you filed with your employer when you started your job. You claimed a filing status (e.g., married filing jointly or single) and other allowances, such as dependents. You can check out the form at irs.gov. After that, I suggest visiting the withholding calculator on the irs.gov site. This calculator will help you figure out how to avoid getting a tax refund check.

You'll need to file a new W-4 when you get a new job, if you got a big refund last year, got married, divorced, or had a child, or if you can no longer claim a dependent that you claimed last year. You can fill out a new W-4 at any time.

2. Know When to Itemize

When you file your income tax return, you choose between using the standard deduction or itemizing all of your deductions. Deductions lower the amount of income that you'll be taxed on, which is a good thing.

If your total itemized deductions are greater than the standard deduction, it pays to itemize. For those of you who don't own a home or significant investments, it might be hard to itemize, as your standard deduction is likely higher than itemized deductions. Was that all Greek to you? Let's use an example to help explain this concept.

Let's take the standard deduction, which in 2009 was:
* Single or married filing separately—$5,700
* Married filing a joint return or qualifying widow/widower—$11,400
* Head of household—$8,350

These numbers change each year. Check out Form 1040 and 1040EZ on irs.gov for current numbers.

Alternately, you can itemize. What kinds of things can you itemize?
* Interest paid on your home mortgage or home equity loan
  Form 1098, which your mortgage lender will send you, will tell you how much interest you paid over the course of the year.
* Points you paid at the closing of the home you bought
  Points can be deducted within the first year you own the home under certain conditions. See IRS Publication 936, Home Mortgage Interest Deduction, for a list of the rules of this deduction.
* Real estate taxes
  Excludes services such as water and sewer that may be part of your real estate tax bill.
* Personal property taxes
* State and local income taxes
* Charitable donations
* Medical expenses
  You get to deduct medical expenses only if they exceed 7.5 percent of your adjusted gross income. See page 207 for a definition of adjusted gross income. Check out IRS Publication 502, Medical and Dental Expenses, for details.

- Job-search expenses

  If you are looking for work in the same field in which you currently work, you can deduct expenses such as printing your resume, postage, and so on.
- See Schedule A (included with the long version of IRS Form 1040) for a complete list of all the deductions you can itemize, or visit irs.gov for a copy of this form.

Now, add up all the items you can itemize. Get a total dollar value. If this dollar value is greater than your standard deduction, you should itemize. For example, let's say you are single and you own a home. You paid $10,000 in mortgage interest last year. So it would make sense for you to itemize in this case because you could deduct $10,000 from your taxable income, whereas if you took the standard deduction, you could only deduct $5,350.

The Tax Deductions and Tips tab at TurboTax.com is great for figuring out all available deductions.

3. Adjust Smartly

Even if you do not itemize your deductions, there are several adjustments you can make to your income that will reduce your taxable income. In other words, even if you take the standard deduction, some items can still be deducted from your taxable income, including:
- Student loan interest

  You might qualify for a deduction, depending on your modified adjusted gross income (MAGI), for interest paid on a student loan used for higher education. In 2008, you qualified for a deduction of up to $2,500 if your MAGI was less than $70,000 ($145,000 if filing a joint return). See page 137 for an explanation of MAGI.
- Moving expenses

  If you have to move more than fifty miles for a new job and are not reimbursed by your employer, you may be able to deduct the cost of moving your things to your new place. To be eligible, you are required to work full-time for at least thirty-nine weeks for the year following your move, and if you are self-employed, at least seventy-eight weeks during the first twenty-four months.
- Deductible IRA and 401(k) contributions

  See Chapter 9.

Visit the Tax Topics section of irs.gov for a full list of adjustments.

4. Give Yourself Some Credit

You can get tax credits for retirement savings contributions, child and dependent care, hybrid car ownership (going green suddenly got way chicer!), and more. Understand what tax credits are available to you and take the appropriate ones. Visit the Tax Topics section of irs.gov for a full list of tax credits. About.com's tax section also has a good list.

5. Claim Exemptions

Exemptions reduce your amount of taxable income, so claim the exemptions that you can. You can usually get one exemption for yourself, one for your husband, and one for each of your kids. In 2009, each exemption was worth $3,650, meaning that with each exemption you could deduct $3,650 from your taxable income. However, those with very high AGIs might not get the entire exemption. You can't claim your exemption if you're the dependent of another person, even if that person doesn't claim an exemption for you. Exemptions are usually claimed on forms 1040, 1040EZ, or 1040A. For more information on exemptions, visit irs.gov.

6. Take Advantage of Tax-Free or Tax-Deferred Benefits from Your Employer (and Other Sources)

If your employer offers a cafeteria plan and flexible spending account (FSA), health insurance, educational assistance programs, retirement plans, stock options, transportation subsidies, and more, it might behoove you to take advantage of these. There are also certain investment vehicles like U.S. Treasury bonds and municipal bonds that provide tax advantages (see page 147), and often, income from these investments is exempt from certain income taxes.

7. Buy a Home (But Only if You Can Really Afford It, Of Course!)

You can deduct mortgage interest and a few other home-related items from your income taxes—see page 210. When you sell a home, you can keep $250,000 if you are single, and $500,000 if you are married in tax-exempt profit. To see how much you'll save each year in taxes by buying a home, check out the Home Ownership Tax Savings calculator from Freddie Mac. You will need to know your federal and state tax rate when you use this calculator.

8. Know When and How to Get Help

Ladies, doing your taxes can be very easy or very hard, depending on your tax situation. If you have complicated investments, own your own business, have a lot of property, have recently had a major life change like a marriage or a divorce or a child, it might be a good idea to have a professional do it. This does not mean that you are dumb—the IRS is just brilliant at making everything harder than it needs to be. For those of you without complicated tax situations, it's not too hard to do your own income taxes. If you qualify for the 1040EZ form, it's actually going to be quite easy to do your taxes—more on that later.

So if you have a pretty simple tax situation, you can file taxes on your own. Plus, there are great online tax preparation sites and software programs that will help you out. I recommend TurboTax online. It prompts you the entire way, and there is a way to do your state taxes on it as well. It asks questions to determine if you can get tax savings. Other programs include TaxACT and TaxCut.

If you need professional help with your taxes, here are a few options.

Tax preparers

Tax preparers have the least amount of training, but they are the cheapest option. They are good for those of you with relatively simple tax situations. There is most likely no need to spend more money for a CPA or enrolled agent if you have a very simple tax situation.

You can find a tax preparer at a firm like H&R Block or Jackson Hewitt. There are also many local and regional firms with fairly low fees that you can use. You can find tax preparers at taxprofessionals.com or just ask friends and family for a recommendation.

Enrolled agents and CPAs

These individuals are more expensive than tax preparers, but they also have more training. They are good for people with more complicated tax situations.

An enrolled agent is a former IRS employee, and a CPA is an extensively trained accountant. CPAs are required to complete continuing education each year to stay certified. With a very complex tax situation, a CPA is probably the way to go, but expect a hefty bill. To find a CPA, check out your local chapter of the American Institute of Certified Public Accountants (AICPA). Make sure you look at his or her qualifications, background, and fees before hiring him or her. It's also worth finding out whether or not the individual has kept up with his or her continuing professional education, as tax laws change frequently. CPAs charge by the hour, usually, so make sure to have all your paperwork in order before you go to him or her. See The Dreaded Paperwork section coming up for a list of what you'll need.

Tax attorney

There's almost no reason for you to need a tax attorney to complete your tax return unless you're dealing with serious legal ramifications from your income taxes. You'll pay a whole lot for a tax attorney, so unless you need him or her, don't bother.

9. Know Where to Find More Information

I don't have to tell you that taxes are complicated, so it's important that you know where to ask questions about them. Better to understand everything than to make major mistakes, which can come back to bite you (and, more important, your wallet) in the butt if you get audited. Some great sites for tax info include About.com Tax Planning, Yahoo.com Tax Center, and SmartMoney.com Tax Guide.

10. Pay Your Taxes on Time and in the Right Way

First of all, don't file late even if you are freaked out that you won't be able to pay what you owe. Either file by the due date or file for an extension. Late filing can cost you up to 25 percent of your total tax bill.

Secondly, beware of paying your taxes via credit card. Yes, the IRS will take a credit card just like Bloomingdale's, but need I remind you of the interest you could potentially incur should you not be able to pay off the balance? And on top of that, you'll need to go through a third-party processor, who will charge you a fee—usually about 2.5 percent of your tax bill—to pay with your card, as the IRS doesn't accept credit card payments directly.

If you really can't afford to pay your taxes, you can set up a payment plan with the IRS. No, they aren't accommodating. They'll charge you a fee (usually from $42 to $105), plus interest, plus a late payment penalty. These penalties plus the interest will add up to about 12 percent annually, but that may still be cheaper than your credit card, in which case, this option may be worth considering. You'll need to fill out IRS Form 9465, which you can find at irs.gov, to get a monthly payment plan.

I recommend electronically filing your taxes if you can. If you are using an online tax preparation program like TurboTax (turbotax.com), TaxACT (taxact.com), or TaxCut (taxcut.com), it will e-file for you. Unless you are having a professional handle your taxes, I recommend using one of these programs as they translate complicated IRS forms into plain English, e-file for you, and more. And they can also help you handle your state income taxes. If you are doing your taxes without the help of software, the IRS lets eligible individuals e-file for free with its Free File program. E-filing is faster and more accurate than mailing in your taxes, and it'll save you paper and postage costs. Plus, you won't have to worry about the forms getting lost in the mail. You can have your taxes debited from your bank account for free. However, if you use your credit card to pay your taxes, you will still be charged a fee. Visit irs.gov/efile for more information on e-filing.

THE DREADED PAPERWORK: WHAT YOU NEED BEFORE YOU (OR SOMEONE ELSE) PREPARES YOUR TAXES

Proof of Income

By the end of January, you should get a Form W-2 from each of your employers, which will show how much you earned, how much of your earnings were taxable, and what taxes were withheld. If you do not receive a W-2, call your employer and ask for it. Should you not get a Form W-2, you can fill out Form 4852, which is downloadable from the IRS Web site. If you're an independent contractor, the company you worked for should send you a Form 1099-MISC. If you're self-employed, you'll need to gather all receipts and documents for business expenses.

You will also need to get statements from your interest-bearing checking and savings accounts, retirement and investment accounts, and other accounts that will be considered when figuring out your taxable income. Interest earnings are typically shown via form 1099-INT. If you have stocks, mutual funds, or MMAs, you should get a Form 1099-DIV for each account.

You'll also want to collect statements on other income such as last year's tax refund or unemployment compensation. Basically, if you received money, you should have documents that show that. If you're missing a statement, call the company that paid you and request a copy.

Proof That You Are Qualified for Deductions, Adjustments, or Credits

Make sure you get statements showing that you are qualified to take deductions, adjustments, or credits. For example, if you want to take a deduction for your student loan interest, you'll want statements from the student loan company showing that you paid it.

I'M FILING MY OWN TAXES. WHAT FORM SHOULD I USE?

You should use the simplest tax form for your needs. This will save you time in preparing your return, and the IRS will be able to process your tax return more quickly. Form 1040EZ is the easiest, followed by Form 1040A. The most complicated is Form 1040. I recommend using an online tax preparation program like TurboTax (turbotax.com), TaxACT (taxact.com) or TaxCut (taxcut.com) to file your taxes. These programs can help you figure out the right form for your needs.

Form 1040EZ

You can use Form 1040EZ, the shortest and easiest federal tax form, if:

- Your total taxable income is under $100,000.
- Your interest income is under $1,500.
- You have income only from wages, interest, and unemployment compensation.
- You and your spouse are under sixty-five years old.
- Your filing status is single or married filing jointly.
- You do not have any adjustments to income.
- You are claiming only the standard deduction.
- You are not claiming any other tax credits besides the Earned Income Tax Credit.

Form 1040A

Most taxpayers qualify to use Form 1040A, often called the short form, although you cannot use Form 1040A if you want to itemize your deductions. This form allows you to claim the most common adjustments to income. You can use this form if:

- Your total taxable income is under $100,000.
- You are any age and any filing status.
- You have capital gains distributions but no other capital gains or losses.

- You have income from wages, interest, dividends, capital gain distributions, IRA or pension distributions, unemployment compensation, or Social Security benefits.
- The only adjustments to your income are: penalty for early withdrawal of savings, IRA contributions, student loan interest, and jury duty pay given to your employer.
- You can claim the following tax credits: child and dependent care credit, credit for the elderly and disabled, education credits, retirement savings contributions credit, child tax credit, earned income credit, telephone excise tax credit.

Form 1040 (the long form)

Any taxpayer can use Form 1040. Even though it takes longer to fill out, Form 1040 can handle any tax situation, no matter how complex. You must use Form 1040 if:

- You have taxable income of $100,000 or more.
- You are itemizing your deductions (such as mortgage interest or charity).
- You have income from a rental, business, farm, S-corporation, partnership, or trust.
- You have foreign wages, paid foreign taxes, or are claiming tax treaty benefits.
- You sold stocks, bonds, mutual funds, or property.
- You are claiming adjustments to income for educator expenses, tuition and fees, moving, expenses, or health savings accounts.

If you have any doubt as to what form you should use, use the 1040.

Pat yourself on the back, girls—you have just finished the most complicated chapter in the book. Yes, the IRS has a way of making things difficult, but then, you've just learned how to get your way (as much as you legally can, anyway) in spite of it. But I imagine many of you are still feeling a little peeved by Uncle Sam. Even when you've done everything in your power to make your tax situation advantageous, you still glance down at your paycheck and want to murder the IRS for taking away all that cash that could be funding your much-needed trip to St. Bart's with your girlfriends, or added to your and your hubby's fund for that gorgeous flat overlooking the park. It's annoying, I get it, so here's a little quote to make you feel better: "The point to remember is that what the government gives, it must first take away," said by John S. Coleman. I like this quote because it helps you look at the bigger tax picture, so you don't end up feeling completely annoyed with and frustrated by the IRS. Try to remember that your tax dollars are funding some really important projects and services, like education; infrastructure, including roads, bridges, and sewer systems (and girls, I assure you, you wouldn't last a minute without flushing toilets); and public safety, like police and firefighters.

That being said, you're certainly not an unlimited ATM for Uncle Sam. You do your part by paying the taxes you owe, but there is no need to give the government more than you have to. (I mean, if you've got extra money that you want to give away, why not fund a charity directly aligned with a cause you support?) Just ask yourself: Do I want the extra cash in my wallet to do with as I wish, or do I want the IRS to have it? I'm guessing the answer to that question will motivate you to go back through this chapter with a fine-tooth comb, looking for where you can take adjustments, exemptions, and credits; figuring out whether to itemize; adjusting your W-4 if needed; considering buying a home; taking advantage of employer benefits; getting professional help if necessary; paying your taxes in full and on time; and simply taking a more active role in doing your homework and putting yourself in a tax situation that nets you the most money. You may have to play within the confines of the system, but come on, when has that ever really stopped you from getting your way, one way or another?

CHAPTER 15

Lift Up Your Love

How to Make Your Relationship Work (Well,
the Money Part Anyway)

So happily ever after is finally in your sights. No more awkward first dates, no more "Can we just be friends," no more obsessing over your "number." Prince Charming has popped the question. And don't deny it: You're already picturing the house with the white picket fence, the Cinderella wedding, the adorable baby girl in her pale pink smocked dress. Ladies, I'm thrilled for you, but before you strap on those perfect white Christian Louboutins and the matching white gown and trot down the aisle, let's get you and your partner on the same page financially.

That's what this chapter will do. First, it provides you with a step-by-step guide to making your relationship work financially, and then gives you information on prenuptial agreements, as well as tips for planning a wedding on a budget and preparing for the cost of a baby. And for those of you who aren't quite ready for the big M, this chapter will help you work out your joint finances, should the two of you decide to move in together. So take your I'm-so-in-love-so-nothing-can-go-wrong blinders off for a few minutes—don't worry, it's just a few minutes, ladies, and you can put them right back on after you follow my advice—and let's get your relationship on the right (financial) track.

SEVEN STEPS FOR A FINANCIALLY SOUND RELATIONSHIP
Step 1: Know All about His (or Her) Finances and Spending Habits
You should go over your credit reports, pull up your FICO scores and examine all your debts (student loans, mortgage, auto, credit cards, etc.), investments, inheritance (what you've already gotten and what you will get), and trust funds (if you have them) together. Remember that when you're married, your financial situations merge (well, at least partially; see below), so it's very important that you know your future spouse's entire financial history. It's a great idea for you and your partner to fill out the Assets, Liabilities, and Monthly Income charts from Chapter 2 and compare them.

Next, is your future hubby a spender, a saver, or somewhere in between? Have him keep a spending diary (see Chapter 3) and look through it. If you guys have different spending and saving tendencies, can't you just already hear the fights coming? ("Wait, you blew half of our savings on a giant plasma screen TV for football season?!") Now, this doesn't mean you shouldn't be together, it just means that you'll have to make financial goals (see below) and a solid plan to achieve them, keeping your spending/saving tendencies in mind. You need to understand your spouse's spending habits so that you can prepare for the situations in which you won't see eye to eye. And when you are working toward your goals, if he has a tendency to scrimp on savings, knowing about it beforehand can help you deal with a problem before it arises.

Here are some suggestions for making it work: If each of you have an income, it's often a good idea to have a joint account for your household and shared expenses and then your own accounts for personal spending. You should contribute to the joint account depending on how much you make—if he makes considerably more than you, you shouldn't have to contribute an equal dollar amount, and vice versa. Sign up for automatic bill pay on that joint account so you don't make late payments, which are a recipe for finger pointing and one of you sleeping alone on the couch. And by the way, financial experts recommend that you keep at least one credit card in your name alone (and pay it off on time, of course). This will protect you in case something happens to your hubby or your marriage—you'll still have credit that's yours and yours alone. Just because you marry doesn't mean you have to merge everything.

Step 2: Talk about Your Financial Goals, Both Short-term And Long-term

Don't just assume that you two will want the same things. I mean, when's the last time you even agreed on what TV show to watch? You may want to buy a house in the 'burbs, while he wants a brand-new Porsche 911. Talk about it. It's okay to agree to disagree sometimes. You don't have to do everything together. You can both work toward individual goals in addition to your common goals. And don't underestimate the importance of compromise: If you can't start doing it now, how are you going to do it when you're both old and gray and the cuteness of that little pouty face you make when you don't get what you want has started to grow thin?

Here are some key goals to consider: paying down debt, saving for retirement, fully insuring yourselves and your stuff, and building up emergency savings. Many other goals can be very important too. Talk about them with your partner. You can use the Financial Goals chart from Chapter 2 to help you here: Fill out one for your individual goals and one for you and your hubby's joint goals.

Step 3: Create a Budget

Create a budget just like you did in Chapter 4, except now it's for both of you. It should help you meet your financial goals and keep within your spending limits. When making this budget, be sure you take into account all the areas where being married might save you money. For example, some insurance companies offer rate breaks to married couples (married people often pay less per person for car insurance than singles) and taxes (see pages 225–226).

Step 4: Determine Who Will Deal with Which Parts of Your Finances

You may decide to share responsibility, you may decide that one of you is better at investing and paying bills. Whatever you decide, just make sure each of you is clear on who will deal with what. Also make sure that one person keeps the other in the loop about all the financial decisions made. And by the way, just because he's a man, does *not* mean that he is better at investing than you. (Think about how great he may think he is at directions, but I know you've driven in circles with him at the wheel more than once.)

Step 5: Understand How Your Marriage Will Affect Your Employer Benefits

Employer benefits may include health benefits, retirement savings plans, life insurance, and more. If your partner receives better benefits than you, consider getting covered under his or her plan (or vice versa).

Step 6: Know the Tax Impact of Marriage

When you get married, your tax situation changes. If both of you make similar incomes, you might get hit with what is called the marriage penalty—a tax situation that forces a married couple to pay a higher tax rate than when both individuals were single. This penalty usually gets harsher—as in, a higher tax rate—the more money you guys earn. If your incomes fall in the 10 percent or 15 percent tax brackets, then this penalty should not affect you. If, however, you guys fall into one of the higher tax brackets, you might get hit with the marriage tax penalty. Page 209 outlines the income requirements for each tax bracket; you can also find them on irs.gov.

Here's an example to help you understand the penalty. A couple, let's call them Ben and Sarah, each have $80,000 per year in taxable income and file their taxes as married filing jointly. This puts them into the 28 percent tax rate bracket, as their combined income exceeds the upper income limit for the 25 percent tax rate of $137,050 in 2009 and thus pushes them into the 28 percent bracket. If, however, Ben and Sarah were single, they would only be in the 25 percent tax rate bracket in 2009 as the upper limit for that bracket was $82,250, and each of their incomes falls within that limit. Ben and Sarah owe more in taxes as a married couple than they would have owed if they could have filed as singles, despite the fact that their income is exactly the same.

However, from a tax perspective, many couples actually benefit from marriage. Couples who have very different incomes often get a marriage bonus, a situation in which marriage leads to a lower tax rate for a couple. These disparate incomes make it more likely that combining them on a joint return will pull some of the higher-earner's income into a lower bracket, which means the couple pays less taxes. Married couples enjoy another bonus as well: When they sell their home, the amount of home-sale profit that is exempt from taxes doubles from $250,000 to $500,000, as long as the couple owns and lives in the house for at least two of the five years before the sale.

Note that when you guys get married, both of you need to file new W-4s with your employers. You'll have the option of filing as married filing jointly or married filing separately. Your choice between the two should be based on the option that makes the most financial sense. Usually married filing jointly is the better option, but it's still worth looking into. The IRS Web site provides all the information you need to figure this out.

Step 7: Consider Life and Disability Insurance

See Chapter 12 for details on how much you'll need now that you are married. If you already have these types of insurance, you might want to change the beneficiary on the plan to be your husband.

WHICH PARTS OF OUR FINANCES MERGE (AND WHICH DON'T) WHEN WE MARRY?

Luckily for those of you who have big-spender fiancés, you will not have to take on any of the debt they racked up before the marriage. But once you are married, it's an entirely different story. You two are pretty much financial Siamese twins at this point: His finances are your finances. If he racks up massive debt on a credit card—even if you had no idea that the credit card even existed and even if he used it to buy his mistress lacy La Perla—the credit card company may come after you for the debt.

THE DREADED PRENUPTIAL AGREEMENT

I'm going to preface this by saying that I have many happily married friends who never signed a prenup. But prenups are not just for the Donald Trumps of the world. No, a prenup is not essential, but it can be very helpful in the event that your marriage—like roughly half of all marriages—goes awry. I know most of you are thinking that having a prenup is just like asking for the marriage to fail. But people change, situations change, and not everything that's amazing today will be so in the future. Look at a prenup as assuming the best will happen, but preparing for the worst.

A prenup is a legal document that dictates how your assets and debts will be handled if you divorce. It can also spell out requirements for child support, education, religious upbringing, and other provisions for your current or future children. Ladies, if you have assets you want to protect—a trust fund, inheritance, business, home, investments, et cetera—or a child or children from a previous marriage, it is a really good idea to have your partner sign a prenup before marrying. Look, he may really be the nicest guy in the world, and you may never get divorced. Just remember, people change and divorce happens, so be careful.

If you decide to get a prenup, both of you will need your own lawyers. To find a lawyer in your area, visit lawyers.findlaw.com. It usually costs around $1,500 to $3,000 to get the agreement. Also check out Legal Zoom.com; for $200 or less, you can fill out a standard prenup form. But if you have major assets or children, it's probably best to have the professionals at a law firm handle this.

AND THE REALLY IMPORTANT PART (THE WEDDING!)

Ladies, I'm kidding about the wedding being the "really important part," though I know for some of you it really is. Ever since you got your first glimpse of Cinderella, you've dreamed of that perfect wedding: You, clad in a flowing cream-lace Vera Wang, ten of your BFFs in azure Nicole Miller off-the-shoulder bridesmaids' dresses, a reception overlooking the crystal-clear Caribbean, Dom flowing freely. Well, ladies, I hope you are marrying a loaded trust fund baby, because that is not going to be cheap.

It's tempting to get into the I'll-have-only-one-wedding-and-I-want-it-to-be-perfect-no-matter-what mentality, but realize that you should have only one marriage, too, and you don't want to enter into it straddled with debt from the wedding. A wedding should be a celebration of your union, not a showcase for how much you spent.

Unless you are marrying Mr. Moneybags (or one of you was born to Mr. and Mrs. Moneybags), you will probably have to create a budget for your wedding. First, know how much you can afford. (And if it's $0, I suggest you either begin saving, or elope in Britney-esque fashion to Las

Vegas.) I do *not* recommend getting yourselves into debt over a wedding. Why don't both of you just start saving now and wait to wed until you can actually afford it?

Once you know how much you can afford, go to Brides.com and click the Planning Tab and then the Budgets and Basics tab to figure out roughly how much each element of your wedding will cost you. The major expenses related to a wedding, courtesy of About.com, and an estimation of the percentage of your budget that these expenses will consume, are the following:

1. Ceremony (6 percent)
   Venue, officiant (priest, rabbi, justice of the peace, etc.), marriage license, musician, other
2. Reception (53 percent)
   Venue, food and drink, rentals (chairs, tables, etc.), gifts to guests, band/DJ
3. Clothing, accessories, makeup, and hair (10 percent)
   Dress, veil, accessories, shoes, tux, cuff links, hair, makeup, other
4. Rings (3 percent—ladies, you can always upgrade later)
5. Flowers (8 percent)
   Ceremony, bride, bridal party, groom party, centerpieces
6. Photography (12 percent)
7. Transportation (2 percent)
   Transportation for wedding party and/or guests, parking
8. Stationery (3 percent)
   Invitations, reply cards, thank-you notes, postage, guest book
9. Gifts (3 percent)
   Bridal and groom parties, parents, welcome baskets

These are very rough estimations of what you'll spend in each category, and some of you may not even have some of these expenses. But you can see that the bulk of your money will probably be spent at the reception. Why? Because the food, drink, and venue costs will probably be really high. As you make your budget, I suggest you make a list of all the elements of the wedding from food to flowers to venue in order of importance to you. As you finalize your budget, this list will help you see the items that you can cut or reduce spending on.

Remember that if you reduce the number of guests, you'll reduce the cost—you haven't seen Aunt Ethel in ten years; does she *really* need to make it onto the guest list? While you are planning this wedding, shop around for better prices. Remember to include the cost of tipping in your budget, because caterers, musicians, limo drivers, and others all should be tipped. Sometimes you can negotiate the prices of items such as venue rental and food costs, especially in this rough economy. You also need to think hard about what you can do without—maybe you can serve three hors d'oeuvres instead of six. Maybe you simply do not have the budget for gifts or transportation or whatever. Ladies, this is not the end of the world—remember, a wedding is about celebrating love, not showing off how much you spent.

My friend Jordana is a great example of how to plan a wedding successfully on a budget. She wanted a destination wedding, which is usually not cheap. But she made it work—within her budget. First, she figured out her priorities—the things that she really cared about having at her wedding. For Jordana, a destination wedding was the big sticking point, but the flowers, food, and invitations were not as important to her. When she made a budget, she ensured that her high-priority items like the right locale were fully funded, while she allotted less money to the less-important items. Jordana kept the guest list to a minimum—yes, that meant not inviting some of people who had invited her to their weddings, but she just told herself, "This is my day." Instead of using an expensive invitation company, Jordana used zazzle.com. She had one of her musician friends make an iPod playlist for the wedding rather than hire a DJ or band. She negotiated with the resort on the prices of the flowers and some of the decorations. Would Jordana have liked an unlimited budget and every single detail to be absolutely just the way she wanted it? Sure, who wouldn't? But you know what, her entire wedding was absolutely perfect in spite of the compromises she chose to make. And even better: It didn't break the bank.

Ten Wedding Cost-Saving Tips

1. Invite fewer guests.
2. Shop around for better prices on everything from caterers to venues to dresses.

   Get a bunch of quotes from many different vendors, and negotiate prices as much as you can. Work the Web for deals. For example, sites like PreOwnedWeddingDresses.com and WoreItOnce.com can save you big bucks on the dress, and sites like budgetinvitations.com and annsbridalbargains.com offer cheaper invitations.
3. Do a buffet or hors d'oeuvres instead of a sit-down dinner.
4. Hold your wedding in the off-season (November through April) or on a less-popular day or time (weekdays, mornings, or afternoons).
5. Think about what's really important to you and spend more on it while spending less in other areas.

   For example, you may decide to splurge on the perfect photos while ordering one less appetizer to be passed around during the reception.
6. Find a low-cost venue.

   The backyard wedding is so in right now—intimate, unpretentious, and lovely. So if you or a friend or family member has a beautiful backyard, do it there instead of paying for a venue. And if you don't want to go that route, apply that dogged-deal finding sense of yours to looking for inexpensive venues.
7. Do-it-yourself, or have friends and family do it.

   All you stylish, crafty chicks, the DIY is perfect for you. With a little Photoshop or design knowledge and a good printer (or take them to Kinkos), you can create invitations yourself on the cheap. You can also make the gifts for your guests, the flower arrangements, do your own hair and makeup, and more. Check out the wedding section on diynetwork.com or do-it-yourself-weddings.com for ideas. And if you aren't the crafty type, tap into the talents of your friends and family. Instead of hiring a DJ or a band, have a

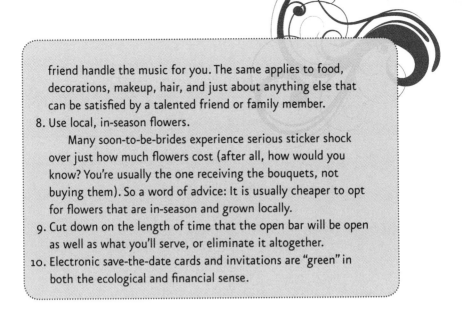

friend handle the music for you. The same applies to food, decorations, makeup, hair, and just about anything else that can be satisfied by a talented friend or family member.

8. Use local, in-season flowers.

Many soon-to-be-brides experience serious sticker shock over just how much flowers cost (after all, how would you know? You're usually the one receiving the bouquets, not buying them). So a word of advice: It is usually cheaper to opt for flowers that are in-season and grown locally.

9. Cut down on the length of time that the open bar will be open as well as what you'll serve, or eliminate it altogether.

10. Electronic save-the-date cards and invitations are "green" in both the ecological and financial sense.

Remember that Cinderella was just a fairy tale. Your wedding does not have to be perfect. This is about the rest of your life, not just the right now. I can guarantee you that starting your life together without being saddled with massive wedding debt is much more liberating than that super-expensive white dress that you couldn't live without (and will never wear again).

PLANNING FOR A BABY

The two of you are thinking about a little bundle of joy. It's one of life's most rewarding journeys (or so I hear), so congrats! But before you embark on this route, let's figure out what a child will probably cost you, so that you can understand the financial impact he or she will have on your life.

You're Pregnant: What Will Be in Your Immediate Future When the Baby Comes?

Here are the top things to consider when planning for the baby.

1. Insurance

Figure out how much of the medical costs for the pregnancy and birth your insurance will cover and budget accordingly. How much more will it cost each month to add your baby to your health insurance policy?

2. Maternity leave

How will you cope financially while you are on maternity leave? Find out your employer's maternity leave policy. If they don't cover you, check your short-term disability insurance policy to see if it does. If you are not covered, start saving now so that you can afford to live comfortably during your maternity leave.

3. Child care

Who will care for your children when you are at work? How much will it cost? Can you afford to stay home with the baby and not work? How will this affect your financial situation?

4. Preparing the home for the baby

To figure out how much this will cost, you will first have to write down all the items you'll need by the time the baby comes, including: clothing, blanket, crib, changing table/pad, diapers, wipes, thermometer, baby monitor, diaper rash cream, toys, pacifier, stroller, car seat, bottles, breast pumps, and all of the appliances and supplies you won't be able to manage without. There are tons of deals online — remember your BBF Google — and many large retailers like overstock.com, diapers.com, walmart.com, and babiesrus.com have good prices. The book *Great Expectations: Baby's First Year* by Sandy Jones and Marcie Jones is also a good resource to help you plan for the new baby.

5. Yearly cost of a child

Figure out what raising a child will cost you each year, and adjust your budget accordingly.

According to the U.S. Department of Agriculture (2004), a family in the middle income tier will spend about $15,000 per year on the child until the kid is age seventeen, not including college costs. The Bankrate Raising a Child calculator will help you figure it out for your personal situation. You will need to budget for these expenses (see Chapter 4). This budget will need to be redone before your little one arrives.

LIVING TOGETHER

Maybe marriage isn't in the cards right now — there's just something about that 'til-death-do-us-part bit that's just a little too, well, final, for you two at the moment — but you've decided to give it a shot and move in together. Here are a few tips the experts recommend:

1. Consider a nonmarital agreement.

   If this sounds a little scary, believe me, it's not—it's just a legal document that spells out how your assets/property and shared expenses will be divvied up if you break up. Now you may think that this sounds ridiculous, and you might think that you'd rather die than bring it up with your partner, but consider how you could benefit from it in the event that your relationship ends and, say, your man never repaid that $800 you loaned him.

   Take my friend Courtney, for example. She had been dating her now ex-boyfriend for about a year when they decided to move in together. We all thought he was amazing, and at the time, so did she. In fact, I remember her telling me that she "could see spending the rest of her life with him." Well, things didn't exactly go as planned. His music career didn't quite work out as he had envisioned it. Courtney, being the sweetheart that she is, loaned him a bunch of money, only to find out that he had been carrying on a relationship with another girl for months! Of course, she threw him out (after hurling all of his clothes onto the lawn—go girl!). Oh, but it gets worse. Not only did he cheat on her and break her heart, he never repaid that big chunk of money he owed her. The lesson: Even the seemingly nicest man or woman can turn out to be a pig, so it's crucial that you protect yourself from this kind of thing. (But not to worry about Courtney—she's now a successful photographer . . . and her ex? Still just struggling along.)

   If you are in a relationship where you buy relatively expensive things together, or if you purchased a home together or will in the future, it's a really good idea to have a nonmarital agreement. If you break up with him or her, you are entitled only to the property or assets in your own name, but the rest of it . . . well, let's just say you could be SOL without this agreement. A lawyer can execute a nonmarital agreement for you. To find a lawyer in your area, visit lawyers.findlaw.com. It usually costs around $1,500 to $3,000 to get a nonmarital agreement executed. So if both of you are pretty broke and don't buy expensive things together, it might not be worth the cost of the lawyer. Just be careful that you guys share expenses in a fair way, if this is the case.

2. Agree upon how you'll deal with shared expenses before you move in together.

   So you're sharing your home, groceries, utilities, and a variety of other expenses. Figure out how you'll pay for these things before you move in together. Maybe you'll have a joint account that you both contribute to that pays for all the household needs, while keeping your own separate accounts for personal spending. Just remember that with a joint account, either of you can clear out the account and walk away. Or maybe you have only separate bank accounts and each of you pays half of all the bills. Or maybe you pay in proportion to your income. Whatever the agreement, decide on it before you move in together to prevent fights and make sure it's fair. If you decide to have separate bank accounts, it's a good idea to pay your share of the bill directly to the company rather than to your partner. This just ensures that there's no way your partner can pocket your money and run—not that he would, but it always pays to be safe.

3. Keep good records when making joint purchases, in the absence of a nonmarital agreement.

If you don't have a non marital agreement and make a large joint purchase together, you need to make sure that your name is somewhere on the title or deed. If it's not an item with a title or deed, you need to be able to prove that you paid for part of the item. Pay by check and make a note on the check, "jointly owned television set," or pay by credit card. Just make sure your method of payment is traceable in case there is ever a dispute. Imagine if you contributed money toward your shared home but his name was the only one on the deed—you could potentially forfeit all your rights to the home.

And there you have it, girls—the basics of making your relationship work, at least the financial side of it. And you know what? The elements that will make your financial relationship work are probably a lot like the elements that make your emotional relationship work: communication, honesty, and hard work. Here's what those elements look like in your financial relationship:

* Communication

You need to communicate with your partner about all aspects of money, from how to divide the financial responsibilities, to spending and savings tendencies, and the need for a prenup or non marital agreement. And communication is a two-way street, requiring both talking *and* listening. Sometimes it can mean compromise and concession. Don't just assume that he knows how you feel about money matters. I mean, really—you and I both know men are not always the best at tuning in to our thoughts and feelings.

* Honesty

    You need to be honest with him about finances, both past and present. He needs to know not only about your past (yes, that means letting him know how your piles of strappy sandals, stacks of handbags, and racks of dresses that constantly cause exclamations like "How can you have nothing to wear? You have so much stuff that we're literally living on top of it," actually came with a giant side of credit card debt), but also about your future—all the things you want out of life that will cost money. Don't be afraid to lay all your goals out on the table—the clapboard house on the shore, the dream of the two of you escaping to a bungalow in Aruba when you're old and gray. And once again, this element is a two-way street: he needs to be honest with you, too.

* Hard work

    Finally, your financial relationship requires hard work. You'll have to make a joint budget and stick to it, even when it takes sacrifice and struggle. You'll have to be vigilant about your spending and savings even when you just don't feel like it. Remember, hard work brings great rewards, whether it's in the form of a lifelong emotional bond or a cushy retirement, a devoted commitment, or your dream house. So keep those financial goals at the top of your mind as your relationship progresses.

Girls, you've done the hard part—landed Mr. Right. And now, by following the advice in this chapter, you can help him become Mr. Right for your pocketbook as well. So here's to happily ever after—for your heart *and* your pocketbook!

Index

About the Author

Catey Hill is the money editor for the *New York Daily News* online. Previously, Hill was the marketing manager at Plum TV and the author of *The Plum Wealth Report*, a specialized blog focusing on the lifestyles and purchasing behaviors of affluent consumers. She first realized her need to kick her shoe habit and get her finances in order when working as the financial marketing manager for *Forbes* magazine. A contributing writer for TheSavvyGal.com and other Web sites and magazines, Hill resides in New York City.